BOOKKEEPER ACCOUNT CLERK

Edited by

Hy Hammer, Chief of
Examining Service Division
New York City Department
of Personnel, (Ret.)

ARCO PUBLISHING, INC.
NEW YORK

Sixth Edition, Third Printing, 1986

Published by Arco Publishing, Inc.
215 Park Avenue South, New York, N.Y. 10003

Copyright © 1983, 1976 by Arco Publishing, Inc.

Library of Congress Cataloging in Publication Data
Hammer, Hy.
  Bookkeeper, account clerk.
  Rev. ed. of: Bookkeeper, account clerk/by David R.
Turner. 4th ed. 1971.
    1. Bookkeeping—Examinations, questions, etc.
2. Accounting—Examinations, questions, etc.   3. Civil
service—United States—Examinations.   I. Turner, David
Reuben, 1915–   . Bookkeeper, account clerk.
II. Title.
HF5661.H15   1982   657'.076   82-11427
ISBN 0-668-05398-4

Printed in the United States of America

CONTENTS

HOW TO USE THIS INDEX
Slightly bend the right-hand edge
of the book. This will expose
the corresponding Parts
which match the index, below.

PART

1

2

3

4

WHAT THIS BOOK WILL DO FOR YOU

ARCO Publishing, Inc. has followed testing trends and methods ever since the firm was founded in 1937. We specialize in books that prepare people for tests. Based on this experience, we have prepared the best possible book to help *you* score high.

To write this book we carefully analyzed every detail surrounding the forthcoming examination . . .
- the job itself
- official and unofficial announcements concerning the examination
- all the previous examinations, many not available to the public
- related examinations
- technical literature that explains and forecasts the examination

CAN YOU PREPARE YOURSELF FOR YOUR TEST?

You want to pass this test. That's why you bought this book. Used correctly, your "self-tutor" will show you what to expect and will give you a speedy brush-up on the subjects tested in your exam. Some of these are subjects not taught in schools at all. Even if your study time is very limited, you should:

- Become familiar with the type of examination you will have.
- Improve your general examination-taking skill.
- Improve your skill in analyzing and answering questions involving reasoning, judgment, comparison, and evaluation.

- Improve your speed and skill in reading and understanding what you read—an important part of your ability to learn and an important part of most tests.

This book will tell you exactly what to study by presenting in full every type of question you will get on the actual test.

This book will help you find your weaknesses. Once you know what subjects you're weak in you can get right to work and concentrate on those areas. This kind of selective study yields maximum test results.

This book will give you the *feel* of the exam. Almost all our sample and practice questions are taken from actual previous exams. On the day of the exam you'll see how closely this book follows the format of the real test.

This book will give you confidence *now,* while you are preparing for the test. It will build your self-confidence as you proceed and will prevent the kind of test anxiety that causes low test scores.

This book stresses the multiple-choice type of question because that's the kind you'll have on your test. You must not be satisfied with merely knowing the correct answer for each question. You must find out why the other choices are incorrect. This will help you remember a lot you thought you had forgotten.

After testing yourself, you may find that you are weak in a particular area. You should concentrate on improving your skills by using the specific practice sections in this book that apply to you.

THE KIND OF WORK YOU WILL BE DOING

Nature of the Work

Every business needs systematic and up-to-date records of accounts and business transactions. Bookkeepers maintain these records in journals, ledgers, and on other accounting forms. They also prepare periodic financial statements showing all money received and paid out. The duties of bookkeepers vary with the size of the business.

In many small firms, there are only *general bookkeepers*. They analyze and record all financial transactions, such as orders and cash sales. They also check money taken in against that paid out to be sure accounts "balance," and calculate the firm's payroll. Although most of this work is done by hand, occasionally bookkeepers use simple office equipment such as adding machines. General bookkeepers also prepare and mail customers' bills and answer the telephone.

In large businesses, a number of bookkeepers and account clerks work under the direction of a head bookkeeper. Bookkeepers often specialize in certain types of work such as preparing statements on a company's income from sales or its daily operating expenses. They sometimes use complex bookkeeping machines to perform these duties. *Account clerks* perform a variety of routine duties. They record details of business transactions, including deductions from payrolls and bills paid and due. They also may type vouchers, invoices, and other financial records.

Places of Employment

Jobs for bookkeepers are found in all kinds of firms, with an especially large number in wholesale and retail trade. One of every three bookkeepers works for a retail store or wholesale firm. In addition, many work in factories, banks, insurance companies, hospitals, and schools.

Training, Other Qualifications, and Advancement

High school graduates who have taken business arithmetic, bookkeeping, and accounting meet the minimum requirements for most bookkeeping jobs. Some employers, however prefer applicants who have completed business courses at a junior college or business school.

Persons also may qualify for bookkeeping jobs through on-the-job training. In some areas, companies cooperate with business schools and high schools in work-study programs. These programs offer part-time experience that helps students get jobs soon after graduation.

Bookkeepers need above average aptitude for working with numbers and a knack for concentrating on details. They should be able to type and operate various office machines. Because they depend on other office workers for information , bookkeepers should be able to work as part of a team.

Newly hired bookkeepers begin by recording routine transactions. They advance to more responsible assignments, such as preparing income statements and operating complex bookkeeping machines. Some workers are promoted to supervisory jobs. Bookkeepers who complete courses in college accounting may become accountants.

Employment Outlook

Thousands of job openings for bookkeepers are expected every year for the occupation is large and turnover is high.

Future employment growth in this occupation will be slowed by the increasing use of electronic data processing and various types of bookkeeping machines. Many machines can process data more accurately, rapidly, and economically than workers doing it by hand. Nevertheless, need for bookkeepers is expected to outpace the impact of labor-saving office machines over the next decade.

Earnings and Working Conditions

Beginning account clerks in private firms average higher salaries than beginning file clerks or typists, but earn less than beginning secretaries or stenographers. Experienced account clerks earn about the same as the average for all nonsupervisory workers in private industry.

Starting salaries are higher for bookkeepers with at least 2 years' work experience or 2 years of college education than for bookkeepers right out of high school.

Working conditions for bookkeepers are similar to those of other office workers in the same firms.

ACCOUNT CLERK

OFFICIAL ANNOUNCEMENT

ACCOUNT CLERK

PROMOTION OPPORTUNITIES: Employees in the title of Account
Clerk are accorded promotion opportunities in the clerical-
administrative occupational group.

MINIMUM REQUIREMENTS: There are no formal education or experience requirements for this position.

DUTIES AND RESPONSIBILITIES: Under direct supervision, with
little latitude for independent or unreviewed action or decision,
performs computations and clerical work of ordinary difficulty
and responsibility related to financial records; performs
related work.

EXAMPLES OF TYPICAL TASKS: Performs computations and posts or
compiles financial data, as directed, for accounting or tax
purposes, or for calculating retirement allowances, balances,
loans, or refunds. Keeps general ledgers and controlling accounts
or subsidiary records used in accounting. Balances or adjusts
accounts. Makes journal entries or entries in registers. Assists
in processing invoices, vouchers, payrolls, fee collection reports,
or applications for retirement allowances, loans, transfers, and
refunds. Writes purchase orders, statements, or bills. Answers
inquiries over phone. Keeps records and makes reports as required.

TESTS: Written, weight 100, 70% required. The written test
will be of the multiple-choice type and may include questions on
arithmetic computations including problems involving ability to
understand basic bookkeeping principles; clerical accuracy;
reading comprehension; chart and table interpretation; coding;
alphabetic and numeric filing; and related areas.

Eligibles will be required to pass a qualifying medical test prior to appointment. Eligibles will be evaluated on the basis of the following medical standard:

1. A candidate may be rejected for any current illness, disease, abnormality, injury, or other disability or condition which will impair his ability to perform the duties of the class of positions.

2. ALCOHOL and DRUGS -- Excessive use of alcohol or abusive use of drugs or chemicals, which interferes with sensorium or other functions, rejects.

3. INFECTIOUS or COMMUNICABLE DISEASES -- Presence of, in an infectious or communicable stage, rejects.

4. VISION (NEAR) -- Inability to read the number 2 line on the Jaeger test chart or equivalent at approximately 30 centimeters, both eyes together, eyeglasses allowed, rejects.

APPLYING FOR CIVIL SERVICE POSITIONS

JOB OPENINGS

About seven million people are employed by our state and local departments and agencies—approximately 1,700,000 by the fifty states and over 5,200,000 by the thousands of local government units and school districts. The employment opportunities cover practically every skill and profession in our complex modern social order. Every year thousands of new jobs are created and tens of thousands of replacements are needed on existing jobs.

Most state and municipal units have recruitment procedures for filling civil service positions. They have developed a number of methods to make job opportunities known. Places where such information may be obtained include:

1. The offices of the State Employment Services. There are almost two thousand throughout the country. These offices are administered by the state in which they are located, with the financial assistance of the Federal government. You will find the address of the one nearest you in your telephone book.

2. Your state Civil Service Commission. Address your inquiry to the capital city of your state.

3. Your city Civil Service Commission—if you live in a large city. It is sometimes called by another name, such as the Department of Personnel, but you will be able to identify it in your telephone directory under the listing of city departments.

4. Your municipal building and your local library.

5. Complete listings are carried by the newspaper *The Chief* (published in New York City) as well as other city and statewide publications devoted to civil service employees. Many local newspapers run a section on regional civil service news.

6. State and local agencies looking for competent employees will contact schools, professional societies, veterans organizations, unions, and trade associations.

7. School Boards and Boards of Education, which employ the greatest proportion of all state and local personnel, should be asked directly for information about job openings.

The Job Announcement

WHAT IT CONTAINS

When a position is open and a civil service examination is to be given for it, a job announcement is drawn up. This generally contains just about everything an applicant has to know about the job.

The announcement begins with the job title and salary. A typical announcement then describes the work, the location of the position, the education and experience requirements, the kind of examination to be given, the system of rating. It may also have something to say about veteran preference and the age limit. It tells which application form is to be filled out, where to get the form, and where and when to file it.

Study the job announcement carefully. It will answer many of your questions and help you decide whether you like the position and are qualified for it.

WHERE THE JOB IS LOCATED

There is no point in applying for a position and taking the examination if you do not want to work where it is situated. The announcement gives you the information. The job may be in your community or hundreds of miles away at the other end of the state.

If a state job, be sure you are willing to work in the area indicated. If you are not, study other announcements that will give you an opportunity to work in a place of your choice.

A civil service job close to your home has as an additional advantage the fact that local residents usually receive preference in appointments.

THE DUTIES

The words *Optional Fields*—sometimes just the word *Options*—may appear on the front page of the announcement. You then have a choice to apply for that particular position in which you are especially interested. This is because the duties of various positions are quite different even though they bear the same broad title. A public relations *clerk,* for example, does different work from a payroll *clerk,* although they are considered broadly in the same general area.

Not every announcement has options. But whether or not it has them, the precise duties are described in detail, usually under the heading: *Description of Work.* Make sure that these duties come within the range of your experience and ability.

THE DEADLINE

Most job requirements give a deadline for filing an application. Others bear the words, *No Closing Date,* at the top of the first page; this means that applications will be accepted until the needs of the agency are met. In some cases a public notice is issued when a certain number of applications have been received.

No application mailed past the deadline date will be considered.

EDUCATION AND EXPERIENCE

Every announcement has a detailed section on education and experience requirements for the particular job and for the optional fields. Make sure that in both education and experience you meet the minimum qualifications. If you do not meet the given standards for one job, there may be others open where you stand a better chance of making the grade.

VETERAN PREFERENCE

If the job announcement does not mention veteran preference, it would be wise to inquire if there is such a provision in your state or municipality. There may be none or it may be limited to disabled veterans. In some jurisdictions widows of veterans are given preference. All such information can be obtained through the agency that issues the job announcement.

WHY YOU MAY BE BARRED

Applicants may be denied examinations and eligibles may be denied appointments for any of the following reasons:

  —intentional false statements;

  —deception or fraud in examination or appointment;

  —reasonable doubt concerning loyalty to the United States;

  —use of intoxicating beverages to excess;

  —criminal, infamous, dishonest, immoral, or notoriously disgraceful conduct.

THE TEST

The announcement describes the kind of test given for the particular position. Please pay special attention to this section. It tells what areas are to be covered in the written test and lists the specific subjects on which questions will be asked. Sometimes sample questions are given.

The test and review material in this Arco book are based on the requirements as given in this section as well as on actual tests.

Usually the announcement states whether the examination is to be assembled or unassembled. In an *assembled* examination applicants *assemble* in the same place at the same time to take a written or performance test. The unassembled examination is one where an applicant does not take a test; instead he is rated on his educaton and experience and whatever records of past achievement he is asked to provide.

The Application Form

On the whole, civil service application forms differ little from state to state and locality to locality. The questions, which have been worked out after years of experimentation, are simple and direct, designed to elicit a maximum of information about you.

Many prospective civil service employees have failed to get a job because of slipshod, erroneous, incomplete, misleading, or untruthful answers. Give the application the serious attention it must have as the first important step toward getting the job you want.

Here, along with some helpful comments, are the questions usually asked on the average application form, although not necessarily in this order.

THE QUESTIONS

Name of examination or kind of position applied for. This information appears in large type on the first page of the job announcement.

Optional job (if mentioned in the announcement). If you wish to apply for an option, simply copy the title from the announcement. If you are not interested in an option, write "None."

Primary place of employment applied for. This would pertain to a state-wide job. The location of the position was probably contained in the announcement. You must consider whether you want to work there. The announcement may list more than one location where the job is open. If you would accept employment in any of the places, list them all; otherwise list the specific place or places where you would be willing to work.

Name and Address. Give in full, including your middle name if you have one, and your maiden name as well if you are a married woman.

Home and Office phones. If none, write "None."

Legal or voting residence. The state in which you vote is the one you list here.

Married or single. If you are a widow or widower, you are considered single.

Birthplace. Changes in the borders of European countries make it difficult for many foreign-born American citizens to know which country to list as the land of their birth. One suggestion is to set down the name of the town and the name of the country which now controls it, together with the name of the country to which it belonged at the time of your birth.

Date of birth. Give the exact day, month, and year.

Lowest grade or pay you will accept. Although the salary is clearly stated in the job announcement, there may be a quicker opening in the same occupation but carrying less responsibility and thus a lower basic entrance salary. You will not be considered for a job paying less than the amount you give in answer to this question.

Will you accept temporary employment if offered you for (a) one month or less, (b) one to four months, (c) four to twelve months? Temporary positions come up frequently and it is important to know whether you are available.

Will you accept less than full-time employment? Part-time work comes up now and then. Consider whether you want to accept such a position while waiting for a full-time appointment.

Were you in active military service in the Armed Forces of the United States? Veterans' preference, if given, is usually limited to active service during the following periods: December 7, 1941 to September 2, 1945; June 26, 1950 to July 27, 1953; January 1, 1963 to March 29, 1973.

Do you claim disabled veterans credit? If you do, you have to show proof of a war-incurred disability. This is done through certification by the Veterans Administration.

Considerable space is allotted on the form for the applicant to tell about all his past employment. Examiners check all such answers closely. DO NOT embroider or falsify your record. If you were ever fired, say so. It is better for you to state this openly than for the examiners to find out the truth from your former employer.

Special qualifications and skills. Even though not directly related to the position for which you are applying, such information as licenses and certificates obtained for teacher, pilot, registered nurses, and so on is wanted. Also, experience in the use of machines and equipment, and a list of whatever other skills you have acquired. Also, published writings, public speaking experience, membership in professional societies, honors and fellowships received.

Education. List your entire educational history, including all diplomas degrees, special courses taken in any accredited or Armed Forces school. Also give your credits toward a college or a graduate degree.

References. The names of people who can give information about you, with their occupations and business and home addresses, are often requested.

Your health. Questions are asked concerning your medical record. You are expected to have the physical and psychological capacity to perform the job for which you are applying. Standards vary, of course, depending on the requirements of the position. A physical handicap will not bar an applicant from a job he can perform adequately.

THE EXAMINATIONS

When you have filled out the application as completely as possible, sign it and send it to the address given on the form. If your examination includes a written test, you must wait until it is scheduled. Shortly before it is to be held, you will be notified where and when to report.

YOU ARE TESTED

Sometimes the date of the written test appears on the job announcement. Sometimes it does not and you must simply wait until you receive notification of the time and place.

The period between the filing of the application and the taking of the test can be of immense value to you. If you use it wisely, it will help you score high.

The most important step you can take in preparing for your test is to study questions on previous tests—or questions similar to those asked on previous tests. The purpose of this book is to acquaint you with the kinds of questions that will be asked and to provide you with review material in the subjects that will be covered. A thorough knowledge of the forms of the actual test as well as of the subject matter will give you a great advantage. There are no substitutes for experience and familiarity.

THE DAY OF THE TEST

The importance of knowing beforehand exactly how to reach the test center and how to get there cannot be stressed enough. Lateness will bar you from taking the test. There is nothing more nerve-wracking than to find yourself in a traffic jam and on the wrong bus with little time to spare. If the test is to take place some distance from your house, make the trip a few days earlier to make sure you know how to get there. On the all-important day give yourself more than enough time. In this way you will avoid the risk of an upsetting experience under circumstances that may affect your final score.

THE ELIGIBLE LIST

When all the parts of the examination have been rated (this may include education, experience, and suitability along with the written test), you are notified of your *numerical* rating. If this is high enough to give you a passing mark, you are placed on the eligible list. Appointments are made from this list.

JOB INFORMATION CENTERS

The Office of Personnel Management offers Federal employment information through a nationwide network of Federal Job Information Centers.

For an answer to your questions about Federal employment, you can visit, write, or call the nearest Federal Job Information Center—the local address and telephone number are listed beside each city.

Some Job Information Centers provide information regarding jobs in other jurisdictions (city, county, or state). Those Intergovernmental Job Information Centers are identified below by a (●)

The Office of Personnel Management invites you to call and talk with our information specialists before writing a letter or filling out a job application. Information specialists can mail you job announcements, application forms, and pamphlets. A call can save you valuable time and effort.

Federal Job Information Centers are open to serve you Monday through Friday, except holidays.

Federal Job Information Centers

ALABAMA
Huntsville:
Southerland Building
806 Governors Dr, N.W. 35801
(205) 453-5070

ALASKA
Anchorage:
Federal Bldg. & U.S. Courthouse
701 C St., P.O. Box 22, 99513
(907) 271-5821

ARIZONA
Phoenix:
522 N. Central Ave. 85004
(602) 261-4736

ARKANSAS
Little Rock:
Federal Bldg. Rm. 1319
700 W. Capitol Ave. 72201
(501) 378-5842

CALIFORNIA
Los Angeles:
Linder Bldg.
845 S. Figueroa 90017
(213) 688-3360
Sacramento:
Federal Bldg., 650 Capitol Mall 95814
(916) 440-3441
San Diego:
880 Front St. 92188
(714) 293-6165
San Francisco:
Federal Bldg., Rm. 1001
450 Golden Ave. 94102
(415) 556-6667

COLORADO
● Denver:
1845 Sherman St., 80203
(303) 837-3506

CONNECTICUT
Hartford:
Federal Bldg., Rm. 717, 450 Main St. 06103
(203) 244-3096

DELAWARE
● Wilmington:
Federal Bldg., 844 King St. 19801
(302) 571-6288

DISTRICT OF COLUMBIA
Metro Area:
1900 E Street, N.W., 20415
(202) 737-9616

FLORIDA
● Miami:
1000 Brickell Ave., Suite 660, 33131
(305) 350-4725
● Orlando:
80 N. Hughey Ave. 32801
(305) 420-6148

GEORGIA
Atlanta:
Richard B. Russell Federal Bldg.,
75 Spring St. SW, 30303
(404) 221-4315

GUAM
Agana:
238 O'Hara St.
Room 308 96910
344-5242

HAWAII
Honolulu (and Island of Oahu):
Federal Bldg. Room 1310
300 Ala Moana Blvd. 96850
(808) 546-8600

IDAHO
Boise:
Box 035, Federal Bldg.,
550 W. Fort Street 83724
(208) 384-1726

ILLINOIS
Chicago:
Dirksen Bldg. Rm. 1322
219 S. Dearborn St. 60604
(312) 353-5136

INDIANA
Indianapolis:
46 East Ohio Street, Room 123, 46204
(317) 269-7161 or 7162

IOWA
Des Moines:
210 Walnut St., Rm. 191, 50309
(515) 284-4546

KANSAS
Wichita:

One-Twenty Bldg., Rm. 101,
120 S. Market St. 67202
(316) 267-6311, ext. 106

In Johnson and Wyandott Counties dial 374-5702

KENTUCKY
Louisville:

Federal Building
600 Federal Pl. 40202
(502) 582-5130

LOUISIANA
New Orleans:

F. Edward Hebert Bldg.,
610 South St., Rm 103 70130
(504) 589-2764

MAINE
Augusta:

Federal Bldg. Rm. 611
Sewall St. & Western Ave. 04330
(207) 622-6171 ext. 269

MARYLAND
Baltimore:

Garmatz Federal Building
101 W. Lombard St. 21201
(301) 962-3822

DC Metro Area:

1900 E St. N.W., 20415
(202) 737-9616

MASSACHUSETTS
Boston:

3 Center Plaza, 02108
(617) 223-2571

MICHIGAN
Detroit:

477 Michigan Ave, Rm. 595, 48226
(313) 226-6950

MINNESOTA
Twin Cities:

Federal Bldg.
Ft. Snelling, Twin Cities, 55111
(612) 725-3355

MISSISSIPPI
Jackson:

100 W. Capitol St. (Suite 102) 39201
(601) 969-4585.

MISSOURI
Kansas City:

Federal Bldg., Rm. 129
601 E. 12th St. 64106
(816) 374-5702

St. Louis:

Federal Bldg., Rm. 1712,
1520 Market St., 63103
(314) 425-4285

MONTANA
Helena:

Federal Bldg. & Courthouse
301 S. Park, Rm. 153 59601
(406) 449-5388

NEBRASKA
Omaha:

U.S. Courthouse and Post Office Bldg.
Rm. 1014, 215 N. 17th St. 68102
(402) 221-3815

NEVADA
● Reno:

Mill & S. Virginia Streets
P.O. Box 3296 89505
(702) 784-5535

NEW HAMPSHIRE
Portsmouth:

Federal Bldg. Rm. 104,
Daniel & Penhallow Streets, 03801
(603) 436-7720 ext. 762

NEW JERSEY
Newark:

Federal Bldg., 970 Broad St. 07102
(201) 645-3673

In Camden, dial (215) 597-7440

NEW MEXICO
Albuquerque:

Federal Bldg. 421 Gold Ave. SW, 87102
(505) 766-2557

NEW YORK
Bronx:

590 Grand Concourse, 10451
(212) 292-4666

Buffalo:

111 W. Huron St, Rm. 35, 14202
(716) 846-4001

Jamaica:

90-04 161st St., Rm. 200, 11432
(212) 526-6192

New York City:

Federal Bldg., 26 Federal Plaza, 10007
(212) 264-0422

Syracuse:

100 S. Clinton St. 13260
(315) 423-5660

NORTH CAROLINA
Raleigh:

Federal Bldg. 310 New Bern Ave.
P.O. Box 25069, 27611
(919) 755-4361

NORTH DAKOTA
Fargo:

Federal Bldg, Rm. 202
657 Second Ave. N. 58102
(701) 237-5771 ext. 363

OHIO
Cleveland:
Federal Bldg., 1240 E. 9th St., 44199
(216) 522-4232

Dayton:
Federal Building Lobby
200 W 2nd St., 45402
(513) 225-2720 and 2854

OKLAHOMA
Oklahoma City:
200 NW Fifth St, 73102
(405) 231-4948

OREGON
Portland:
Federal Bldg., Lobby (North)
1220 SW Third St. 97204
(503) 221-3141

PENNSYLVANIA
● Harrisburg:
Federal Bldg., Rm. 168, 17108
(717) 782-4494
Philadelphia:
Wm. J. Green, Jr. Fed. Bldg,
600 Arch Street, 19106
(215) 597-7440
Pittsburgh:
Fed. Bldg. 1000 Liberty Ave., 15222
(412) 644-2755

PUERTO RICO
San Juan:
Federico Degetau Federal Bldg.
Carlos E. Chardon St.,
Hato Rey, P.R. 00918
(809) 753-4209, ext. 209

RHODE ISLAND
Providence:
Federal & P.O. Bldg., Rm. 310
Kennedy Plaza 02903
(401) 528-4447

SOUTH CAROLINA
Charleston:
Federal Bldg., 334 Meeting St., 29403
(803) 724-4328

SOUTH DAKOTA
Rapid City:
Rm. 201, Federal Building
U.S. Court House, 515 9th St. 57701
(605) 348-2221

TENNESSEE
Memphis:
Federal Bldg., 167 N. Main St. 38103
(901) 521-3956

TEXAS
Dallas:
Rm. 1C42, 1100 Commerce St., 75242
(214) 749-7721
El Paso:
Property Trust Bldg.—Suite N302
2211 E. Missouri Ave. 79903
(915) 543-7425
Houston:
702 Caroline Street, 77002
(713) 226-5501
San Antonio:
643 E. Durango Blvd., 78205
(512) 229-6600

UTAH
Salt Lake City:
350 South Main St. Rm 484, 84101
(801) 524-5744

VERMONT
Burlington:
Federal Bldg., Rm. 614
P.O. Box 489
Elmwood Ave. & Pearl St., 05402
(802) 862-6712

VIRGINIA
Norfolk:
Federal Bldg., Rm. 220,
200 Granby Mall, 23510
(804) 441-3355
D.C. Metro Area:
1900 E Street, N.W. 20415
(202) 737-9616

WASHINGTON
● Seattle:
Federal Bldg., 915 Second Ave. 98174
(206) 442-4365

WEST VIRGINIA
● Charleston:
Federal Bldg., 500 Quarrier St. 25301
(304) 343-6181, ext. 226

WISCONSIN
Milwaukee:
Plankinton Bldg., Rm. 205,
161 W. Wisconsin Ave. 53203
(414) 244-3761

WYOMING
Cheyenne:
2120 Capitol Ave., Rm. 304
P.O. Box 967 82001
(307) 778-2220, ext. 2108

TECHNIQUES OF STUDY AND TEST-TAKING

Although a thorough knowledge of the subject matter is the most important factor in succeeding on your exam, the following suggestions could raise your score substantially. These few pointers will give you the strategy employed on tests by those who are most successful in this not-so-mysterious art. It's really quite simple. Do things right . . . right from the beginning. Make these successful methods a habit. Then you'll get the greatest dividends from the time you invest in this book.

PREPARING FOR THE EXAM

1. *Budget your time.* Set aside definite hours each day for concentrated study. Keep to your schedule.

2. *Study alone.* You will concentrate better when you work by yourself. Keep a list of questions you cannot answer and points you are unsure of to talk over with a friend who is preparing for the same exam. Plan to exchange ideas at a joint review session just before the test.

3. *Eliminate distractions.* Disturbances caused by family and neighbor activities (telephone calls, chit-chat, TV programs, etc.) work to your disadvantage. Study in a quiet, private room.

4. *Use the library.* Most colleges and universities have excellent library facilities. Some institutions have special libraries for the various subject areas: physics library, education library, psychology library, etc. Take full advantage of such valuable facilities. The library is free from those distractions that may inhibit your home study. Moreover, research in your subject area is more convenient in a library since it can provide more study material than you have at home.

5. *Answer all the questions in this book.* Don't be satisfied merely with the correct answer to each question. Do additional research on the other choices which are given. You will broaden your background and be more adequately prepared for the "real" exam. It's quite possible that a question on the exam which you are going to take may require you to be familiar with the other choices.

6. *Get the "feel" of the exam.* The sample questions which this book contains will give you that "feel" since they are virtually the same as those you will find on the test.

7. *Take the Sample Tests as "real" tests.* With this attitude, you will derive greater benefit. Put yourself under strict examination conditions. Tolerate no interruptions while you are taking the sample tests. Work steadily. Do not spend too much time on any one question. If a question seems too difficult go to the next one. If time permits, go back to the omitted question.

8. *Tailor your study to the subject matter. Skim or scan.* Don't study everything in the same manner. Obviously, certain areas are more important than others.

9. *Organize yourself.* Make sure that your notes are in good order—valuable time is unnecessarily consumed when you can't find quickly what you are looking for.

10. *Keep physically fit.* You cannot retain information well when you are uncomfortable, headachy, or tense. Physical health promotes mental efficiency.

HOW TO TAKE AN EXAM

1. *Get to the Examination Room about Ten Minutes Ahead of Time.* You'll get a better start when you are accustomed to the room. If the room is too cold, or too warm, or not well ventilated, call these conditions to the attention of the person in charge.

2. *Make Sure that You Read the Instructions Carefully.* In many cases, test-takers lose credits because they misread some important point in the given directions—example: the *incorrect* choice instead of the *correct* choice.

3. *Be Confident.* Statistics conclusively show that high scores are more likely when you are prepared. It is important to know that you are not expected to answer every question correctly. The questions usually have a range of difficulty and differentiate between several levels of skill.

4. *Skip Hard Questions and Go Back Later.* It is a good idea to make a mark on the question sheet next to all questions you cannot answer easily, and to go back to those questions later. First answer the questions you are sure about. Do not

panic if you cannot answer a question. Go on and answer the questions you know. Usually the easier questions are presented at the beginning of the exam and the questions become gradually more difficult.

If you do skip ahead on the exam, be sure to skip ahead also on your answer sheet. A good technique is periodically to check the number of the question on the answer sheet with the number of the question on the test. You should do this every time you decide to skip a question. If you fail to skip the corresponding answer blank for that question, all of your following answers will be wrong.

Each student is stronger in some areas than in others. No one is expected to know all the answers. Do not waste time agonizing over a difficult question because it may keep you from getting to other questions that you can answer correctly.

5. *Guess If You Are Not Sure.* No penalty is given for guessing when these exams are scored. Therefore, it is better to guess than to omit an answer

6. *Mark the Answer Sheet Clearly.* When you take the examination, you will mark your answers to the multiple-choice questions on a separate answer sheet that will be given to you at the test center. If you have not worked with an answer sheet before, it is in your best interest to become familiar with the procedures involved. Remember, knowing the correct answer is not enough! If you do not mark the sheet correctly, so that it can be machine-scored, you will not get credit for your answers!

In addition to marking answers on the separate answer sheet, you will be asked to give your name and other information, including your social security number. As a precaution bring along your social security number for identification purposes.

Read the directions carefully and follow them exactly. If they ask you to print your name in the boxes provided, write only one letter in each box. If your name is longer than the number of boxes provided, omit the letters that do not fit. Remember, you are writing for a machine; it does not have judgment. It can only record the pencil marks you make on the answer sheet.

Use the answer sheet to record all your answers to questions. Each question, or item, has four or five answer choices labeled (A), (B), (C), (D), (E). You will be asked to choose the letter that stands for the best answer. Then you will be asked to mark your answer by blackening the appropriate space on your answer sheet. Be sure that each space you choose and blacken with your pencil is *completely* blackened. The machine will "read" your answers in terms of spaces blackened. Make sure that only one answer is clearly blackened. If you erase an answer, erase it completely and mark your new answer clearly. The machine will give credit only for clearly marked answers. It does not pause to decide whether you really meant (B) or (C).

Make sure that the number of the question you are being asked on the question sheet corresponds to the number of the question you are answering on the answer sheet. It is a good idea to check the numbers of questions and answers frequently. If you decide to skip a question, but fail to skip the corresponding answer blank for that question, all your answers after that will be wrong.

7. *Read Each Question Carefully.* The exam questions are not designed to trick you through misleading or ambiguous alternative choices. On the other hand, they are not all direct questions of factual information. Some are designed to elicit responses that reveal your ability to reason, or to interpret a fact or idea. It's up to you to read each question carefully, so you know what is being asked. The exam authors have tried to make the questions clear. Do not go astray looking for hidden meanings.

8. *Don't Answer Too Fast.* The multiple-choice questions which you will meet are not superficial exercises. They are designed to test not only your memory but also your understanding and insight. Do not place too much emphasis on speed. The time element is a factor, but it is not all-important. Accuracy should not be sacrificed for speed.

9. *Materials and Conduct at the Test Center.* You need to bring with you to the test center your Admission Form, your social security number, and several No. 2 pencils. Arrive on time as you may not be admitted after testing has begun. Instructions for taking the tests will be read to you by the test supervisor and time will be called when the test is over. If you have questions, you may ask them of the supervisor. Do not give or receive assistance while taking the exams. If you do, you will be asked to turn in all test materials and told to leave the room. You will not be permitted to return and your tests will not be scored.

PART ONE

Sample Examinations for Practice

SAMPLE ANSWER SHEET FOR EXAMINATION I

1 Ⓐ Ⓑ Ⓒ Ⓓ   17 Ⓐ Ⓑ Ⓒ Ⓓ   33 Ⓐ Ⓑ Ⓒ Ⓓ   49 Ⓐ Ⓑ Ⓒ Ⓓ   65 Ⓐ Ⓑ Ⓒ Ⓓ

2 Ⓐ Ⓑ Ⓒ Ⓓ   18 Ⓐ Ⓑ Ⓒ Ⓓ   34 Ⓐ Ⓑ Ⓒ Ⓓ   50 Ⓐ Ⓑ Ⓒ Ⓓ   66 Ⓐ Ⓑ Ⓒ Ⓓ

3 Ⓐ Ⓑ Ⓒ Ⓓ   19 Ⓐ Ⓑ Ⓒ Ⓓ   35 Ⓐ Ⓑ Ⓒ Ⓓ   51 Ⓐ Ⓑ Ⓒ Ⓓ   67 Ⓐ Ⓑ Ⓒ Ⓓ

4 Ⓐ Ⓑ Ⓒ Ⓓ   20 Ⓐ Ⓑ Ⓒ Ⓓ   36 Ⓐ Ⓑ Ⓒ Ⓓ   52 Ⓐ Ⓑ Ⓒ Ⓓ   68 Ⓐ Ⓑ Ⓒ Ⓓ

5 Ⓐ Ⓑ Ⓒ Ⓓ   21 Ⓐ Ⓑ Ⓒ Ⓓ   37 Ⓐ Ⓑ Ⓒ Ⓓ   53 Ⓐ Ⓑ Ⓒ Ⓓ   69 Ⓐ Ⓑ Ⓒ Ⓓ

6 Ⓐ Ⓑ Ⓒ Ⓓ   22 Ⓐ Ⓑ Ⓒ Ⓓ   38 Ⓐ Ⓑ Ⓒ Ⓓ   54 Ⓐ Ⓑ Ⓒ Ⓓ   70 Ⓐ Ⓑ Ⓒ Ⓓ

7 Ⓐ Ⓑ Ⓒ Ⓓ   23 Ⓐ Ⓑ Ⓒ Ⓓ   39 Ⓐ Ⓑ Ⓒ Ⓓ   55 Ⓐ Ⓑ Ⓒ Ⓓ   71 Ⓐ Ⓑ Ⓒ Ⓓ

8 Ⓐ Ⓑ Ⓒ Ⓓ   24 Ⓐ Ⓑ Ⓒ Ⓓ   40 Ⓐ Ⓑ Ⓒ Ⓓ   56 Ⓐ Ⓑ Ⓒ Ⓓ   72 Ⓐ Ⓑ Ⓒ Ⓓ

9 Ⓐ Ⓑ Ⓒ Ⓓ   25 Ⓐ Ⓑ Ⓒ Ⓓ   41 Ⓐ Ⓑ Ⓒ Ⓓ   57 Ⓐ Ⓑ Ⓒ Ⓓ   73 Ⓐ Ⓑ Ⓒ Ⓓ

10 Ⓐ Ⓑ Ⓒ Ⓓ   26 Ⓐ Ⓑ Ⓒ Ⓓ   42 Ⓐ Ⓑ Ⓒ Ⓓ   58 Ⓐ Ⓑ Ⓒ Ⓓ   74 Ⓐ Ⓑ Ⓒ Ⓓ

11 Ⓐ Ⓑ Ⓒ Ⓓ   27 Ⓐ Ⓑ Ⓒ Ⓓ   43 Ⓐ Ⓑ Ⓒ Ⓓ   59 Ⓐ Ⓑ Ⓒ Ⓓ   75 Ⓐ Ⓑ Ⓒ Ⓓ

12 Ⓐ Ⓑ Ⓒ Ⓓ   28 Ⓐ Ⓑ Ⓒ Ⓓ   44 Ⓐ Ⓑ Ⓒ Ⓓ   60 Ⓐ Ⓑ Ⓒ Ⓓ   76 Ⓐ Ⓑ Ⓒ Ⓓ

13 Ⓐ Ⓑ Ⓒ Ⓓ   29 Ⓐ Ⓑ Ⓒ Ⓓ   45 Ⓐ Ⓑ Ⓒ Ⓓ   61 Ⓐ Ⓑ Ⓒ Ⓓ   77 Ⓐ Ⓑ Ⓒ Ⓓ

14 Ⓐ Ⓑ Ⓒ Ⓓ   30 Ⓐ Ⓑ Ⓒ Ⓓ   46 Ⓐ Ⓑ Ⓒ Ⓓ   62 Ⓐ Ⓑ Ⓒ Ⓓ   78 Ⓐ Ⓑ Ⓒ Ⓓ

15 Ⓐ Ⓑ Ⓒ Ⓓ   31 Ⓐ Ⓑ Ⓒ Ⓓ   47 Ⓐ Ⓑ Ⓒ Ⓓ   63 Ⓐ Ⓑ Ⓒ Ⓓ   79 Ⓐ Ⓑ Ⓒ Ⓓ

16 Ⓐ Ⓑ Ⓒ Ⓓ   32 Ⓐ Ⓑ Ⓒ Ⓓ   48 Ⓐ Ⓑ Ⓒ Ⓓ   64 Ⓐ Ⓑ Ⓒ Ⓓ   80 Ⓐ Ⓑ Ⓒ Ⓓ

ACCOUNT CLERK

SAMPLE EXAMINATION I

The time allowed for the entire examination is 4 hours. In order to create the climate of the test to come, that's precisely what you should allow yourself . . . no more, no less. Use a watch and keep a record of your time, especially since you may find it convenient to take the test in several sittings.

Questions 1 through 5 are based on the extracts from Federal income tax withholding and social security tax tables shown below. These tables indicate the amounts which must be withheld from the employee's salary by his employer for Federal income tax and for social security. They are based on weekly earnings.

INCOME TAX WITHHOLDING TABLE						
The wages are		And the number of withholding allowances is				
At least	But less than	5	6	7	8	9	10 or more
		The amount of income tax to be withheld shall be				
$190	$200	$7.90	$5.00	$2.10	0	0	0
$200	$210	$9.40	$6.50	$3.60	.80	0	0
$210	$220	$10.90	$8.00	$5.10	$2.30	0	0
$220	$230	$12.50	$9.50	$6.60	$3.80	.90	0
$230	$240	$14.30	$11.00	$8.10	$5.30	$2.40	0
$240	$250	$16.10	$12.60	$9.60	$6.80	$3.90	$1.00
$250	$260	$17.90	$14.40	$11.10	$8.30	$5.40	$2.50
$260	$270	$19.70	$16.20	$12.70	$9.80	$6.90	$4.00
$270	$280	$21.50	$18.00	$14.50	$11.30	$8.40	$5.50
$280	$290	$23.30	$19.80	$16.30	$12.90	$9.90	$7.00
$290	$300	$25.10	$21.60	$18.10	$14.70	$11.40	$8.50

SOCIAL SECURITY TAX TABLE					
Wages		Tax to be withheld	Wages		Tax to be withheld
At least	But less than		At least	But less than	
$220.08	$220.22	$14.64	$221.58	$221.72	$14.74
$220.23	$220.37	$14.65	$221.73	$221.87	$14.75
$220.38	$220.52	$14.66	$221.88	$222.02	$14.76
$220.53	$220.67	$14.67	$222.03	$222.17	$14.77
$220.68	$220.82	$14.68	$222.18	$222.32	$14.78
$220.83	$220.97	$14.69	$222.33	$222.47	$14.79
$220.98	$221.12	$14.70	$222.48	$222.62	$14.80
$221.13	$221.27	$14.71	$222.63	$222.67	$14.81
$221.28	$221.42	$14.72	$222.68	$222.82	$14.82
$221.43	$221.57	$14.73	$222.83	$222.87	$14.83

1. If an employee has a weekly wage of $241.50 and claims 6 withholding allowances, the amount of income tax to be withheld is

   (A) $11.00   (B) $12.60   (C) $17.90   (D) $9.60

2. An employee had wages of $222.00 for one week. With eight withholding allowances claimed, how much income tax will be withheld from his salary?

   (A) $2.30   (B) $3.80   (C) 0   (D) $9.50

3. How much social security tax will an employee with weekly wages of $220.25 pay?

   (A) $14.66   (B) $14.64   (C) $14.65   (D) $14.67

4. Mr. Wise earns $222.50 a week and claims seven withholding allowances. What is his take-home pay after income tax and social security tax are deducted?

   (A) $199.70   (B) $201.10   (C) $210.20   (D) $200.60

5. If a City employee pays $14.73 in social security tax and claims eight withholding allowances, the amount of income tax that should be withheld from his wages is

   (A) $8.10   (B) $3.80   (C) $6.80   (D) $5.30

6. A fundamental rule of bookkeeping states that an individual's assets equal his liabilities plus his proprietorship (ASSETS = LIABILITIES + PROPRIETORSHIP). Which of the following statements logically follows from this rule?

   (A) ASSETS = PROPRIETORSHIP - LIABILITIES.
   (B) LIABILITIES = ASSETS + PROPRIETORSHIP.
   (C) PROPRIETORSHIP = ASSETS - LIABILITIES.
   (D) PROPRIETORSHIP = LIABILITIES + ASSETS.

7. Mr. Martin's assets consist of the following:

> Cash on hand: $ 5,233.74
> Automobile: $ 3,206.09
> Furniture: $ 4,925.00
> Government Bonds: $ 5,500.00
> House: $36,690.85

What are his total assets?

(A) $54,545.68   (B) $54,455.68   (C) $55,455.68   (D) $55,555.68

8. If Mr. Mitchell has $627.04 in his checking account and then writes three checks for $241.75, $13.24 and $102.97, what will be his new balance?

(A) $257.88   (B) $269.08   (C) $357.96   (D) $369.96

9. An employee's net pay is equal to his total earnings less all deductions. If an employee's total earnings in a pay period are $497.05, what is his net pay if he has the following deductions: Federal income tax, $90.32; FICA, $33.05 State tax, $18.79; City tax, $7.25; Pension, $1.88?

(A) $345.16   (B) $354.17   (C) $345.67   (D) $345.76

10. A petty cash fund had an opening balance of $85.75 on December 1, 198–. Expenditures of $23.00, $15.65, $5.23, $14.75 and $26.38 were made out of this fund during the first 14 days of the month. Then on December 17 another $38.50 was added to the fund. If additional expenditures of $17.18, $3.29 and $11.64 were made during the remainder of the month, what was the final balance of the petty cash fund at the end of December?

(A) $6.93   (B) $7.13   (C) $46.51   (D) $91.40

Answer questions 11 through 15 on the basis of the following instructions.

The chart below is used by the loan division of a City retirement system for the following purposes: (1) to calculate the monthly payment a member must pay on an outstanding loan; (2) to calculate how much a member owes on an outstanding loan after he has made a number of payments.

To calculate the amount a member must pay each month in repaying his loan, look at Column II on the chart. You will notice that each entry in Column II corresponds to a number appearing under the "Months" column; for example, 1.004868 corresponds to 1 month, 0.503654 corresponds to 2 months, etc. To calculate the amount a member must pay each month, use the following procedure: multiply the amount of the loan by the entry in Column II which corresponds to the number of months over which the loan will be paid back. For example, if a loan of $200 is taken out for six months, multiply $200 by 0.169518, the entry in Column II which corresponds to six months.

In order to calculate the balance still owed on an outstanding loan, multiply the monthly payment by the number in Column I which corresponds to the number of monthly payments which remain to be paid on the loan. For example, if a member is supposed to pay $106.00 a month for twelve months, after seven payments, five monthly payments remain. To calculate the balance owed on the loan at this point, multiply the $106.00 monthly payment by 4.927807, the number in Column I that corresponds to five months.

MONTHS	COLUMN I	COLUMN II
1	0.995156	1.004868
2	1.985491	0.503654
3	2.971029	0.336584
4	3.951793	0.253050
5	4.927807	0.202930
6	5.899092	0.169518
7	6.865673	0.145652
8	7.827572	0.127754
9	8.784811	0.113833
10	9.737414	0.102697
11	10.685402	0.093586
12	11.628798	0.085993
13	12.567624	0.079570
14	13.501902	0.074064
15	14.431655	0.069292

11. If Mr. Carson borrows $1,500 for eight months, how much will he have to pay back each month?

(A) $187.16   (B) $191.63   (C) $208.72   (D) $218.65

12. If a member borrows $2,400 for one year, the amount he will have to pay back each month is

(A) $118.78   (B) $196.18   (C) $202.28   (D) $206.38

13. Mr. Elliot borrowed $1,700 for a period of fifteen months. Each month he will have to pay back

(A) $117.80   (B) $116.96   (C) $107.79   (D) $101.79

14. Mr. Aylward is paying back a thirteen-month loan at the rate of $173.13 a month. If he has already made six monthly payments, how much does he owe on the outstanding loan?

(A) $1,027.39   (B) $1,178.75   (C) $1,188.65   (D) $1,898.85

15. A loan was taken out for 15 months, and the monthly payment was $104.75. After two monthly payments, how much was still owed on this loan?

(A) $515.79   (B) $863.89   (C) $1,116.76   (D) $1,316.46

16. One year the ABC Corporation had a gross income of $125,500.00. Of this, it paid 60% for overhead. The following year the gross income increased by $6,500 and the cost of overhead increased to 61% of gross income. How much more did it pay for overhead in the second year than in the first?

    (A) $1,320.00   (B) $5,220.00   (C) $7,530.00   (D) $8,052.00

17. After one year, Mr. Richards paid back a total of $1,695.00 as payment for a $1,500.00 loan. All the money paid over $1,500.00 was simple interest. The interest charge was most nearly

    (A) 13%   (B) 11%   (C) 9%   (D) 7%

18. A checking account has a balance of $253.36. If deposits of $36.95, $210.23, and $7.34 and withdrawals of $117.35, $23.37 and $15.98 are made, what is the new balance of the account?

    (A) $155.54   (B) $351.18   (C) $364.58   (D) $664.58

19. The Weelkes Realty Company spends 27% of its income on rent . If it earns $97,254.00, the amount it pays for rent is

    (A) $26,258.58   (B) $26,348.58   (C) $27,248.58   (D) $27,358.58

20. Twelve percent simple annual interest on $1,218.09 is most nearly

    (A) $145.08   (B) $145.17   (C) $146.08   (D) $146.17

21. Assume that the XYZ Company has $10,402.72 cash on hand. If it pays $699.83 of this for rent, the amount of cash on hand would be

    (A) $9,792.89   (B) $9,702.89   (C) $9,692.89   (D) $9,602.89

22. On January 31, Mr. Warren's checking account had a balance of $933.68. If he deposited $36.40 on February 2, $126.00 on February 9, and $90.02 on February 16 and wrote no checks during this period, what was the balance of his account on February 17?

    (A) $680.26   (B) $681.26   (C) $1,186.10   (D) $1,187.00

Questions 23 through 32 below present the identification numbers, initials, and last names of employees enrolled in a city retirement system. You are to choose the option (A, B, C, or D) that has the identical identification number, initials and last name as those given in each question.

SAMPLE QUESTION:

B145698 JL Jones

A) B146798 JL Jones
B) B145698 JL Jonas
C) P145698 JL Jones
D) B145698 JL Jones

The correct answer is D. Only option D shows the identification number, initials and last name exactly as they are in the sample question. Options A, B and C have errors in the identification number or last name.

23.   J297483 PL Robinson

A) J294783 PL Robinson
B) J297483 PL Robinson
C) J297483 PI Robinson
D) J297843 PL Robinson

24.   S497662 JG Schwartz

A) S497662 JG Schwarz
B) S497762 JG Schwartz
C) S497662 JG Schwartz
D) S497663 JG Schwartz

25.   G696436 LN Alberton

A) G696436 LM Alberton
B) G696436 LN Albertson
C) G696346 LN Albertson
D) G696436 LN Alberton

26.   R774923 AD Aldrich

A) R774923 AD Aldrich
B) R744923 AD Aldrich
C) R774932 AP Aldrich
D) R774932 AD Allrich

27.   N239638 RP Hrynyk

A) N236938 PR Hrynyk
B) N236938 RP Hrynyk
C) N239638 PR Hrynyk
D) N239638 RP Hrynyk

28.   R156949 LT Carlson

A) R156949 LT Carlton
B) R156494 LT Carlson
C) R159649 LT Carlton
D) R156949 LT Carlson

29. **T**524697 MN Orenstein

    A) T524697 MN Orenstein
    B) T524967 MN Orinstein
    C) T524697 NM Ornstein
    D) T524967 NM Orenstein

30. L346239 JD Remsen

    A) L346239 JD Remson
    B) L364239 JD Remsen
    C) L346329 JD Remsen
    D) L346239 JD Remsen

31. P966438 SB Rieperson

    A) P996438 SB Reiperson
    B) P966438 SB Reiperson
    C) R996438 SB Rieperson
    D) P966438 SB Rieperson

32. D749382 CD Thompson

    A) P749382 CD Thompson
    B) D749832 CD Thomsonn
    C) D749382 CD Thompson
    D) D749823 CD Thomspon

33. Multiplying a number by .75 is the same as

    (A) multiplying it by 2/3   (C) multiplying it by 3/4
    (B) dividing it by 2/3   (D) dividing it by 3/4

34. In City Agency A, 2/3 of the employees are enrolled in a retirement system. City Agency B has the same number of employees as Agency A, and 60% of these are enrolled in a retirement system. If Agency A has a total of 660 employees, how many more employees does it have enrolled in a retirement system than does Agency B?

    (A) 36   (B) 44   (C) 56   (D) 66

35. Net Worth is equal to Assets minus Liabilities. If, at the end of the year, a textile company had assets of $98,695.83 and liabilities of $59,238.29, what was its net worth?

    (A) $38,478.54   (B) $38,488.64   (C) $39,457.54   (D) $48,557.54

Assume that each of the capital letters in the table below represents the name of an employee enrolled in a city employees' retirement system. The number directly beneath the letter represents the agency for which the employee works, and the small letter directly beneath represents the code for the employee's account.

Name of Employee	L	O	T	Q	A	M	R	N	C
Agency	3	4	5	9	8	7	2	1	6
Account Code	r	f	b	i	d	t	g	e	n

In each of the following questions 36 through 45, the agency code numbers and the account code letters in Columns 2 and 3 should correspond to the capital letters in Column 1 and should be in the same consecutive order. For each question, look at each column carefully and mark your answer as follows:

If there are one or more errors in Column 2 only, mark your answer A.
If there are one or more errors in Column 3 only, mark your answer B.
If there are one or more errors in Column 2 and one or more errors in Column 3, mark your answer C.
If there are no errors in either column, mark your answer D.

The following sample question is given to help you understand the procedure.

SAMPLE QUESTION:

Column 1	Column 2	Column 3
T Q L M O C	5 8 3 7 4 6	b i r t f n

In Column 2, the second agency code number (corresponding to letter Q) should be "9", not "8". Column 3 is coded correctly to Column 1. Since there is an error only in Column 2, the correct answer is A.

	Column 1	Column 2	Column 3
36.	Q L N R C A	9 3 1 2 6 8	i r e g n d
37.	N R M O T C	1 2 7 5 4 6	e g f t b n
38.	R C T A L M	2 6 5 8 3 7	g n d b r t
39.	T A M L O N	5 7 8 3 4 1	b d t r f e
40.	A N T O R M	8 1 5 4 2 7	d e b i g t
41.	M R A L O N	7 2 8 3 4 1	t g d r f e
42.	C T N Q R O	6 5 7 9 2 4	n d e i g f
43.	Q M R O T A	9 7 2 4 5 8	i t g f b d
44.	R Q M C O L	2 9 7 4 6 3	g i t n f r
45.	N O M R T Q	1 4 7 2 5 9	e f t g b i

Questions __46__ through __50__ are to be answered solely on the basis of the following passage.

A city may issue its own bonds or it may purchase bonds as an investment. Bonds may be issued in various denominations, and the face value of the bond is its par value. Before purchasing a bond, the investor desires to know the rate of income that the investment will yield. In computing the yield on a bond, it is assumed that the investor will keep the bond until the date of maturity, except for callable bonds which are not considered in this passage. To compute exact yield is a complicated mathematical problem, and scientifically prepared tables are generally used to avoid such computation. However, the approximate yield can be computed much more easily. In computing approximate yield, the accrued interest on the date of purchase should be ignored, because the buyer who pays accrued interest to the seller receives it again at the next interest date. Bonds bought at a premium (which cost more) yield a lower rate of income than the same bonds bought at par (face value), and bonds bought at a discount (which cost less) yield a higher rate of income than the same bonds bought at par.

46. An investor bought a $10,000 City bond paying 6% interest. Which of the following purchase prices would indicate that the bond was bought at a premium?

    (A) $9,000   (B) $9,400   (C) $10,000   (D) $10,600

47. One year, a particular $10,000 bond paying 7 1/2% sold at fluctuating prices. Which of the following prices would indicate that the bond was bought at a discount?

    (A) $9,800   (B) $10,000   (C) $10,200   (D) $10,750

48. A certain group of bonds was sold in denominations of $5,000, $10,000, $20,000, and $50,000. In the following list of four purchase prices, which one is most likely to represent a bond sold at par value?

    (A) $10,500   (B) $20,000   (C) $22,000   (D) $49,000

49. When computing the approximate yield on a bond, it is desirable to

    (A) assume the bond was purchased at par
    (B) consult scientifically prepared tables
    (C) ignore accrued interest on the date of purchase
    (D) wait until the bond reaches maturity.

50. Which of the following is most likely to be an exception to the information provided in the above passage?

    (A) Bonds purchased at a premium.
    (B) Bonds sold at par.
    (C) Bonds sold before maturity.
    (D) Bonds which are callable.

Questions 51 through 56 consist of computations of addition, subtraction, multiplication, and division. For each question, do the computation indicated, and choose the correct answer from the four choices given.

51. Add   8936   (A) 45371   (C) 46371
                7821   (B) 45381   (D) 46381
                8953
                4297
                9785
                6579

52. Subtract   95,432   (A) 27,836   (C) 27,936
                67,596   (B) 27,846   (D) 27,946

53. Multiply   987   (A) 854609   (C) 855709
                867   (B) 854729   (D) 855729

54. Divide   59)321439.0   (A) 5438.1   (C) 5448.1
                                        (B) 5447.1   (D) 5457.1

55. Divide   .057)721   (A) 12,648.0   (C) 12,649.0
                                        (B) 12,648.1   (D) 12,649.1

56. Add   1/2 + 5/7 =   (A) 1 3/14   (C) 1 5/14
                                        (B) 1 2/7   (D) 1 3/7

57. If the total number of employees in one city agency increased from 1,927 to 2,006 during a certain year, the percentage increase in the number of employees for that year is most nearly

     (A) 4%   (B) 5%   (C) 6%   (D) 7%

58. During a single fiscal year, which totaled 248 workdays, one Account Clerk verified 1,488 purchase vouchers. Assuming a normal work week of five days, what is the average number of vouchers verified by the Account Clerk in a one-week period during this fiscal year?

     (A) 25   (B) 30   (C) 35   (D) 40

59. If the City Department of Purchase bought 190 manual typewriters for $79.35 each and 208 manual typewriters for $83.99 each, the total price paid for these manual typewriters is

     (A) $31,581.30   (B) $32,546.42   (C) $33,427.82   (D) $33,586.30

Answer questions <u>60</u> through <u>64</u> on the basis of the information given in the paragraph below.

Since discounts are in common use in the commercial world and apply to purchases made by government agencies as well as business firms, it is essential that individuals in both public and private employment who prepare bills, check invoices, prepare payment vouchers, or write checks to pay bills have an understanding of the terms used. These include cash or time discount, trade discount, and discount series. A cash or time discount offers a reduction in price to the buyer for the prompt payment of the bill and is usually expressed as a percentage with a time requirement, stated in days, within which the bill must be paid in order to earn the discount. An example would be 3/10, meaning a 3% discount may be applied to the bill if the payment is forwarded to the vendor within ten days. On an invoice the cash discount terms are usually followed by the net terms, which is the time in days allowed for ordinary payment of the bill. Thus, 3/10, Net 30 means that full payment is expected in thirty days if the cash discount of 3% is not taken for having paid the bill within ten days. When the expression Terms Net Cash is listed on a bill it means that no deduction for early payment is allowed. A trade discount is normally applied to list prices by a manufacturer to show the actual price to retailers so that they may know their cost and determine markups that will allow them to operate competitively and at a profit. A trade discount is applied by the seller to the list price and is independent of a cash or time discount. Discounts may also be used by manufacturers to adjust prices charged to retailers without changing list prices. This is usually done by series discounting and is expressed as a series of percentages. To compute a series discount, such as 40%, 20%, 10%, first apply the 40% discount to the list price, then apply the 20% discount to the remainder, and finally apply the 10% discount to the second remainder.

60. According to the above passage, trade discounts are

(A) applied by the buyer
(B) independent of cash discounts
(C) restricted to cash sales
(D) used to secure rapid payment of bills.

61. According to the above passage, if the sales terms 5/10, Net 60 appear on a bill in the amount of $100 dated December 5, 198- and the buyer submits his payment on December 15, 198-, his proper payment should be

(A) $60   (B) $90   (C) $95   (D) $100.

62. According to the above passage, if a manufacturer gives a trade discount of 40% for an item with a list price of $250 and the terms are Net Cash, the price a retail merchant is required to pay for this item is

(A) $250   (B) $210   (C) $150   (D) $100.

63. According to the above passage, a series discount of 25%, 20%, 10% applied to a list price of $200 results in an actual price to the buyer of

(A) $88   (B) $90   (C) $108   (D) $110.

64. According to the above passage, if a manufacturer gives a trade discount of 50% and the terms are 6/10, Net 30, the cost to a retail merchant of an item with a list price of $500 and for which he takes the time discount is

(A) $220   (B) $235   (C) $240   (D) $250.

Questions 65 through 72 each show in Column I the information written on five cards (lettered j, k, l, m, n) which have to be filed. You are to choose the option (lettered A, B, C, or D) in Column II which best represents the proper order of filing according to the information, rules, and sample question given below.

A file card record is kept of the work assignments for all the employees in a certain bureau. On each card is the employee's name, the date of work assignment, and the work assignment code number. The cards are to be filed according to the following rules:

First: File in alphabetical order according to employee's name.

Second: When two or more cards have the same employee's name, file according to the assignment date beginning with the earliest date.

Third: When two or more cards have the same employee's name and the same date, file according to the work assignment number beginning with the lowest number.

Column II shows the cards arranged in four different orders. Pick the option (A, B, C, or D) in Column II which shows the correct arrangement of the cards according to the above filing rules.

SAMPLE QUESTION:

Column I

(j) Cluney 4/8/80 (486503)
(k) Roster 5/10/79 (246611)
(l) Altool 10/15/80 (711433)
(m) Cluney 12/18/80 (527610)
(n) Cluney 4/8/80 (486500)

Column II

(A) k, l, m, j, n
(B) k, n, j, l, m
(C) l, k, j, m, n
(D) l, n, j, m, k

The correct way to file the cards is:

(l) Altool 10/15/80 (711433)
(n) Cluney 4/8/80 (486500)
(j) Cluney 4/8/80 (486503)
(m) Cluney 12/18/80 (527610)
(k) Roster 5/10/79 (246611)

The correct filing order is shown by the letters l, n, j, m, k. The answer to the sample question is the letter (D), which appears in front of the letters l, n, j, m, k in Column II.

Now answer the following questions using the same procedure.

	Column I			Column II

65.
- (j) Smith 3/19/79 (662118)
- (k) Turner 4/16/75 (481349)
- (1) Terman 3/20/80 (210229)
- (m) Smyth 3/20/80 (481359)
- (n) Terry 5/11/77 (672128)

(A) j, m, 1, n, k
(B) j, 1, n, m, k
(C) k, n, m, 1, j
(D) j, n, k, 1, m

66.
- (j) Ross 5/29/80 (396118)
- (k) Rosner 5/29/80 (439281)
- (1) Rose 7/19/80 (723456)
- (m) Rosen 5/29/81 (829692)
- (n) Ross 5/29/80 (399118)

(A) 1, m, k, n, j
(B) m, 1, k, n, j
(C) 1, m, k, j, n
(D) m, 1, j, n, k

67.
- (j) Sherd 10/12/81 (552368)
- (k) Snyder 11/12/81 (539286)
- (1) Shindler 10/13/80 (426798)
- (m) Scherld 10/12/81 (552386)
- (n) Schneider 11/12/81 (798213)

(A) n, m, k, j, 1
(B) j, m, 1, k, n
(C) m, k, n, j, 1
(D) m, n, j, 1, k

68.
- (j) Carter 1/16/80 (489636)
- (k) Carson 2/16/79 (392671)
- (1) Carter 1/16/79 (486936)
- (m) Carton 3/15/78 (489639)
- (n) Carson 2/16/79 (392617)

(A) k, n, j, 1, m
(B) n, k, m, 1, j
(C) n, k, 1, j, m
(D) k, n, 1, j, m

69.
- (j) Thomas 3/18/79 (763182)
- (k) Tompkins 3/19/80 (928439)
- (1) Thomson 3/21/80 (763812)
- (m) Thompson 3/18/79 (924893)
- (n) Tompson 3/19/79 (928793)

(A) m, 1, j, k, n
(B) j, m, 1, k, n
(C) j, 1, n, m, k
(D) 1, m, j, n, k

70.
- (j) Breit 8/10/79 (345612)
- (k) Briet 5/21/76 (837543)
- (1) Bright 9/18/75 (931827)
- (m) Breit 3/7/74 (553984)
- (n) Brent 6/14/80 (682731)

(A) m, j, n, k, 1
(B) n, m, j, k, 1
(C) m, j, k, 1, n
(D) j, m, k, 1, n

71.
- (j) Roberts 10/19/78 (581932)
- (k) Rogers 8/9/76 (638763)
- (1) Rogerts 7/15/73 (105689)
- (m) Robin 3/8/68 (287915)
- (n) Rogers 4/2/80 (736921)

(A) n, k, 1, m, j
(B) n, k, 1, j, m
(C) k, n, 1, m, j
(D) j, m, k, n, 1

72.
(j)	Hebert	4/28/76	(719468)	(A) n, k, j, m, l
(k)	Herbert	5/8/75	(938432)	(B) j, l, n, k, m
(1)	Helbert	9/23/78	(832912)	(C) l, j, k, n, m
(m)	Herbst	7/10/77	(648599)	(D) l, j, n, k, m
(n)	Herbert	5/8/75	(487627)	

73. In order to pay its employees, the Ajax Company obtained bills and coins in the following denominations:

Denomination	$20	$10	$5	$1	$.50	$.25	$.10	$.05	$.01
Number	317	122	38	73	69	47	39	25	36

What was the total amount of cash obtained?

(A) $7,874.76   (B) $7,878.00   (C) $7,889.25   (D) $7,924.35

74. G. Allison receives a weekly gross salary (before deductions) of $198.75. Through weekly payroll deductions of $6.59, he is paying back a loan he took from his pension fund. If other fixed weekly deductions amount to $61.38, how much pay would Mr. Allison take home over a period of 33 weeks?

(A) $3,815.64   (B) $4,125.23   (C) $4,315.74   (D) $6,558.75

75. Mr. Robertson is a city employee enrolled in a city retirement system. He has taken out a loan from the retirement fund and is paying it back at the rate of $14.90 every two weeks. In eighteen weeks, how much money will he have paid back on the loan?

(A) $268.20   (B) $152.80   (C) $134.10   (D) $67.05

76. One year the Aubrey Book Company had the following expenses: rent, $6,500; overhead, $52,585; inventory, $35,700; and miscellaneous, $1,275. If all of these expenses went up 18% the following year, what would the new total be?

(A) $17,290.80   (B) $78,769.20   (C) $96,060.00   (D) $113,350.80

77. Ms. Hollander had a gross salary of $355.36, paid once every two weeks. If the deductions from each pay check are $62.72, $25.13, $6.29, and $1.27, how much money would Ms. Hollander take home in eight weeks?

(A) $1,039.80   (B) $1,421.44   (C) $2,079.60   (D) $2,842.88

78. Mr. Jones had a net income of $9,550. If he spent 34% on rent and household expenses, 3% on house furnishings, 25% on clothes and 36% on food, how much was left for savings and other expenses?

(A) $98.00   (B) $191.00   (C) $324.70   (D) $980.00

79. Mr. Edwards can pay back a loan of $1,800 from a city employees' retirement system if he pays back $36.69 every two weeks for two full years. At the end of the two years, how much more than the original $1,800 he borrowed will Mr. Edwards have paid back?

    (A) $53.94　　　　(B) $107.88　　　　(C) $190.79　　　　(D) $214.76

80. Mr. Nelson is a city employee, receiving a yearly gross salary (salary before deductions) of $10,400. Every two weeks the following deductions are taken out of his salary: Federal Income Tax, $81.32; FICA, $22.13; State Tax, $14.86; City Tax, $6.97; Health Insurance, $1.57. If Mr. Nelson's salary and deductions remained the same for a full calendar year, what would his net salary (gross salary less deductions) be in that year?

    (A) $3,298.10　　　　(B) $7,101.90　　　　(C) $9,372.75　　　　(D) $10,273.15

Answer Key

1.B	11.B	21.B	31.D	41.D	51.C	61.C	71.D
2.B	12.D	22.C	32.C	42.C	52.A	62.C	72.B
3.C	13.A	23.B	33.C	43.D	53.D	63.C	73.A
4.B	14.C	24.C	34.B	44.A	54.C	64.B	74.C
5.B	15.D	25.D	35.C	45.D	55.D	65.A	75.C
6.C	16.B	26.A	36.D	46.D	56.A	66.C	76.D
7.D	17.A	27.D	37.C	47.A	57.A	67.D	77.A
8.B	18.B	28.D	38.B	48.B	58.B	68.C	78.B
9.D	19.A	29.A	39.A	49.C	59.B	69.B	79.B
10.B	20.D	30.D	40.B	50.D	60.B	70.A	80.B

SAMPLE ANSWER SHEET FOR EXAMINATION II

Part 1

1 Ⓐ Ⓑ Ⓒ Ⓓ Ⓔ	11 Ⓐ Ⓑ Ⓒ Ⓓ Ⓔ	21 Ⓐ Ⓑ Ⓒ Ⓓ Ⓔ	31 Ⓐ Ⓑ Ⓒ Ⓓ Ⓔ	41 Ⓐ Ⓑ Ⓒ Ⓓ Ⓔ
2 Ⓐ Ⓑ Ⓒ Ⓓ Ⓔ	12 Ⓐ Ⓑ Ⓒ Ⓓ Ⓔ	22 Ⓐ Ⓑ Ⓒ Ⓓ Ⓔ	32 Ⓐ Ⓑ Ⓒ Ⓓ Ⓔ	42 Ⓐ Ⓑ Ⓒ Ⓓ Ⓔ
3 Ⓐ Ⓑ Ⓒ Ⓓ Ⓔ	13 Ⓐ Ⓑ Ⓒ Ⓓ Ⓔ	23 Ⓐ Ⓑ Ⓒ Ⓓ Ⓔ	33 Ⓐ Ⓑ Ⓒ Ⓓ Ⓔ	43 Ⓐ Ⓑ Ⓒ Ⓓ Ⓔ
4 Ⓐ Ⓑ Ⓒ Ⓓ Ⓔ	14 Ⓐ Ⓑ Ⓒ Ⓓ Ⓔ	24 Ⓐ Ⓑ Ⓒ Ⓓ Ⓔ	34 Ⓐ Ⓑ Ⓒ Ⓓ Ⓔ	44 Ⓐ Ⓑ Ⓒ Ⓓ Ⓔ
5 Ⓐ Ⓑ Ⓒ Ⓓ Ⓔ	15 Ⓐ Ⓑ Ⓒ Ⓓ Ⓔ	25 Ⓐ Ⓑ Ⓒ Ⓓ Ⓔ	35 Ⓐ Ⓑ Ⓒ Ⓓ Ⓔ	45 Ⓐ Ⓑ Ⓒ Ⓓ Ⓔ
6 Ⓐ Ⓑ Ⓒ Ⓓ Ⓔ	16 Ⓐ Ⓑ Ⓒ Ⓓ Ⓔ	26 Ⓐ Ⓑ Ⓒ Ⓓ Ⓔ	36 Ⓐ Ⓑ Ⓒ Ⓓ Ⓔ	46 Ⓐ Ⓑ Ⓒ Ⓓ Ⓔ
7 Ⓐ Ⓑ Ⓒ Ⓓ Ⓔ	17 Ⓐ Ⓑ Ⓒ Ⓓ Ⓔ	27 Ⓐ Ⓑ Ⓒ Ⓓ Ⓔ	37 Ⓐ Ⓑ Ⓒ Ⓓ Ⓔ	47 Ⓐ Ⓑ Ⓒ Ⓓ Ⓔ
8 Ⓐ Ⓑ Ⓒ Ⓓ Ⓔ	18 Ⓐ Ⓑ Ⓒ Ⓓ Ⓔ	28 Ⓐ Ⓑ Ⓒ Ⓓ Ⓔ	38 Ⓐ Ⓑ Ⓒ Ⓓ Ⓔ	48 Ⓐ Ⓑ Ⓒ Ⓓ Ⓔ
9 Ⓐ Ⓑ Ⓒ Ⓓ Ⓔ	19 Ⓐ Ⓑ Ⓒ Ⓓ Ⓔ	29 Ⓐ Ⓑ Ⓒ Ⓓ Ⓔ	39 Ⓐ Ⓑ Ⓒ Ⓓ Ⓔ	49 Ⓐ Ⓑ Ⓒ Ⓓ Ⓔ
10 Ⓐ Ⓑ Ⓒ Ⓓ Ⓔ	20 Ⓐ Ⓑ Ⓒ Ⓓ Ⓔ	30 Ⓐ Ⓑ Ⓒ Ⓓ Ⓔ	40 Ⓐ Ⓑ Ⓒ Ⓓ Ⓔ	50 Ⓐ Ⓑ Ⓒ Ⓓ Ⓔ

Part 2

51. _____	55. _____	59. _____	63. _____	67. _____	71. _____
52. _____	56. _____	60. _____	64. _____	68. _____	72. _____
53. _____	57. _____	61. _____	65. _____	69. _____	73. _____
54. _____	58. _____	62. _____	66. _____	70. _____	74. _____

BOOKKEEPER

SAMPLE EXAMINATION II

The time allowed for the entire examination is 3 hours. In order to create the climate of the test to come, that's precisely what you should allow yourself . . . no more, no less. Use a watch and keep a record of your time, especially since you may find it convenient to take the test in several sittings.

Part 1

1. Of the following taxes, the one which is levied most nearly in accordance with ability to pay is
   (A) an excise tax
   (B) an income tax
   (C) a general property tax
   (D) a sales tax

2. When a check has been lost, the bank on which it is drawn should ordinarily be notified and instructed to
   (A) stop payment on the check
   (B) issue a duplicate of the check
   (C) charge the account of the drawer for the amount of the check
   (D) certify the check

3. The amounts of the transactions recorded in a journal are transferred to the general ledger accounts by a process known as

   (A) auditing
   (B) balancing
   (C) posting
   (D) verifying

4. Sales minus cost of goods sold equals
   (A) net profit
   (B) gross sales
   (C) gross profit
   (D) net sales

5. The chief disadvantage of single-entry bookkeeping is that it
   (A) is too difficult to operate
   (B) is illegal for income tax purposes
   (C) provides no possibility of determining net profits
   (D) furnishes an incomplete picture of the business

6. The phrase "3%—10 days" on an invoice ordinarily means that
   (A) 3% of the amount must be paid each 10 days
   (B) the purchaser is entitled to only ten days credit
   (C) a discount of 3% will be allowed for payment in 10 days
   (D) the entire amount must be paid in 10 days or a penalty of 3% of the amount due will be added

7. A firm which voluntarily terminates business, selling its assets and paying its liabilities, is said to be in
   (A) receivership
   (B) liquidation
   (C) depletion
   (D) amortization

8. Many business firms provide a petty cash fund from which to pay for small items in order to avoid the issuing of many small checks. If this fund is replenished periodically to restore it to its original amount, the fund is called
   (A) an imprest fund
   (B) a debenture fund
   (C) an adjustment fund
   (D) an expense reserve fund

9. Many business firms maintain a book of original entry in which all bills to be paid are recorded. This book is known as a
   (A) purchase returns journal
   (B) subsidiary ledger
   (C) voucher register
   (D) notes payable register

10. A trial balance will *not* indicate that an error has been made in
    (A) computing the balance of an account
    (B) entering an amount in the wrong account
    (C) carrying forward the balance of an account
    (D) entering an amount on the wrong side of an account

11. When an asset is depreciated on the straight-line basis, the amount charged off for depreciation
    (A) is greater in the earlier years of the asset's life
    (B) is greater in the later years of the asset's life
    (C) varies each year according to the extent to which the asset is used during the year
    (D) is equal each full year of the asset's life

12. The essential nature of an asset is that
    (A) it must be tangible
    (B) it must be easily converted into cash
    (C) it must have value
    (D) its cost must be included in the profit and loss statement

13. A controlling account
    (A) contains the totals of the accounts used in preparing the balance sheet at the end of the fiscal period
    (B) contains the totals of the individual amounts entered in the accounts of a subsidiary ledger during the fiscal period
    (C) contains the totals of all entries in the General Journal during the fiscal period
    (D) contains the totals of the accounts used in preparing the profit and loss statement for the fiscal period

14. A trial balance is a
    (A) list of the credit balances in all accounts in a General Ledger
    (B) list of all General Ledger accounts and their balances
    (C) list of the asset accounts in a General Ledger and their balances
    (D) list of the liability accounts in a General Ledger and their balances

15. An accounting system which records revenues as soon as they are earned and records liabilities as soon as they are incurred regardless of the date of payment, is said to operate on
    (A) an accrual basis
    (B) a budgetary basis
    (C) an encumbrance basis
    (D) a cash basis

16. The term "current assets" usually includes such things as
    (A) notes payable
    (B) machinery and equipment
    (C) furniture and fixtures
    (D) accounts receivable

17. The one of the following which is never properly considered a negotiable instrument is
    (A) an invoice
    (B) a bond
    (C) a promissory note
    (D) an endorsed check

18. A statement of the assets, liabilities and net worth of a business is called
    (A) a trial balance
    (B) a budget
    (C) a profit and loss statement
    (D) a balance sheet

19. A subsidiary ledger contains accounts which show
    (A) details of contingent liabilities of undetermined amount
    (B) totals of all asset accounts in the General Ledger
    (C) totals of all liability accounts in the General Ledger
    (D) details of an account in the General Ledger

20. Modern accounting practice favors the valuation of the inventories of a going concern at
    (A) current market prices, if higher than cost
    (B) cost or market, whichever is lower
    (C) estimated selling price
    (D) probable value at forced sale

Questions 21 to 35 consist of a list of some of the accounts in a general ledger.

Indicate whether each account listed generally contains a debit or credit balance by putting the letter D (for debit balance) or the letter C (for credit balance) in the correspondingly numbered space on your answer sheet for each account listed. For example, for the account Cash which generally contains a debit balance, you would give the letter D as your answer.

21. Sales Taxes Collected
22. Social Security Taxes Paid by Employer
23. Deposits from Customers
24. Freight Inward
25. Sales Discount
26. Withholding Taxes Payable
27. W. Jones, Drawings
28. Office Salaries
29. Merchandise Inventory
30. W. Jones, Capital
31. Purchases Returns
32. Unearned Rent Income
33. Reserve for Bad Debts
34. Depreciation of Machinery
35. Insurance Prepaid

Questions 36 to 50 consist of a list of some of the accounts in a General Ledger. For the purpose of preparing financial statements, each of these accounts is to be classified into one of the following five major classifications, lettered A to E as follows:

    (A) Assets
    (B) Liabilities
    (C) Proprietorship
    (D) Income
    (E) Expense

You are to indicate the classification to which each account belongs by printing the correct letter, A, B, C, D or E, in the correspondingly numbered space on your answer sheet. For example, for the account Furniture and Fixtures, which is an asset account, you would print the letter A.

36. Notes Receivable
37. Sales
38. Wages Payable
39. Office Salaries
40. Capital Stock Authorized
41. Goodwill
42. Capital Surplus
43. Office Supplies Used
44. Interest Payable
45. Prepaid Rent
46. Interest Cost
47. Accounts Payable
48. Prepaid Insurance
49. Merchandise Inventory
50. Interest Earned

Answer Key

1. B	6. C	11. D	16. D	21. C	26. C	31. C	36. A	41. A	46. E
2. A	7. B	12. C	17. A	22. D	27. D	32. C	37. D	42. C	47. B
3. C	8. A	13. B	18. D	23. C	28. D	33. C	38. B	43. C	48. A
4. C	9. C	14. B	19. D	24. D	29. D	34. D	39. E	44. B	49. A
5. D	10. B	15. A	20. B	25. D	30. C	35. D	40. C	45. A	50. D

Part 2

(Each question in Part II is double weight. Detailed explanatory answers of Questions 51 to 74 will be found at the end of the test.)

Below is a list of accounts in our general ledger with a number in front of each account:

1. Accounts Receivable
2. Accounts Payable
3. Bad Debts Expense
4. Cash
5. Delivery Equipment
6. Depreciation of Delivery Equipment
7. Discount on Purchases
8. Discount on Sales
9. Furniture and Fixtures
10. Insurance Prepaid
11. Interest Cost
12. Interest Income
13. J. Klein, Capital
14. J. Klein, Drawings
15. Notes Receivable
16. Notes Receivable Discounted
17. Notes Payable
18. Purchases
19. Purchases Returns
20. Reserve for Bad Debts
21. Reserve for Depreciation of Delivery Equipment
22. Sales
23. Sales Returns
24. Sales Taxes Payable

Using the number in front of each account title (using only the accounts listed), make journal entries for the transactions given below in questions 51 to 65. Do not write the names of the accounts on your answer sheet. Simply indicate in the correspondingly numbered space on your answer sheet, the numbers of the accounts to be debited or credited. Always give the number or numbers of accounts to be *debited* first, then give the number or numbers of accounts to be *credited*. For example, if Delivery Equipment is to be debited and Cash and Accounts Payable are to be credited, write on your answer sheet 5—4, 2 *(use a dash to separate the debits from the credits)*.

51. M. Landes, a customer, sent us a check for $392, the payment for a $400 invoice less a 2% discount.

52. We bought a safe costing $600 and paid $200 in cash and gave a 60-day note for the balance.

53. We returned damaged goods to A. Wilson and received a credit memorandum from him for $35.

54. We sold merchandise to J. Brill on account for $300 and also charged him $9 for Sales Tax.

55. B. Fried's 60-day note for $500, which was discounted by us at our bank last month, was paid by him today.

56. We accepted A. Wilson's trade acceptance for $1,200 for merchandise bought from him last week.

57. H. Marks & Company sent us a check for $12 for a discount we had failed to take when we paid him last week.

58. We took home merchandise for our own use amounting to $35.

59. We paid our 60-day note in favor of S. Berg for $700 plus interest of $7.

60. We paid an insurance bill today, amounting to $270, for a three-year policy for fire insurance on the furniture and fixtures.

61. H. Kahn sent us a check for $380 and returned $20 in merchandise in settlement of our invoice of $400 of last month.

62. We inherited $5,000 and invested it in the business.

63. We discounted at the bank M. Lipton's interest bearing note for $1,000, given to us by him last month, and received credit for $1,003 from the bank.

64. We set up a Reserve for Bad Debts of $1,500 at the end of the year.

65. We set up depreciation amounting to $400, on the delivery equipment.

You are to answer Questions 66 to 75 by putting the numerical answer to each question in the correspondingly numbered space on your answer sheet. Do all calculations on the scratch paper furnished you. Put only the answer, in ink, on the answer sheet. Note that only the answers you put on the answer sheet will be rated.

66. A certain correctly totalled Cash Receipts Journal contained the following columns: Net Cash, Accounts Receivable, Sales Discounts, and General. At the end of January the totals of the columns were as follows: Net Cash, $15,255.75; Accounts Receivable, $11,145.85; Sales Discounts (not given); General, $4,375.30.

What was the total of the Sales Discounts column?

67. A certain correctly totalled Cash Payments Journal contained the following columns: Net Cash, Accounts Payable, Purchase Discounts, General. At the end of January the totals of the columns were as follows: Net Cash, $11,247.60; Accounts Payable (not given); Purchase Discounts, $346.70; General, $4,740.65.

What was the total of the Accounts Payable column?

68. On January 1, the debit balance of the Accounts Receivable account in a General Ledger was $7,134.65. For the month of January, the Sales Journal total amounted to $6,347.30; the Accounts Receivable column in the Cash Receipts Journal amounted to $5,260.85; the total of the Returned Sales Journal for January amounted to $239.50; and the General column in the Cash Receipts Journal showed that $800 had been received in January on notes received from customers and entered in previous months.

What was the balance in the Accounts Receivable account at the end of January?

69. On January 1, the balance of the Accounts Payable account in a General Ledger was $5,264.75. At the end of January, the Purchase Journal showed a total of $8,190.42; the Cash Payments Journal showed a total for the Accounts Payable column amounting to $5,170.40; the Returned Purchases Journal for January amounted to $469.72 and the General Journal showed that $1,275 in notes had been given to creditors in January.

What was the balance in the Accounts Payable account at the end of January?

70. In a certain city the tax rate on real estate was $42.50 per thousand of assessed valuation. An apartment house in that city is assessed for $125,000.

How much must the owner of the house pay for the real estate tax?

71. In a certain business, the cash sales for the year were $38,000 and the charge sales were $70,000. The gross profit on all sales was $29,160.

What was the percent of gross profit for the year?

72. One year, a man employed 40 persons. His total payroll for that year amounted to $120,650. He was obliged to pay 3.625% as employer's share of union health benefits on all earnings of his employees up to $4,800 per employee. Ten of his employees earned $5000 each that year. All the others earned less than $4,800 each.

How much did this employer have to pay as employer's share of union health benefits on employees' salaries for that year?

73. On December 31, 198—, A. Brill's capital was $12,600. His partner, W. Simon, had a capital of $21,000. They were to share profits in proportion to balances in their respective Capital accounts at the end of the year. The net profit for the year amounted to $15,200.

What was A. Brill's share of the profits?

74. On December 31st, you discounted a customer's 60 day non-interest bearing note at your bank. The face of the note was $1,020 and it was dated December 7th. The discount rate was 6%.

What was the amount of the net proceeds? (use 360-day year.)

Explanatory Answers

Part 2

51. 4, 8–1. The asset Cash and the expense, Discount on Sales, are increased; the asset, Accounts Receivable, is decreased.

52. 9–4, 17. The asset, Furniture and Fixtures, was increased; to do this, another asset, Cash, was decreased and the liability, Notes Payable, increased.

53. 2–19. This reduces the liability, Accounts Payable and increases the income (or negative expense) account, Purchases Returns.

54. 1–22, 24. The receivables asset is increased by $309; but only $300 of this is sales income, and $9 is recorded as a liability to pay taxes.

55. 16–15. Fried's payment removes our liability to the bank for the discounted note as well as our asset of the note receivable from Fried.

56. 2–17. The account payable liability was removed, and replaced by the liability to pay a note.

57. 4–7. The asset Cash is increased; so is the income account, Discount on Purchases.

58. 14–18. The Drawings account is debited for the reduction of owner's equity in the business; Purchases is credited because it represents merchandise purchased for sale and included the original purchase of this merchandise, as a debit.

59. 17, 11–4. A liability, Notes Payable, is reduced by $700; the expense, Interest Cost, is increased by $7; the asset Cash is reduced by $707.

60. 10–4. The Prepaid Insurance asset is increased by the three-year premium amount; the asset Cash is decreased. (When the books are closed at the end of the year, the part of the premium covering the current year will be transferred to an insurance expense account and Prepaid Insurance reduced by that amount.)

61. 4, 23–1. Cash is increased by $380; the expense (or negative income) account, Sales Returns, is increased by $20; Accounts Receivable is reduced by $400.

62. 4, 13. The asset Cash is increased, as is the owner's equity represented by the J. Klein, Capital, account.

63. 4–16, 12. Cash is increased by $1,003; we are assuming a contingent liability (Notes Receivable Discounted) to pay the bank if Lipton does not, $1,000; and are receiving interest so far accumulated on the note. (Notice that we make no entry affecting the Notes Receivable account in which Lipton's note to us is included. When Lipton pays the bank, which will inform us of the payment, our entry will be similar to the one in question 55.

64. 3–20. The estimated losses are debited to the Bad Debts Expense account and increase the credit balance in the Reserve account which serves to adjust the value of the asset Accounts Receivable.

65. 6–21. The estimated reduction in value of the asset is recorded in the expense (Depreciation) account as a debit; it also increases the amount in the Reserve account which adjusts the value of the Delivery Equipment assets.

66. $265.40. The Cash Receipts Journal *debit* columns are for cash and the expense account, Sales Discount. The *credit* columns are for reductions of Accounts Receivable and credits to miscellaneous General Ledger accounts. The debits and credits must be equal as follows:

Cash, DR	15,255.75	
Sales Discount, DR	265.40	15,521.15
		debit totals
Accounts Receivable, CR	11,145.85	
General Ledger, CR	4,375.30	15,521.15
		credit totals

67. $6,853.65. The Cash Payments Journal *debit* columns are for reductions in Accounts Payable and debits to miscellaneous General Ledger accounts. The *credit* columns are for cash paid out and income resulting from taking purchase discounts. Debits and credits equate as follows:

Accounts Payable, DR	6,853.65	
General Ledger, DR	4,740.65	11,594.30
		debit totals
Purchase Discounts, CR	346.70	
Cash, CR	11,247.60	11,594.30
		credit totals

68. The debit balance in Accounts Receivable is $7,981.60, as follows:

Jan. 1 Balance	7,134.65	
31 Sales	6,347.30	
Total debits	13,481.95	
Jan. 31 Cash Rec.	5,260.85	
31 Ret. Sales	239.50	
Total credits	5,500.35	

The General column showing $800 receipts against customers' *notes* does not enter into the figures above, since these were receipts against notes *taken and entered* in previous months, at which time they would have decreased Accounts Receivable and increased Notes Receivable. Since the question does not mention any notes received in *January* to settle any accounts receivable, we must assume there were none.

69. The credit balance in Accounts Payable is $6,540.05, as follows:

Jan. 31 Cash Paym.	5,170.40	
31 Ret. Purch.	469.72	
31 Gen. Journal	1,275.00	
Total debits	6,915.12	
Jan. 1 Balance	5,264.75	
31 Purchases	8,190.42	
Total credits	13,455.17	

Note the difference between this question and #68 with respect to current month's notes issued to settle open accounts. The $1,275.00 debit is offset by a corresponding credit to Notes Payable.

70. $5,312.50. ($42.50, the rate per thousand, times 125, the number of thousands of dollars of assessed value).

71. $$\frac{\text{Gross profit}}{\text{Total sales}} \quad \frac{\$ 29,160}{\$108,000} = 27\%$$

72. $4,301.06, as follows:

Total gross payroll	$120,650
Deduct: Not subjected to payment (10 employees × $200 each, excess earnings over $4,800)	2,000
Payroll subject to payment	$118,650

Employer's share is $118,650 × 3.625%, or $4,301.06.

73.

A Brill, Capital	$12,600	37.5%
W. Simon, Capital	21,000	62.5%
Total capital	$33,600	100.0%

Brill's share of profits = 37.5% of $15,200 = $5,700
Simon's share of profits = 62.5% of $15,200 = 9,500
Total profit $15,200

74. 24 days (December 31 minus December 7) of the 60 days to maturity have expired. The bank discounts the note for the remaining 36 days, the period for which it is lending us the money. Using the 6% 60-day method, we know that interest on $1,020 for 60 days is $10.20. Since 36 days is 6/10 of 60, 36 days' interest is 6/10 of $10.20, or $6.12, which the bank deducts from the $1,020.00 face, giving a net proceeds of $1,013.88.

SAMPLE ANSWER SHEET FOR EXAMINATION III

1. _____
2. _____
3. _____
4. _____
5. _____
6. _____
7. _____
8. _____
9. _____
10. _____
11. _____
12. _____
13. _____
14. _____
15. _____
16. _____
17. _____
18. _____
19. _____
20. _____
21. _____
22. _____
23. _____

24. _____
25. _____
26. _____
27. _____
28. _____
29. _____
30. _____
31. _____
32. _____
33. _____
34. _____
35. _____
36. _____
37. _____
38. _____
39. _____
40. _____
41. _____
42. _____
43. _____
44. _____
45. _____
46. _____

47. _____
48. _____
49. _____
50. _____
51. _____
52. _____
53. _____
54. _____
55. _____
56. _____
57. _____
58. _____
59. _____
60. _____
61. _____
62. _____
63. _____
64. _____
65. _____
66. _____
67. _____
68. _____
69. _____

70. _____
71. _____
72. _____
73. _____
74. _____
75. _____
76. _____
77. _____
78. _____
79. _____
80. _____
81. _____
82. _____
83. _____
84. _____
85. _____
86. _____
87. _____
88. _____
89. _____
90. _____

BOOKKEEPER

SAMPLE EXAMINATION III

The time allowed for the entire examination is 3 hours. In order to create the climate of the test to come, that's precisely what you should allow yourself . . . no more, no less. Use a watch and keep a record of your time, especially since you may find it convenient to take the test in several sittings.

The material following refers to the first 25 questions.

1. Below you will find the general ledger balances on February 28, 1980, in the books of A. Morton.

2. Following it you will find all the entries on the books of A. Morton for the month of March of the same year.

3. You are to supply the new balances for the accounts called for at the end of March 31 of that year.

4. Note should be taken that the accounts have not been arranged in the customary trial balance form.

The correct balances in the general ledger of A. Morton on February 28 were as follows:

Cash	$4336
Accounts Receivable	8165
Notes Receivable	2200
Furniture and Fixtures	9000

Merchandise Inventory	
1/1/80	4175
Accounts Payable	5560
Notes Payable	1500
Reserve for Depreciation of	
Furniture and Fixtures	1800
A. Morton, Capital	14162
A. Morton, Drawing	900
Purchases	42600
Freight In	36
Rent	1750
Light	126
Telephone	63
Salaries	4076
Shipping Expenses	368
Sales	53200
Sales Discount	637
Purchase Discount	596
City Sales Tax	
Collected	804
Social Security Taxes	
Payable	96
Withholding Taxes Payable	714

CASH RECEIPTS

Date	Name	Net Cash	Accounts Receivable	Sales Discount	Miscellaneous Account	Amount
1980						
3/1	S. Klein	6027.00	6150.00	123.00		
3/3	L. Brown	1015.00			Notes Rec.	1000.00
					Int. Income	15.00
3/10	M. Sanders	3969.00	4050.00	81.00		
3/17	Rebuilt Desk Co.	45.00			Furn. & Fixt.	45.00
3/24	J. Walters	2910.00	3000.00	90.00		
3/31	Corn Exch. Bank	3000.00			Notes Pay.	3000.00
		16966.00	13200.00	294.00		4060.00

CASH DISBURSEMENTS

Date	Name	Net Cash	Accounts Payable	Purchase Discount	Soc. Sec. Tax	Withhold. Tax	Miscellaneous Account	Amount
3/1	Bliss Realty Co.	875.					Rent	875.
3/4	United Utilities	54.					Light	54.
3/10	C. Lamont	2891.	2950.	59.				
3/15	Payroll	747.			26.	175.	Sal.	948
3/19	Rebuilt Desk Co.	115.					Furn. Fix.	115.
3/26	Winchel & Co.	3686.	3800.	114.				
3/30	Corn Exch. Bank	1218.					Notes Pay.	1200.
							Int. Cost	18.
3/31	Payroll	733.			22.	171.	Sal.	926.
3/31	A. Morton	600.					Drawings	600.
		10919.	6750.	173.	48.	346.		4736.

SALES BOOK

Date	Name	Accounts Receivable	Sales	City Sales Tax
3/3	L. Brown	6850.00	6665.00	185.00
3/10	J. Walters	5730.00	5730.00	
3/16	M. Sanders	3100.00	3007.00	93.00
3/25	Willis & Co.	7278.00	7069.00	209.00
3/30	S. Rayburn	2190.00	2190.00	
		25148.00	24661.00	487.00

PURCHASE BOOK

Date	Name	Accounts Payable	Purchases	Freight In	Miscellaneous Account	Amount
3/4	Winchel & Co.	5212.00	5070.00	142.00		
3/11	Barton & Co.	320.00			(Insurance Prepaid)	320.00
3/16	A. Field	6368.00	6179.00	189.00		
3/19	Smith Delivery	22.00			(Shipping Expense)	22.00
3/23	Western Telephone	29.00			Telephone	29.00
3/26	C. Lamont	3000.00	3000.00			
3/29	Bird & Bird	7531.00	7168.00	363.00		
		22482.00	21417.00	694.00		371.00

Questions 1-25, referring to the above material, follow this section.

Supply the balances of the following accounts on March 31, 1980, after all posting has been done for March. (Do all work on scratch paper.) Put answers in the appropriate spaces on Answer Sheet. Give amounts only.

1. Cash
2. Accounts Receivable
3. Notes Receivable
4. Insurance Prepaid
5. Furniture and Fixtures
6. Accounts Payable
7. Notes Payable
8. Reserve for Depreciation of Furniture and Fixtures
9. A. Morton, Capital
10. A. Morton, Drawing
11. Purchases
12. Freight In
13. Rent
14. Light
15. Telephone
16. Salaries
17. Shipping Expenses
18. Sales
19. Sales Discount
20. Purchase Discount
21. City Sales Tax Collected
22. Social Security Taxes Payable
23. Withholding Taxes Payable
24. Interest Income
25. Interest Cost

Mr. Jones has a complete set of books—Cash Journals, Purchase and Sales Journals, and a General Journal. Below you will find the General Journal used by Mr. Jones. Under the heading of each money column you will find a letter of the alphabet. Following the General Journal, there is a series of transactions. You are to determine the correct entry for each transaction and then show on your answer paper in the appropriate space the columns to be used. For example, if a certain transaction results in an entry of $100 in the Notes Receivable Column (on the left side) and an entry of $100 in the General Ledger Column (on the right side), in the appropriate space on your answer paper you should write A, D. If the record of the transaction requires the use of more than two columns, your answer should contain more than two letters. *Do not put the amounts on your answer paper.* The *letters* of the columns to be used are sufficient. If a transaction requires no entry in the General Journal write "None" in the appropriate space on your answer paper even though a record would be made in some other journal. You may, if you wish, use the journal for scratch work. However, your rating will be determined solely by what you write on the answer paper provided.

GENERAL JOURNAL

Notes Receivable	Accounts Payable	General Ledger	L. F.		General Ledger	Accounts Receivable	Notes Payable
A	B	C			D	E	F

26. We sent Philips & Co. a 30-day trade acceptance for $500 for merchandise sold him today. They accepted it.

27. The proprietor, Mr. Jones, returned $100 in cash to be deposited, representing Traveling Expenses he had not used.

28. An entry in the Purchase Journal last month for a purchase invoice from S. Taylor for $647 was erroneously entered in the Purchase Journal as $746 and posted as such.

29. A check of $200 received from Mr. Bernstein was erroneously credited to account of L. Bergman.

30. In posting the totals of the Cash Receipts Journal last month, an item of bank discount of $30 on our note for $1500 discounted for 60 days was included in the total posted to the sales discount account.

31. J. Murphy paid his note of $600 and interest of $12 and his account was credited for $612.

32. Mr. Low informed us he could not pay his invoice of $2000 due today. Instead he sent us his 30 day note for $2000 for 30 days bearing interest at 6% per annum.

33. The proprietor, Mr. Jones, drew $75 to buy his son a U.S. Bond.

34. Mr. Klein wrote to us that we overcharged him on an invoice last week. Sent him a credit memorandum for $40.

35. Returned $120 worth of merchandise to Libby & Co. and received their credit memorandum.

Below you will find a list of accounts with a number before each:

1. Cash
2. Accounts Receivable
3. Notes Receivable
4. Notes Receivable Discounted
5. Furniture and Fixtures
6. Delivery Equipment
7. Insurance Prepaid
8. Depreciation on Del. Equipment
9. Bad Debts
10. Purchases
11. Discount on Purchases
12. Sales
13. Discount on Sales
14. Accounts Payable
15. Notes Payable
16. Interest Cost
17. Reserve for Depreciation on Delivery Equipment
18. Reserve for Bad Debts
19. Sales Taxes Collected
20. J. Holt, Capital
21. J. Holt, Drawing
22. Interest Income
23. Purchase Returns

Using the number in front of each account title (using no accounts not listed), make journal entries for the transactions given below. Do not write the names of the accounts on your answer paper. Simply indicate in the proper space on your answer paper, the numbers of the accounts to be debited or credited. Always give the number or numbers of accounts to be debited first, then give the number or numbers of accounts to be credited. For example, if furniture and fixtures and delivery equipment are to be debited and cash and notes payable are to be credited in a certain transaction, then write on your answer paper 5, 6—1, 15 (use a dash to separate the debits from the credits).

Item

36. A. Manville, a customer, went into bankruptcy owing us $600. We received a check for $200.

37. Later in the month we are informed that there is no possibility of collecting the balance from A. Manville. There is a sufficient balance in the Reserve for Bad Debts to take care of the above.

38. Set up the Depreciation on the Delivery Equipment for the year amounting to $240.

39. Discounted H. Cohn's note for $500 today and received $490 in proceeds.

40. Mr. Holt, the proprietor, invested $2000 in the business.

41. Paid our note due to Willard & Co. today for $800 with interest of $16.

42. Accepted Boyle's trade acceptance for $1500 for merchandise bought today.

43. Create a Reserve for Bad Debts of $2000 at the end of the year.

44. Returned to Willard & Co.—$30 worth of damaged merchandise for credit. They allowed it.

45. F. Frank claimed a discount of $12 which we had failed to allow him. He had already paid his bill. Sent him check for $12.

46. On one sale during the month we had failed to collect the Sales Tax of $15. Wrote to the customer and he sent us a check for $15.

47. H. Cohen paid his note due today which we had discounted two months ago.

48. Bought a new safe for $875 from Marvin & Co., terms 2/10, n/60 days. Agreed to pay them in 60 days.

49. Bought merchandise during the month amounting to $17,500—all on account.

50. On Dec. 31, paid for a Fire Insurance policy to run for 3 years from that date—premium was $480.

51. The following information was taken from the ledger of Walter Lee on Dec. 31, 1980 after adjusting entries had been posted to the ledger.

Sales Income	$60000
Sales Returns	3500
Mdse. Purchases	42000
Inventory 1/1/80	9400
Sales Taxes Payable	360
Freight Inward	225
Inventory 12/31/80	7640
Insurance Unexpired	163

Find the gross profit on Sales for the year.

52. On March 31 your bank sent you a statement of account. You compared the cancelled checks with the stubs in your check book and found the following:

Check #34—$56.00 had not been paid by the bank.

Check #44—$38.00 had been paid by the bank as $38.89 because the amount on the check did not agree with your stub in the check book.

Check #52—$76.50 had not been returned by the bank though the check had been certified.

Check #57—$127.42 had not been paid by the bank.

What total amount would you deduct from the balance on the bank's statement as checks outstanding?

53. On April 30, Mr. Klein received his statement of account from the bank. A comparison of the bank statement and your check book revealed the following: Check book balance $5640; this included a deposit of $325 on the last day of April which had not been entered on the bank statement. You also find the following:

    Check #69—$89 had not been paid
    by the bank.
    Check #70—Paid by the bank as
    $47.55, had been en-
    tered in your check
    book as $45.57.
    Check #76—$114.30 had not been
    paid by the bank.

    The bank statement included a debit memo of $4.00 for excessive activity during the month.
    What was the balance on the bank statement?

54. An invoice dated Jan. 15th for merchandise you bought added up to $876.00. The terms were 3/10, n/60 *f.o.b. destination.* When the goods arrived you paid freight amounting to $8.50. On Jan. 20 you returned goods billed at $26 and received credit therefor. You paid the bill on January 24. What was the amount of your check?

55. Income taxes paid by residents of a certain state are based on the balance of taxable income at the following rates:
    2% on first $1000 or less
    3% on 2nd and 3rd $1000
    4% on 4th and 5th $1000
    5% on 6th and 7th $1000
    6% on 8th and 9th $1000
    7% on all over $9000

    What would be the normal income tax to be paid by a resident of that state whose taxable balance of income was $6750?

56. A salesman's yearly gross earnings came to $8820. His rate of Commission was 5% of his sales to customers after deducting returns by customers. During that same year his customers returned 10% of the goods they purchased. What were his yearly total sales before deducting returns?

57. On December 31, the insurance account contained a debit for $144 for a three fire insurance policy dated Aug. 1. What amount should be listed on the balance sheet of Dec. 31?

58. A partnership began business on Jan. 1st with the partners' investments of $26,000. During the year, the partners drew $18,500 for personal use. On Dec. 31st, the assets of the firm were $46,300 and the liabilities were $15,600. What was the firm's net profit for the year? Write P or L before your answer.

59. The rent income account of a real estate firm showed a total balance of $75,640 at the end of 1979. Of this amount $3545 represented prepaid 1980 rents. The account also included entries for 1979 rents due from tenants, but not yet collected, amounting to $2400. What amount should be listed on the profit and loss statement as rent income for 1979?

60. You discounted a customer's note for $7200 at your bank at the rate of 6% and received net proceeds of $7182. How many days did the note have to run from date of discount to date of maturity? (Use 360 days to the year.)

Below you will find a list of ledger accounts. Indicate whether an account is generally listed in the Trial Balance as a *Debit* or as a *Credit* by putting the letter D or the letter C in the correct space on your answer sheet for each account listed.

61. Sales
62. Land
63. Notes Payable
64. Traveling expenses
65. Purchases
66. Buildings
67. Merchandise Inventory
68. Machinery and Equipment
69. Notes Receivable
70. Bonds Payable
71. Advertising
72. Delivery expense
73. Cash
74. Accounts Payable
75. Interest on Bonds
76. Real Estate Taxes
77. Accounts Receivable
78. John Smith, Proprietor
79. Sales Discount
80. Withholding Taxes
81. Depreciation
82. Prepaid Insurance
83. Reserve for Deprec. on Bldgs.
84. Rent Income
85. Reserve for Bad Debts
86. John Smith, Drawing Account
87. Sales Returns
88. Bad Debts
89. Purchase Discount
90. Reserve for Deprec. on Mach. & Equip.

Explanatory Answers

ANSWERS 1 THROUGH 25

The chief danger in this type of problem lies in carelessness. It is easy to miss noticing an item in the month's transactions or to add incorrectly a figure in arriving at any of the twenty-five answers required. If scratch paper work is organized as described below, proof that your answers are correct can be built up while arriving at the separate answers. The follow scratch-work procedure will result in the format of answers as given:

A. List, in the item order called for by the answer sheet, the starting balances given for each account, in the proper debit or credit position. Allow space for writing one or two lines of figures between any item and the one following it. Check off each balance on the question sheet as you list it. List also any starting balances given but not required by the answer sheet (as, for example, Merchandise Inventory in the problem at hand).

B. Take a trial balance. If you placed each starting balance in the proper debit or credit position, the debit and credit sides will equal each other. You then know you have a proper start for the answer to every item.

C. Post to the scratch work the totals of the special columns from the journals and the individual entries in the miscellaneous columns, making a check mark against each item on the question sheet as you post it.

D. When you have made sure all items have been posted, figure the ending debit or credit balance for each account and enter it in the proper debit or credit column.

E. Take a trial balance of the ending balances. If debit and credit totals equal each other, write your ending balances on the answer sheet. Check to make sure you have made no copying errors.

Item Account	Journal	Date	Feb. 28 Balance and Entries Dr	Cr	March 31 Balance Dr	Cr
1. Cash	Bal.	2/28	4,336			
	Receipts	3/31	16,966			
	Disbursements	3/31		10,919	10,383	
2. Accounts Receivable	Bal.	2/28	8,165			
	Sales	3/31	25,148			
	Receipts	3/31		13,200	20,113	
3. Notes Receivable	Bal.	2/28	2,200			
	Receipts	3/31		1,000	1,200	
4. Insurance Prepaid						
	Purchases	3/11	320		320	
5. Furniture & Fixt.	Bal.	2/28	9,000			
	Receipts	3/17		45		
	Disbursements	3/19	115		9,070	
6. Accounts Payable	Bal.	2/28		5,560		
	Disbursements	3/31	6,750			
	Purchases	3/31		22,482		21,292

Item Account	Journal	Date	Feb. 28 Balance and Entries Dr	Cr	March 31 Balance Dr	Cr
7. Notes Payable	Bal.	2/28		1,500		
	Receipts	3/31		3,000		
	Disbursements	3/31	1,200			3,300
8. Reserve for Depreciation —Furn. & Fixt.	Bal.	2/28		1,800		1,800
9. A. Morton, Capital	Bal.	2/28		14,162		14,162
10. A. Morton, Drawing	Bal.	2/28	900			
	Disbursements	3/31	600		1,500	
11. Purchases	Bal.	2/28	42,600			
	Purchases	3/31	21,417		64,017	
12. Freight In	Bal.	2/28	36			
	Purchases	3/31	694		730	
13. Rent	Bal.	2/28	1,750			
	Disbursements	3/31	875		2,625	
14. Light	Bal.	2/28	126			
	Disbursements	3/ 4	54		180	
15. Telephone	Bal.	2/28	63			
	Purchases	3/23	29		92	
16. Salaries	Bal.	2/28	4,076			
	Disbursements	3/15	948			
	Disbursements	3/31	926		5,950	
17. Shipping Expense	Bal.	2/28	368			
	Purchases	3/19	22		390	
18. Sales	Bal.	2/28		53,200		
	Sales	3/31		24,661		77,861
19. Sales Discount	Bal.	2/28	637			
	Receipts	3/31	294		931	
20. Purchase Discount	Bal.	2/28		596		
	Disbursements	3/31		173		769
21. City Sales Tax Collected	Bal. Sales	2/28 3/31		804 487		1,291
22. Social Security Taxes Payable	Bal. Disbursements	2/28 3/31		96 48		144
23. Withholding Taxes Payable	Bal. Disbursements	2/28 3/31		714 346		1,060
24. Interest Income	Receipts	3/ 3		15		15
25. Interest Cost	Disbursements	3/30	18		18	
Feb. 28 balance included in statement of problem, but not called for above:						
Merchandise Inventory			4,175	4,175	4,175	
Ending balances for March 31:					121,694	121,694

Note that the February 28 account balances stated, if arranged in proper debit or credit position, will balance with debit and credit totals, each being $78,432.

ANSWERS 26 TO 35

26. A, E. A $300 note receivable is set up to replace the account receivable.

27. None. The entry would be made in the Cash Receipts Journal debiting cash and crediting Traveling Expense—to offset an entry which must have been made in the Cash Disbursements Journal when the money was given to Mr. Jones.

28. B. D. A debit of $99 to Accounts Payable (to reduce $746 to $647) and a like credit to Purchases are made to correct this error.

29. C, E. The account debited is also Accounts Receivable. The only purpose of this entry is to explain the transfer of the $200 credit in Bergman's account to Bernstein's. A transfer made, even with cross-references, in the subsidiary ledger accounts alone would, especially in this case, create the impression of mishandling of funds. Ledger postings should be made only from books of original entry (journals).

30. C, D. Debit Sales Discount and credit Interest Income to remove the erroneous credit to the former and place it in the proper account.

31. C, D. If, as stated, Accounts Receivable was credited (erroneously) with $612, this error must be corrected by a General Journal entry *debiting* Accounts Receivable with $612 to

offset the error, crediting *Notes* Receivable with $600 to reflect payment of the note, and crediting Interest Income with $12 to record the receipt of earned interest.

32. A, E. This sets up a $2,000 note receivable to replace the $2,000 account receivable.

33. None. This would be a Cash Disbursements Journal entry debiting Mr. Jones' Drawings account and crediting Cash.

34. C, E. Since there is no Sales Returns and Allowances Journal, this type of entry would be made in the General Journal, debiting Sales Returns and Allowances (or Sales) and crediting Accounts Receivable.

35. B, D. In the absence of a Purchase Returns and Allowances Journal, this is also a General Journal entry. Debit Accounts Payable and credit Purchase Returns and Allowances (or Purchases).

ANSWERS 36 TO 60

36. 1-2. At this time, we simply debit Cash and credit Accounts Receivable for $200, leaving a $400 balance in Manville's account. See item 37.

37. 18-2. We now write off the remaining $400 by debiting the Reserve for Bad Debts account and crediting Accounts Receivable. The Reserve is built up by debiting Bad Debts expense and crediting the Reserve for *anticipated* losses. An *actual* loss is charged against the Reserve if the Reserve credit balance is, as stated here, at least as large as the actual loss.

38. 8-17. Debit the Depreciation expense account for the portion of cost write-off and credit the Reserve account used to show the accumulated reduction as an adjustment of the fixed asset costs on the balance sheet.

39. 1, 16-4. Cash is debited for $490, Interest Cost for $10, and our contingent liability of $500 for a note receivable discounted is set up as a credit, in case Mr. Cohn fails to pay his note to the bank.

40. 1-20. Cash is debited and J. Holt's Capital account is credited for this investment of $2,000.

41. 15, 16-1. Debit Notes Payable, $800, to record payment of the liability, debit Interest Cost $16 to record the expense, and credit Cash for the $816 paid out.

42. 14-15. Our acceptance created a Note Payable liability of $1,500 to wipe out an Accounts Payable liability of like amount.

43. 9-18. We are recording our estimate of anticipated losses by debiting the Bad Debts account and crediting the Reserve account.

44. 14-23. Accounts Payable is reduced by a debit recording the allowance of this return, and the income (or negative expense) account, Purchase Returns, is credited.

45. 13-1. The expense (or negative income) account Sales Discount is debited and Cash credited for $12.

46. 1-19. Cash is debited and the $15 credited to Sales Taxes Collected, representing liability to pay the taxes to the government.

47. 4-3. The payment of the note removes our contingent liability to pay the discounted note if Cohen had not paid it, and also requires that we credit the Notes Receivable asset account to record its payment.

48. 5-14. The $875 cost of the safe is debited to the Furniture and Fixtures account and set up as a current liability in Accounts Payable.

49. 10-14. Debit Purchases and credit Accounts Payable for $17,500.

50. 7-1. This prepaid expense of $480 is debited to the asset account, Insurance Prepaid, as Cash is credited.

51. $12,515, determined as follows:

Sales Income	$60,000	
Deduct Sales Returns	3,500	
Net Sales		$56,500
Deduct Cost of Goods Sold:		
Inventory, Jan. 1	$ 9,400	
Add:		
Purchases	42,000	
Freight In	225	
Cost of Goods Available for Sale	$51,625	
Deduct Inventory, Dec. 31	7,640	
Cost of Goods Sold		43,985
Gross Profit on Sales		$12,515

52. $183.42, consisting of Check #34 for $56.00 and #57 for $127.42. The check book balance would have to be adjusted by subtracting the 89¢ difference between the incorrect checkbook stub and the actual amount of the check, #44. Bank statement and checkbook would be in agreement on check #52, which would appear on the statement as a deduction as of the day it was certified.

53. $5,512.32, determined as follows:

Check book balance	$5,640	
Deduct deposit not on bank statement	325	$5,315
Add: Checks outstanding: #69 $ 89.		
#76 114.30		203.30
		$5,518.30
Other deductions:		
Checkbook error— check #70 for $47.55 recorded as 45.57	$1.98	
Bank service charge	4.00	5.98
		$5,512.37

54. $816.00, determined as follows:

Original purchase		$876.00
Deduct return of		26.00
Net purchase		850.00
Deductions:		
3% discount on $850 = $25.50		
Freight paid	8.50	34.00
Amount of check		$816.00

The deduction of $8.50 for payment of freight is made because the terms f.o.b. destination mean that the seller pays the transportation charges. Since the purchaser paid them, he is entitled to recover them from the seller.

55. $247.50, determined as follows:

On first $1,000 of taxable income	2%, or	$ 20
On the next $2,000 of taxable income	3%, or	60
On the next $2,000 of taxable income	4%, or	80
On remaining $1,750 of taxable income	5%, or	87.50
On total $6,750 of taxable income total tax of		$247.50

56. $196,000, computed as follows: $8,820 represents 5% of $176,400. Since these are net sales after returns of 10% of goods originally sold,

$$\frac{\$176,400}{\text{sales before returns}} = \frac{90\%}{100\%}$$

or sales before returns $= \dfrac{\$176,400}{90\%} =$ $196,000.

57. $124, computed as follows: Five months of the three years prepayment have expired (August through December). This means that 31/36ths of the asset value of $144 remains unexpired on December 31.

$$\frac{31}{36} \times \$144 = \$124.$$

58. P, $23,200. The partners capital accounts, if consolidated, would look like this on December 31 after closing the books:

Drawings,	$18,500
Jan. 1 balance	$26,000
Profits	23,200
showing a credit balance of	$30,700
which, when added to the stated liabilities of	15,600
equals the stated assets of	$46,300

59. $72,095, based on
    Rent income per account balance $75,640
    Deduct prepayments of 1980 rent   3,545
                                    $72,095

So long as the profit and loss statement is on an accrual, rather than cash, basis, the $2,400 in uncollected 1979 rents would simply appear on the balance sheet as accounts receivable, but *not* enter into any adjustment of income on the profit and loss statement.

60. 15 days. Since 6% for 60 days on $7,200 is $72.00, and the bank charged $18, or ¼ of $72.00, for discounting $7,200 at 6%, the discount period was ¼ of 60 days, or 15 days.

Answer Key 61 to 90

61. C	69. D	77. D	85. C
62. D	70. C	78. C	86. D
63. C	71. D	79. D	87. D
64. D	72. D	80. C	88. D
65. D	73. D	81. D	89. C
66. D	74. C	82. D	90. C
67. D	75. D*	83. C	
68. D	76. D*	84. C	

*It is assumed that when a payment of taxes or of bond interest is made the bookkeeper will charge the expense account, so that during the year the expense account will have a debit balance most of the time. The liability accounts for bond interest or taxes will normally be created at the end of a fiscal period and may be reversed at the beginning of a new year. For this reason the answer to Questions 75 and 76 is preferably D.

SAMPLE ANSWER SHEET FOR EXAMINATION IV

1. _____
2. _____
3. _____
4. _____
5. _____
6. _____
7. _____
8. _____
9. _____
10. _____
11. _____
12. _____
13. _____
14. _____
15. _____
16. _____
17. _____
18. _____
19. _____
20. _____

21. _____
22. _____
23. _____
24. _____
25. _____
26. _____
27. _____
28. _____
29. _____
30. _____
31. _____
32. _____
33. _____
34. _____
35. _____
36. _____
37. _____
38. _____
39. _____
40. _____

41. _____
42. _____
43. _____
44. _____
45. _____
46. _____
47. _____
48. _____
49. _____
50. _____
51. _____
52. _____
53. _____
54. _____
55. _____
56. _____
57. _____
58. _____
59. _____
60. _____

61. _____
62. _____
63. _____
64. _____
65. _____
66. _____
67. _____
68. _____
69. _____
70. _____
71. _____
72. _____
73. _____
74. _____
75. _____
76. _____
77. _____
78. _____
79. _____
80. _____

SAMPLE ANSWER SHEET FOR EXAMINATION IV

SAMPLE EXAMINATION IV

The time allowed for the entire examination is 3 hours. In order to create the climate of the test to come, that's precisely what you should allow yourself . . . no more, no less. Use a watch and keep a record of your time, especially since you may find it convenient to take the test in several sittings.

NOTE: The first 60 items have a weight of 2 each. The last 20 items have a weight of 1 each.

Below you will find the Cash Receipts Journal and the Cash Payments Journal of John Walker, merchant in New York City. Under the heading of each money column of the Journals, there is a letter of the alphabet. Following the Journals there is a series of transactions. You are to determine the entry for each transaction and then show on your answer paper in the appropriate space, the columns to be used. For example: if a certain transaction entered in the Cash Receipts Journal results in an entry of $100 in the General Ledger Column and $100 in the Net Cash Column, in the appropriate space on your answer paper you should write: A, E. If the record of the transaction requires the use of more than two columns, your answer should contain more than two letters. Do not put the amounts on your answer paper. The letters of the columns in the Cash Journals to be used are sufficient. If a transaction requires no entry in the Cash Journals, write "None" in the appropriate space on your answer paper even though a record would be made in some other journal.

You may, if you wish, use the journals for scratch work. However, your rating will be determined by what you write on the answer sheet provided.

CASH RECEIPTS JOURNAL

Date	Account Credited	Explanation	F	General Ledger	Accounts Receivable	Cash Sales	Discount on Sales	Net Cash
				A	B	C	D	E

CASH PAYMENTS JOURNAL

Date	Account Debited	Explana-tion	F	General Ledger	Accounts Payable	Soc. Sec. Taxes Payable	Withold. Taxes Payable	Disc. on Purch.	Net Cash
				F	G	H	I	J	K

Item

1. Cash Sales amounted to $280.

2. Paid employees salaries for the week. The check amounted to $346 after deducting $4.00 for Social Security Taxes and $30 for Income Taxes withheld.

3. A check received in the mail from R. Walters was in payment of a bill of $150, terms 2/10, n/30. The customer had taken the discount.

4. The proprietor, Mr. Walker, took merchandise valued at $30 from the stock room for his personal use.

5. Prepaid $15 freight on shipment of goods to H. Lane, a customer, and charged his account.

6. Sent a check for $250 to P. Packer to apply on account.

7. Drew a check for $75 to start a Petty Cash fund.

8. H. Wall sent us a check for $700 in payment of his 60 day note for $700. The note was interest bearing (6%) but he failed to pay us the interest. We deposited the $700 check and wrote to him requesting an additional check.

9. Paid rent for month $180.

10. Received a check for $70 from K. London to apply on account.

11. H. Wall sent us a check for the interest due on note (see item 8).

12. Paid our 30 day note for $460 due today which we had given to G. Thompson.

13. Accepted a trade acceptance drawn by R. Sparks on us for invoice of $722.

14. Borrowed at our bank on our $1500 note. Net proceeds $1485. (The Bookkeeper used only one journal to make a complete and correct entry. You are to do likewise.)

15. Received a check for $60 from W. Saks, a creditor, refunding our overpayment to him on our account.

16. A check from H. Low which was deposited by us last month was returned to us marked "insufficient funds." The check amounted to $55 and had been sent to us to settle his account.

17. Drew a sight draft on R. Coe for overdue account of $120. Left draft at bank for collection.

18. Paid $26 freight on goods purchased from W. Lincoln of Chicago, terms f.o.b. Chicago.

19. Mailed a credit memorandum to E. Stern for return of defective merchandise sold him on account for $65.

20. The proprietor, John Walker, drew $90 cash for personal use.

21. Received a money order for $110 from B. Kiner for invoice of merchandise charged to him.

22. Mr. Walker, proprietor, drew $1200 from his personal savings account and invested the entire sum in his business.

23. Issued check to Clark & Co. in payment of invoice amounting to $500. Discount of 3% was taken.

24. Received a 30 day non interest bearing note for $610 from A. Allen for merchandise sold him today.

25. Sent a check for $51 to Collector of Internal Revenue for Social Security taxes collected for the past three months.

Below you will find the General Journal used by D. Prince, wholesaler. Under the heading of each money column you will find a letter of the alphabet. Following the General Journal, there is a series of transactions. You are to determine the correct entry for each transaction and then show on your answer paper in the appropriate space, the columns to be used. For example, if a certain transaction results in an entry of $100 in the Notes Receivable Column (on the left side) and an entry of $100 in the General Ledger Column (on the right side), in the appropriate space on your answer paper you should write A, D. If the record of the transaction requires the use of more than two columns, your answer should contain more than two letters. Do not put the amounts on your answer paper. The letters of the columns to be used are sufficient. If a transaction requires no entry in the General Journal write "None" in the appropriate space on your answer paper even though a record would be made in some other journal. You may, if you wish, use the journal for scratch work. However, your rating will be determined solely by what you write on the answer paper provided.

GENERAL JOURNAL

Notes Receivable	Accounts Payable	General Ledger	L. F.		General Ledger	Accounts Receivable	Notes Payable
A	B	C			D	E	F

Item

26. Issued a credit memorandum for $68 to J. Winston for goods returned to us

27. P. Jones sent us his 60 day note for $750 in full settlement of his account.

28. Sent a 60 day note to J. O'Connor for invoice of $375 less 2%.

29. H. Owens sent us a credit memorandum for overcharge of $75 on invoice.

30. Mailed a 30 day draft to W. Kinder, a customer, for his acceptance amounting to $375 for invoice of goods sold him yesterday.

31. A Hocker, a customer, went out of business owing us $170. The claim is considered worthless.

32. The proprietor requested the bookkeeper to provide a reserve of $500 for expected losses on customers' accounts.

33. P. Winston sent us a $350 bank draft in full settlement of his account.

34. Accepted a 30 day trade acceptance drawn by A. Hall for bill of goods amounting to $316 purchased by us last week.

35. Mr. D. Prince, the proprietor, takes his brother L. Prince, into the busi-

ness as an equal partner. Mr. L. Prince invests merchandise worth $3500 in the business and becomes a partner.

Below you will find a list of accounts from the ledger of R. Lincoln. There is a letter of the alphabet before each account.
A. Accounts Payable
B. Accounts Receivable
C. Cash
D. Delivery Expense
E. Discount on Purchases
F. Freight Inward
G. Interest Cost
H. Purchases
I. Notes Receivable
J. Notes Receivable Discounted
K. Notes Payable
L. Office Supplies
M. R. Lincoln, Personal
N. Petty Cash
O. Purchase Returns
P. Sales Discount
R. Sales Returns
S. Sales Income

Using the letter in front of each account title (using no accounts not listed), make journal entries for the transactions given below. Do not write the names of the accounts on your answer paper. Simply indicate in the proper space on your answer paper, the letters of the accounts to be debited or credited. Always give the letter or letters of accounts to be debited first, then give the letter or letters of accounts to be credited. For example, if Office Supplies and Delivery Expenses are to be debited and Notes Payable and Cash are to be credited in a certain transaction, then write on your answer paper L, D; K, C.

36. Paid the Fox Transportation Co. $15 by check for express charges on goods delivered to us.

37. Accepted a 30 day trade acceptance for $850 drawn on us by Allen & Co.

38. Returned damaged goods to H. Parker and he sent us a credit memorandum for $47.

39. John Smith's 30 day note for $800, which was discounted by us at our bank last month, was paid by him today.

40. Paid our 60 day note due today in favor of S. Paul for $600 with interest. The check amounted to $606.

41. The total of the Notes Payable column in the General Journal amounted to $450 at the end of last month. It was posted in error to the Notes Receivable Discounted account. Make the correction entry.

42. Issued a check to J. News in settlement of invoice $500 less 2%.

43. Paid Stern Brothers $5.00 by check for four reams of paper for office use.

44. Sent a check for $48 to Gregory's Garage for storage, gasoline, oil and service on auto trucks.

45. Drew a check for $100 to establish a Petty Cash fund.

46. A. Black, a customer, settled his account of $400 by sending us a check for $100 and a 30 day note for the balance.

47. J. Walters failed to deduct a discount of $400 by sending us a check for $100 and a 30 day note for the balance.

48. Donated to the Salvation Army merchandise out of stock costing the proprietor $75.

49. At the end of the year the Sales Returns account had a balance of $225. Make the entry to close this account.

50. At the end of the year the Freight Inward account had a balance of $450. Make the entry to close this account.

In the next 10 items, place the correct answer on your answer paper in the appropriate space. Take particular care with your figures.

51. On Dec. 31,   a bookkeeper prepared a Profit and Loss Statement in which the following are some of the items listed:

Sales	$ 50,000
Purchases	45,000
Inventory 1/1/	7,500
Sales Returns	400
Gross Profit	15,000
Selling Expense	3,200

Find the Inventory of Merchandise on Dec. 31.

52. A. Landers invested $5000 in cash in a new business. At the end of the year he finds he has $2500 in cash, $1000 in furniture, $1800 in merchandise on which he owes $750. During the year, Mr. Landers drew $2400 for his own use.

What was his profit or loss for the year? (Write P or L before the figure.)

53. Wm. Abbott purchased a machine for $2600. The estimated life of the machine was five years. At the end of five years the machine could be sold for scrap for $400. Find the depreciation charge at the end of the first six months of use.

54. On Jan 1, A. Menton's Capital was $2400. His partner, P. King, had a Capital of $6000. Their agreement provided for dividing profits in proportion to Capital. During the year the Net Profit was $12,480. What was A. Menton's share of the Net Profit?

55. On Dec. 31,   J. Klein's ledger, after all closing entries, contained the following balances:

Cash	$ 5,000
Merchandise Inventory	1,500

Accounts Receivable	8,000
Notes Receivable	2,000
Deferred Expense	300
Furniture and Fixtures	1,200
Accounts Payable	4,000
Reserve for Bad Debts	600
Notes Receivable Discounted	800
Reserve for Depreciation of Furniture and Fixtures	900

What was J. Klein's Capital on Dec. 31.

56. An employer paid $160 in Social Security taxes during the current year at the rate of 1% on taxable wages. He expects to employ more persons in the coming year and pay out 50% more in taxable wages than he did this year. What will be his Social Security costs at the new rate of 1-1/2% in the coming year?

57. On June 17 you discounted a customer's 60 day note at your bank. The face of the note was $840 and it was dated June 5, discount rate 6%. What was the amount of the net proceeds?

58. On June 18 you sold I. Cohen of Chicago merchandise. The invoice totalled $684 which included $38 freight which you had prepaid. Terms were 2, 10, n/30, f.o.b., New York. If Mr. Cohen pays you on June 27, what should be the correct amount of the check?

59. A bankrupt firm agrees to pay its creditors 30 cents on the dollar. It pays Klein & Co. $12,600. What was Klein & Co's loss?

60. A salesman earned $15,600 this year. His commissions were at the rate of 7-1/2% of Sales. What were his sales for the year?

NOTE: Each item 61-80 has a weight of 1 each.

The bookkeeper of Walters Co. began to take a trial balance of his General Ledger on Dec. 31. Before he had completed his trial balance you were permitted to examine his work. If a balance is in the correct column write "C" in the appropriate space on your answer paper. If a balance is in the wrong column write "W" in the appropriate space on your answer paper.

Caution: Since the trial balance is not complete do not attempt to strike a balance of the figures given in the question.

Walter Co.
Trial Balance, Dec. 31.

61.	Merchandise Inventory, Jan. 1.	16,000	
62.	Freight Inward	150	
63.	Petty Cash		75
64.	Interest Income	70	
65.	Notes Receivable	4,000	
66.	Sales		17,000
67.	Sales Discount		170
68.	Purchase Returns	250	
69.	Auto Trucks	9,000	
70.	Reserve for Depreciation of Furniture	770	
71.	Bad Debts		160
72.	Sales Taxes Collected	225	
73.	Sales Returns		485
74.	Reserve for Bad Debts		500
75.	Deposits with Landlord		150
76.	Accrued interest on Notes Receivable		50
77.	Income from Commissions		900
78.	Purchase Discounts		110
79.	Depreciation of Furniture		225
80.	Notes and Acceptances from Customers		780

Answer Key

1. C, E	17. None	33. None	47. P, C	63. W
2. F, H, I, K	18. F, K	34. B, F	48. M, H or M, S	64. W
3. B, D, E	19. None	35. C, D	49. S, R	65. C
4. None	20. F, K	36. F, C	50. H, F	66. C
5. F, K	21. B, E	37. A, K	51. 17900	67. W
6. G, K	22. A, E	38. A, O	52. P 1950	68. W
7. F, K	23. G, J, K	39. J, I	53. 220	69. C
8. A, E	24. None	40. K, G, C or G	54. 3565.71 or	70. W
9. F, K	25. F, K or H, K	41. J, K	3565.72	71. W
10. B, E	26. C, E or	42. A, C, E or	55. 11700	72. W
11. A, E	None	A, E, C	56. 360	73. W
12. F, K	27. A, E	43. L, C	57. 833.28	74. C
13. None	28. B, D, F	44. D, C	58. 671.08	75. W
14. A, D, E or	29. B, D or None	45. N, C	59. 29400	76. W
A, A, E	30. None	46. I, C; B or	60. 208000	77. C
15. A, E	31. C, E	C, I; B or	61. C	78. C
16. F, K	32. C, D	I, C; B, B or	62. C	79. W
		C, I; B, B		80. W

SAMPLE ANSWER SHEET FOR EXAMINATION V

1 Ⓐ Ⓑ Ⓒ Ⓓ   19 Ⓐ Ⓑ Ⓒ Ⓓ   37 Ⓐ Ⓑ Ⓒ Ⓓ   55 Ⓐ Ⓑ Ⓒ Ⓓ

2 Ⓐ Ⓑ Ⓒ Ⓓ   20 Ⓐ Ⓑ Ⓒ Ⓓ   38 Ⓐ Ⓑ Ⓒ Ⓓ   56 Ⓐ Ⓑ Ⓒ Ⓓ

3 Ⓐ Ⓑ Ⓒ Ⓓ   21 Ⓐ Ⓑ Ⓒ Ⓓ   39 Ⓐ Ⓑ Ⓒ Ⓓ   57 Ⓐ Ⓑ Ⓒ Ⓓ

4 Ⓐ Ⓑ Ⓒ Ⓓ   22 Ⓐ Ⓑ Ⓒ Ⓓ   40 Ⓐ Ⓑ Ⓒ Ⓓ   58 Ⓐ Ⓑ Ⓒ Ⓓ

5 Ⓐ Ⓑ Ⓒ Ⓓ   23 Ⓐ Ⓑ Ⓒ Ⓓ   41 Ⓐ Ⓑ Ⓒ Ⓓ   59 Ⓐ Ⓑ Ⓒ Ⓓ

6 Ⓐ Ⓑ Ⓒ Ⓓ   24 Ⓐ Ⓑ Ⓒ Ⓓ   42 Ⓐ Ⓑ Ⓒ Ⓓ   60 Ⓐ Ⓑ Ⓒ Ⓓ

7 Ⓐ Ⓑ Ⓒ Ⓓ   25 Ⓐ Ⓑ Ⓒ Ⓓ   43 Ⓐ Ⓑ Ⓒ Ⓓ   61 Ⓐ Ⓑ Ⓒ Ⓓ

8 Ⓐ Ⓑ Ⓒ Ⓓ   26 Ⓐ Ⓑ Ⓒ Ⓓ   44 Ⓐ Ⓑ Ⓒ Ⓓ   62 Ⓐ Ⓑ Ⓒ Ⓓ

9 Ⓐ Ⓑ Ⓒ Ⓓ   27 Ⓐ Ⓑ Ⓒ Ⓓ   45 Ⓐ Ⓑ Ⓒ Ⓓ   63 Ⓐ Ⓑ Ⓒ Ⓓ

10 Ⓐ Ⓑ Ⓒ Ⓓ   28 Ⓐ Ⓑ Ⓒ Ⓓ   46 Ⓐ Ⓑ Ⓒ Ⓓ   64 Ⓐ Ⓑ Ⓒ Ⓓ

11 Ⓐ Ⓑ Ⓒ Ⓓ   29 Ⓐ Ⓑ Ⓒ Ⓓ   47 Ⓐ Ⓑ Ⓒ Ⓓ   65 Ⓐ Ⓑ Ⓒ Ⓓ

12 Ⓐ Ⓑ Ⓒ Ⓓ   30 Ⓐ Ⓑ Ⓒ Ⓓ   48 Ⓐ Ⓑ Ⓒ Ⓓ   66 Ⓐ Ⓑ Ⓒ Ⓓ

13 Ⓐ Ⓑ Ⓒ Ⓓ   31 Ⓐ Ⓑ Ⓒ Ⓓ   49 Ⓐ Ⓑ Ⓒ Ⓓ   67 Ⓐ Ⓑ Ⓒ Ⓓ

14 Ⓐ Ⓑ Ⓒ Ⓓ   32 Ⓐ Ⓑ Ⓒ Ⓓ   50 Ⓐ Ⓑ Ⓒ Ⓓ   68 Ⓐ Ⓑ Ⓒ Ⓓ

15 Ⓐ Ⓑ Ⓒ Ⓓ   33 Ⓐ Ⓑ Ⓒ Ⓓ   51 Ⓐ Ⓑ Ⓒ Ⓓ   69 Ⓐ Ⓑ Ⓒ Ⓓ

16 Ⓐ Ⓑ Ⓒ Ⓓ   34 Ⓐ Ⓑ Ⓒ Ⓓ   52 Ⓐ Ⓑ Ⓒ Ⓓ

17 Ⓐ Ⓑ Ⓒ Ⓓ   35 Ⓐ Ⓑ Ⓒ Ⓓ   53 Ⓐ Ⓑ Ⓒ Ⓓ

18 Ⓐ Ⓑ Ⓒ Ⓓ   36 Ⓐ Ⓑ Ⓒ Ⓓ   54 Ⓐ Ⓑ Ⓒ Ⓓ

ACCOUNT CLERK

SAMPLE EXAMINATION V

The time allowed for the entire examination: 3 hours

In order to create the climate of the actual exam, that's exactly what you should allow yourself . . . no more, no less. Use a watch to keep a record of your time, since it might suit your convenience to try this practice exam in several short takes.

1. The accounts in a general ledger are best arranged

   (A) in alphabetical order   (B) according to the frequency with which each account is used   (C) according to the order in which the headings of the columns in the cash journals are arranged   (D) according to the order in which they are used in preparing financial statements.

2. A physical inventory is an inventory obtained by

   (A) an actual count of the items on hand   (B) adding the totals of the stock record cards   (C) deducting the cost of goods sold from the purchases for the period   (D) deducting the purchases from the sales for the period.

3. A fixed asset is an asset that

   (A) is held primarily for sale to customers   (B) is used in the conduct of the business until worn out or replaced   (C) is readily convertible into cash   (D) has no definite value.

4. The gross profit on sales for a period is determined by

   (A) subtracting the cost of goods sold from the sales   (B) subtracting the sales returns and the discounts on sales from the gross sales   (C) subtracting the sales from the purchases for the period   (D) finding the difference between the inventory of merchandise at the beginning of the period and the inventory of merchandise at the end of the period.

5. The term "auditing" refers to the

   (A) entering of amounts from the journals into the general ledger
   (B) reconciliation of the accounts in a subsidiary ledger with the
   controlling account in the general ledger   (C) preparation of a trial
   balance of the accounts in the general ledger   (D) examination of the
   general ledger and other records of a concern to determine its true
   financial condition.

6. A voucher register is a

   (A) type of electric cash register   (B) list of customers whose accounts
   are past due   (C) list of the assets of a business   (D) book in which
   bills to be paid are recorded.

7. The method of depreciation which deducts an equal amount each full year
   of an asset's life is called

   (A) sum-of-years digits depreciation   (B) declining balance depreciation
   (C) straight-line depreciation   (D) service-hours depreciation.

8. When two business corporations join their assets and liabilities to form
   a new corporation, the procedure is called

   (A) a merger   (B) a liquidation   (C) a receivership   (D) an exchange.

9. The profit and loss statement prepared for a retail store does not
   ordinarily show

   (A) the cost of goods sold   (B) depreciation of fixtures and equipment
   (C) expenditures for salaries of employees   (D) the net worth of the
   proprietor.

10. The phrase "2%/10 net 30 days" on an invoice ordinarily means that
    (A) 2% of the amount must be paid within 30 days   (B) the purchaser must add
    2% to the amount of the invoice if he fails to pay within 30 days   (C) the
    entire amount must be paid within 30 days   (D) the purchaser may deduct 2%
    from the amount if he pays within 30 days.

11. The essential characteristic of a C.O.D. sale of merchandise is that the

    (A) purchaser pays for the merchandise upon its receipt by him   (B) seller
    guarantees the merchandise to be as specified by him   (C) merchandise is
    delivered by a common carrier   (D) purchaser is permitted to pay for the
    merchandise in convenient installments.

12. If the drawer of a check makes an error in writing the amount of the check, he
    should
    (A) erase the error and insert the correct amount   (B) cross out the error and
    insert the correct amount   (C) destroy the check and prepare another one
    (D) write the correct amount directly above the incorrect one.

13. The cost of goods sold by a retail store is properly determined by
    (A) adding the closing inventory to the total of the opening inventory and the
    purchases for the year   (B) deducting the closing inventory from the total of
    the opening inventory and the purchases for the year   (C) deducting the total
    of the opening and closing inventories from the purchases for the year
    (D) adding the total of the opening and closing inventories to the purchases
    for the year.

14. The purpose of the Drawing account in the general ledger of an individual enterprise is to show the
(A) salaries paid to the employees (B) amounts paid to independent contractors for services rendered (C) amounts taken by the proprietor for his personal use (D) total of payments made for general expenses of the business.

15. A controlling account is an account which contains
(A) the totals of all the expense accounts in the general ledger (B) the total of the amounts entered in the accounts in a subsidiary ledger (C) the total of the depreciation on fixtures claimed in all preceding years
(D) all totals of the income and expense accounts before closing to the Profit and Loss account.

16. The account Unearned Rental Income is usually considered
(A) an asset account (B) a nominal account (C) a capital account
(D) a liability account.

17. The account Discount on Purchases is properly closed directly to the
(A) Accounts Payable account (B) Sales account (C) Purchases account
(D) Fixtures account.

18. The primary purpose of a trial balance is to determine
(A) that all transactions have been entered in the journals (B) the accuracy of the totals in the general ledger (C) the correctness of the amounts entered in the journals (D) that amounts have been posted to the proper accounts in the general ledger

19. The Surplus account of a corporation is ordinarily used to record
(A) the actual amount subscribed by stockholders (B) the amount of profits earned by the corporation (C) any excess of current assets over current liabilities
(D) the total of the fixed assets of the corporation.

Questions 20 to 34 consist of a list of some of the accounts in the general ledger of a corporation which operates a retail store. Indicate whether each account listed contains generally a debit or credit balance by marking the letter D (for debit balance) or the letter C (for credit balance) in the correspondingly numbered row on your answer sheet for each account listed. For example, for the account Cash which generally contains a debit balance, you would mark the letter D as your answer.

20. Rent Expense

21. Allowance for Depreciation of Fixtures

22. Sales Returns and Allowances

23. Security Deposit for Electricity

24. Accrued Salaries Payable

25. Dividends Payable

26. Petty Cash Fund

27. Notes Receivable Discounted

28. Surplus

29. Capital Stock Authorized

30. Insurance Expense

31. Sales for Cash

32. Purchase Discounts

33. Automobile Delivery Equipment

34. Bad Debts Expense

Questions 35 to 49 consist of a list of some of the accounts in a general ledger. For the purpose of preparing financial statements, each of these accounts is to be classified into one of the following four major classifications, lettered A to D as follows:

(A) Assets   (B) Liabilities   (C) Income   (D) Expense

You are to indicate the classification to which each belongs by marking the appropriate letter, A, B, C or D in the correspondingly numbered row on your answer sheet. For example, for the account Merchandise Inventory, which is an asset account, you would mark the letter A as your answer.

35. Purchases

36. Prepaid Interest

37. Cash in Bank

38. Depreciation of Fixtures

39. Accounts Receivable

40. Mortgage Payable

41. Accrued Interest Receivable

42. Bad Debts Expense

43. Insurance Expired

44. Treasury Stock

45. Investments

46. Loan to Partner

47. Unearned Rent Received

48. Petty Cash Fund

49. Loss on Sale of Equipment

Each of questions 50 to 59 consists of a typical transaction of our business followed by the debit and credit (amounts omitted) of the journal entry for that transaction. For each of these questions, the debit and credit given may be appropriately classified under one of the following four categories:

(A) the debit of the journal entry is correct but the credit is incorrect

(B) the debit of the journal entry is incorrect but the credit is correct

(C) both the debit and the credit of the journal entry are correct

(D) both the debit and the credit of the journal entry are incorrect

Examine each question carefully. Then, in the correspondingly numbered row on your answer sheet, mark as your answer the letter preceding the category which is the best of the four suggested above.

Example: We purchased a desk for cash.
Debit: Office Equipment
Credit: Account Payable

In this example, the debit is correct but the credit is incorrect. Therefore, you should mark A as your answer.

50. We sent a check for $500 to W. Brown in payment for an invoice for that amount.
Debit: Cash
Credit: Accounts Receivable

51. We took merchandise, amounting to $35, for our own use.
Debit: Proprietor, Personal
Credit: Purchases

52. John Smith's 90 day note for $350, which was discounted by us at our bank last month, was paid by him today.
Debit: Notes Receivable Discounted
Credit: Accounts Receivable

53. We sold merchandise to J. Brown on account for $275.
Debit: Accounts Payable
Credit: Sales

54. We returned damaged merchandise to J. Howard and received a credit memorandum from him for $28.

Debit: Accounts Payable
Credit: Sales Returns and Allowances

55. We paid our 30 day note given to Mr. Jones for $650 without interest.
Debit: Notes Receivable
Credit: Cash

56. We sent William Green a check for $10.50 for a discount he had forgotten to take when he paid us for merchandise this week.
Debit: Sales Discounts
Credit: Cash

57. The bank loaned us $1000 and we invested it in the business.
Debit: Cash
Credit: Loan Receivable

58. We recorded depreciation for the year on our office equipment.
Debit: Reserve for Depreciation of Office Equipment
Credit: Depreciation of Office Equipment

59. One of our customers, Edward Thomas, was declared a bankrupt and his debt of $25 to us was cancelled.
Debit: Reserve for Bad Debts
Credit: Accounts Receivable

60. A merchant purchased a stock of goods and priced these goods so as to gain 40% on the cost to him. If the merchant sold these goods for $840, the cost of these goods to him was

   (A) $504   (B) $600   (C) $336   (D) $710.

61. If the interest at 6% for one full year on a principal sum amounts to $12, the principal sum is

   (A) $100   (B) $72   (C) $240   (D) $200.

62. On September 17, a business man discounted a customer's 90 day non-interest bearing note at his bank. The face of the note was $960 and it was dated August 28. The discount rate was 5%. Using a 360 day year, the amount in cash that the business man received from the bank was most nearly
   (A) $866.67   (B) $950.67   (C) $952.00   (D) $948.80.

63. A certain correctly totalled cash receipts journal contained the following columns: Net Cash Debit, Accounts Receivable, Sales Discounts, and General. At the end of April, the totals of the columns were as follows: Net Cash Debit, $18,925.15; Accounts Receivable (not given); Sales Discounts, $379.65; General, $5,639.25. The total of the Accounts Receivable column was
   (A) $13,285.90   (B) $12,906.25   (C) $24,184.75   (D) $13,665.55.

64. During its first year of operation, a retail store had cash sales of $49,000 and installment sales of $41,000. If 12% of the amount of these installment sales were collected in that year, the total amount of cash received from sales for that year was
   (A) $10,800   (B) $51,720   (C) $53,920   (D) $59,850.

65. W. Jones and A. Brown formed a partnership and agreed to share profits in proportion to their initial capital investments. W. Jones invested $15,000 and A. Brown invested $12,500. If the profits for the year were $16,500, A. Brown's share of the profits was
   (A) $8,250   (B) $7,500   (C) $9,000   (D) $8,500.

66. In a certain city the yearly tax rate on real estate was $48.75 per thousand dollars of assessed valuation. If an apartment house in that city was assessed for $185,000, the real estate tax payable by the owner of that house was most nearly

    (A) $9,018.75 (B) $8,939.50 (C) $8,757.75 (D) $9,515.25.

67. A correctly totalled cash payments journal contained the following columns: Net Cash, Accounts Payable, Purchase Discounts, General. At the end of April, the totals of the columns were as follows: Net Cash, $18,375.60; Accounts Payable, $16,981.19; Purchase Discounts (not given); General, $1,875.37. The total of the Purchase Discounts column was

    (A) $240.48 (B) $3,269.78 (C) $480.96 (D) $3,151.27.

68. On January 1, the credit balance of the Accounts Payable account in a general ledger was $9,139.87. For the month of January, the Purchase Journal total amounted to $3,467.81; the Accounts Payable column in the Cash Disbursements Journal amounted to $2,935.55; the total of the Returned Purchases Journal for January amounted to $173.15; and the Miscellaneous column in the Cash Disbursements Journal showed that $750 had been paid in January on notes given to creditors and entered in previous months. The balance in the Accounts Payable account at the end of January was

    (A) $8,748.98 (B) $9,498.98 (C) $10,248.98 (D) $8,434.46.

69. The bank statement received from his bank by a business man showed a certain balance for the month of June. This bank statement showed a service charge of $5.19 for the month. He discovered that a check drawn by him in the amount of $83.75 and returned by the bank had been entered on the stub of his check book as $38.75. He also found that two checks which he had issued, #29 for $37.18 and #33 for $18.69, were not listed on the statement and had not been returned by the bank. The balance in his check book before he reconciled it with the balance shown on the bank statement was $8917.91. The balance on the bank statement was

    (A) $8933.97 (B) $8923.59 (C) $8811.85 (D) $9013.59.

Answer Key

1. D	9. D	18. B	27. C	36. A	45. A	54. A	63. D
2. A	10. C	19. B	28. C	37. A	46. A	55. B	64. C
3. B	11. A	20. D	29. C	38. D	47. B	56. C	65. B
4. A	12. C	21. C	30. D	39. A	48. A	57. A	66. A
5. D	13. B	22. D	31. C	40. B	49. D	58. D	67. C
6. D	14. C	23. D	32. C	41. A	50. D	59. C	68. B
7. C	15. B	24. C	33. D	42. D	51. C	60. B	69. B
8. A	16. D	25. C	34. D	43. D	52. A	61. D	
	17. C	26. D	35. D	44. A	53. B	62. B	

PART TWO

Bookkeeping and Accounting Practice

2

APPLYING ACCOUNTING AND BOOKKEEPING PRINCIPLES

Practice Set Material

PURPOSE

The object of supplying these transactions is to give practice in applying accounting principles and do bookkeeping by making journal entries, posting them and closing the books through four successive stages of a business.

1. John Smith goes into business (July Transactions).
2. The business grows and the books are expanded (August Transactions).
3. John Smith takes in a partner (September Transactions).
4. The partnership incorporates (October Transactions).

MATERIALS NEEDED

50 Sheets of Journal Ruled Paper (Letter Size 8 1/2" x 11").
100 Sheets of Ledger Ruled Paper (Letter Size 8 1/2" x 11").
20 Sheets of 10 or 20 column Ruled Paper (Letter Size 8 1/2" x 11").
1 Loose Leaf Prong Binder
The paper and binder can be obtained at any stationery store, but be sure that the holes in the paper match the binder. Colored paper (with or without tabs) can be used as a separation sheet between the Journal, Ledger, etc.

EXPLANATION

It was necessary to assume an abnormal growth and expansion of the business in order to list transactions which would bring into practice all the accounting principles within four consecutive months. Also, to make the principles clear, short cuts used in actual business practice could not be used. Some of these practices are noted and explained below. (For purposes of simplicity, sales, wages and other figures are lower than in actual practice, and payroll taxes have been omitted.)

NOTES ON BUSINESS PRACTICES

(a) Although in the practice set all accounts have been ruled and the balances brought down, in actual practice it is not customary to rule off the asset, liability and capital accounts until they are actually closed out.

(b) While the reserve for bad debts in the practice set has been computed on the basis of net sales including both charge and cash sales, the custom in business is to determine the reserve on a percentage of charge sales only.

(c) In actual practice the Sales Journal is seldom written up. Instead, the duplicates of the customers' sales invoices are filed in a binder. Postings to the individual accounts in the Accounts Receivable Subsidiary Ledger are made directly from the duplicate copy of the invoices. The total of the invoices for the month are debited to the Accounts Receivable Control Account in the General Ledger, and credited to Sales. The same procedure is used for Sales Returns and Allowances. In this case, posting is made directly from duplicates of the Credit Memos issued to Customers; (usually a colored paper is used).

(d) Where it is the practice of a firm to pay most of its bills in full at the time of settlement, considerable time and labor is saved by the use of a Voucher Register. This eliminates the Accounts Payable Subsidiary Ledger. Except for the addition of a few extra columns the Voucher Register is similar to the Purchase Journal.

A form for a Voucher Register follows:

Month of _____ 19__   Page _

Line No.	Date	Voucher No.	Vendor	Terms	Cr. Amount	Paid by Check #	Dr. DISTRIBUTION			
							Mdse.	Adver.	Ins.	etc.
1										
2										
3										
4										
etc.										

Vendors are instructed to render their invoices in duplicate. When received, the invoices are checked, approved, entered and distributed. Where it is practical all invoices from one vendor are clipped together, totaled and entered as one voucher. On both the original and duplicate a Voucher # is entered, and the page and line number of entry. Thus, $\frac{1}{25}$ means that the invoice or invoices were entered on page 1, line 25 of the voucher register. After entry, the invoices are placed in a file under the date on which they are to be paid. When the invoices are paid the check number is entered on the corresponding page and line number. The original invoices are filed alphabetically, and the duplicates, numerically, by voucher number.

1. SINGLE PROPRIETORSHIP

This section exemplifies the use of a General Journal (Book No. 1) and a Ledger (Book No. 2). Transactions for John Smith are to be recorded for July. At the end of one month, special journals and subsidiary ledgers are placed into operation for Mr. Smith.

Following are the transactions for John Smith, who begins business as a hardware dealer on July 1. Each transaction is to be journalized and posted to the proper account in the ledger. An explanation is to accompany each Journal entry. Number each Journal entry, beginning with "1".

July 1. Mr. Smith invests cash, $40,000.00. Pays rent for the month, $375.00. Pays for advertising in a local paper, $25.00. Purchases merchandise on account from the Brown Wholesale Co., $1,000.00. Buys furniture for the store for cash, $1,750.00.

July 2. Purchases additional furniture for the store from Clark & Co. on account $200.00. Sells to Macy & Co. on account $66.25, and to Spalding & Co. on account $54.00. Cash sales for the day, $355.25.

July 3. Purchases merchandise from Hamilton Supply Co., on account $4,185.00. Sells on account to Spalding & Co. $30.00 and to John Pollard $64.50. Macy & Co. returns $16.25 of merchandise purchased July 2. Cash sales $383.50.

July 5. Smith buys a used automobile delivery truck for cash, $3,625.00. He pays for a license for the truck, $125.00. Pays for gasoline, $15.50. Sells on account to Macy & Co. $85.00. Pays Brown Wholesale Co. for merchandise purchased on July 1. Cash sales for the day, $412.25. Smith purchases the store building in which he is located for $30,000.00, giving a mortgage for $15,000.00 and paying the balance in cash, with the rent of $375.00 paid on July 1 being taken by the seller as payment on the building.

July 6. Macy & Co. pays his account in full. Sells on account to William Dickson, $51.50. Pays Clark & Co. for furniture purchased on July 2. Pays Hamilton Supply Co. for purchases of July 3. Pays wages of clerk for the week, $150.00. Cash sales, $289.45. Hereafter cash sales will be summarized by weeks to avoid repetition.

July 8. Sells on account to Robert Black, $55.00, and to Henry Kelley, $31.35. Pays for repairs to building, cash $355.00. Buys merchandise for cash, $750.00.

July 9. Pays $35.00 for advertising in a local paper. Sells on account to Macy & Co. $95.00 and to George Cornwell $29.45.

July 10. Purchases merchandise from the Fulton Supply Co. on account, $385.00. Pays cash for building repairs, $17.50.

July 11. Returns $35.00 of merchandise to the Fulton Supply Co. George Cornwell returns $5.45 of merchandise purchased on July 9. Robert Black pays $15.00 on account.

July 12. Sells to Selden Hawley on account, $66.00. Purchases an accounting machine for cash, $750.00.

July 13. Cash sales for the week, $1,498.00. Pays wages for the week $150.00.

July 15. Pays for advertising in local paper, $60.00. Buys merchandise on account from White & Co. $313.75. Sells on account to George Cornwell $30.00; to Henry Kelly $15.00.

July 16. Returns $50.00 of merchandise to White & Co. Sells on account to Robert Black, $30.00, to Henry Kelly, $22.00.

July 17. Buys merchandise for cash, $469.00.

July 18. Sells on account to George Cornwell, $35.00, to Selden Hawley, $36.50. Pays for repairs to delivery truck, $31.00.

July 19. Buys merchandise for cash, $270.00.

July 20. Smith donates $50.00 to the Red Cross. George Cornwell pays $15.00 on account. Buys merchandise on account from the Brown Durrell Co., $436.00. Cash Sales for the week, $1,576.20. Pays wages for the week, $150.00.

July 22. Sells on account to William Dickson, $30.00; to Henry Kelly, $15.00 Buys merchandise for cash $415.60.

July 23. Pays for truck repairs, $10.00.

July 24. Buys merchandise on account from Brown Durrell Co., $991.50.

July 25. Returns merchandise to Brown Durrell Co., $65.25. Henry Kelly pays $25.00 on account.

July 26. Sells on account to Robert Black, $202.50; to George Cornwell, $60.00.

July 27. Cash sales for the week, $1,691.00. Pays wages for the week, $150.00.

July 29. Henry Kelly pays $15.00 on account.

July 31. Cash Sales for July 29-31 are $489.50.

ASSIGNMENT

(1) The student should take a trial balance of the Ledger at this point.

(2) Prepare a work sheet taking the following adjustments into consideration:

Adjustments:

(a) The merchandise inventory, July 31, is $3,436.50.
(b) Set up a Reserve for Bad Debts of $50.00 for month of July.
(c) Accrued Interest on the Mortgage is $62.50 for month of July.
(d) Set up a Reserve for Depreciation of Delivery Equipment for $75.00 for July.
(e) Set up a Reserve for Depreciation of Furniture and Fixtures for $50.00 for July.
(f) Set up a Reserve for Depreciation of Buildings for $100.00 for July.
(g) Accrued wages are $75.00.

(3) Journalize and post the adjusting entries.

(4) Journalize and post the closing entries.

(5) Prepare a Balance Sheet in account form. (Exhibit A)

(6) Prepare a Statement of Profit and Loss for the month of July. (Exhibit B)

(7) Rule and balance all accounts.

2. THE BOOKS ARE EXPANDED

John Smith's business has grown in sufficient volume to expand the bookkeeping system. Beginning on Aug. 1, the following books will be installed in addition to the General Journal (GJ) (Book No. 1) and the General Ledger (GL) (Book No. 2) used for the July transactions.

Cash Journal (CJ) (Book No. 3) containing Cash Receipts (CR) and the Cash Disbursements (CD)
Sales Journal (SJ) (Book No. 4) containing also Sales Returns and Allowances (SRJ)
Purchase Journal (PJ) (Book No. 5) containing also Purchase Returns (PRJ)
Petty Cash Journal (PCJ) (Book No. 6)
Accounts Receivable Ledger or Customer's Ledger (CL) (Book No. 7)
Accounts Payable Ledger or Creditor's Ledger (CrL) (Book No. 8)

NOTE: The letters, in parenthesis, identify the book from which the entries are made when posting is done in your Practical Set.

Following are the transactions for John Smith, who entered the hardware business, as a single proprietor on July 1.

Aug. 1. Purchases merchandise on account from Whitney & Co., $1,000.00, terms 2/10/n/30; purchases merchandise from Hicks & Co. on account, $1,500.00, terms 2/10/n/30. Pays $10.00 for advertisement in the Local Times. Buys store supplies from the Carter Paper Co. for $125.00 and pays cash for them. The invoice rendered for purchase of merchandise from Whitney & Co. requires the approval of some one authorized by the proprietor, which, after going through the usual routine, is entered in the Cash Disbursement Journal. Subsequent invoices for purchase should be treated in the same manner.

Aug. 3. Returns merchandise to Whitney & Co., $50.00. Sells on account to H.C. Young, $250.00; to H.S. Darby, $125.00; to E.W. Russell, $36.00; to H.C. Taylor, $75.00. Cash Sales $1,511.70 Cash Sales will be summarized weekly.

Aug. 5. Sells on account to W.S. Lee, $165.00; to E.W. Russell, $91.50, to H.S. Roy, $120.00. Pays A.L. Jones $40.00 for repairs to store building.

Aug. 6. Buys merchandise from Robinson & Co., on account, $3,000.00, terms 2/10/n/60. Buys merchandise from Pierce & Co., on account $2,500.00, terms 2/10/n/30; pays the account today. Sells on account to E.C. Griffin, $175.00; to G.C. Doyle, $85.00.

Aug. 7. H.S. Roy returns merchandise, $15.00. Sells on account to H.C. Evans, $80.00; H.S. Roy, $30.00. Pays the General Delivery Co. $85.00 for delivery expenses to date.

Aug. 8. Pays the Whitney & Co. invoice, taking the discount. Pays the Hicks & Co. invoice, taking the discount. Purchases merchandise from the Harper Wholesale Co., on account, $1,750.00, terms n/30. Sells on account to Frank Snyder, $90.00.

Aug. 9. Sells on account to E.W. Russell, $60.00, to W.S. Lee, $85.00. Pays the Local Times $50.00 for advertisement. Purchases supplies from the Edwards Co., cash, $50.00.

Aug. 10. Sells on account to George Crane, $498.00. Cash sales, $2,727.40.

Aug. 12. W.S. Lee returns merchandise, $10.00.

Aug. 13. Sells on account to George Crane, $20.00. A voucher for $250.00 is prepared together with a check for a similar amount for the establishment of a petty cash fund. The check is cashed.

Aug. 14. Pays Robinson & Co. for purchases of August 6. Purchases merchandise from Western Wholesale Co., on account, $3,600.00, terms 2/10/n/30. Pays R.K. Frost $30.00 for repairs to the building. Sells on account to E.W. Russell, $80.00; to H.S. Kirby, $43.75. Purchases supplies, $5.00, and pays $10.00 for advertising, both sums being paid out of petty cash. Enter the two items, putting both sums in the Total column; carry them to the proper distribution columns, also. Pays W.C. Worth two weeks wages, $500.00.

Aug. 15. Sells on account to H.C. Young $663.55. Pays $7.50 out of petty cash for special delivery of Young's order. Sells on account to H.L. Pratt, $50.00, to H.S. Kirby, $ 66.35. Purchases merchandise, $10.00, paying for it out of petty cash.

Aug. 16. Purchases a typewriter from the Underwood Co., for cash, $375.00. Purchases a Billing machine from the Remington Co., on account $875.00, terms n/30. Sells on account to H.L. Pratt, $30.00, to H.S. Gibbs $20.00. H.C. Young pays $250.00 on account.

Aug. 17. Purchases merchandise from the Herrick Supply Co. on account, $350.00, terms 2/20/n/60. Pays the Local Times $75.00 for advertising. Cash Sales, $2,361.50.

Aug. 19. H.S. Darby pays $75.00 on account. Pays $15.00 out of petty cash for supplies. Pays $5.00 out of petty cash for repairs to the store fixtures. Pays $25.00 out of petty cash for merchandise. E.W. Russell pays $60.00 on account.

Aug. 20. Pays $7.50 out of petty cash for repairs to store fixtures.

Aug. 21. Sells on account to E.J. Kemp, $185.00; to E.W. Russell, $50.00. C.C. Doyle pays $55.00 on account. Pays General Delivery Co. $150.00 for delivery services. Pays Western Wholesale Co. for purchases of August 14.

Aug. 22. Sells on account to H.C. Evans, $86.50; to H.S. Roy, $36.50. E.J. Kemp returns $50.00 of his purchases of January 21. Purchases merchandise on account from Grimes & Co., $190.00, terms 2/30/n/60. Pays $11.50 out of petty cash for supplies.

Aug. 23. Buys table for the office from the Hartley Co., cash, $150.00. Sells on account to H.S. Roy $15.00; to E.W. Russell $27.00. Pays $8.75 out of petty cash for advertising.

Aug. 24. Sells on account to E.W. Russell, $70.00; to G.C. Doyle, $200.00. Cash sales, $2,305.50.

Aug. 26. Pays Harper Wholesale Co. for purchases of August 8. G.C. Doyle returns merchandise, $27.50.

Aug. 27. Sells on account to G.C. Doyle, $75.00; to H.S. Roy, $55.00. Pays $15.00 out of petty cash for merchandise.

Aug. 28. E.W. Russell pays $125.00 on account.

Aug. 29. Pays the Local Times $90.00 for advertising. Purchases merchandise from the Sanford & Co., on account, $500.00, terms n/30. Pays W.C. Worth wages for two weeks, $500.00.

Aug. 30. Purchases merchandise on account from Wilson & Co., $2,000.00, terms 2/10/n/30. Sells on account to H.G. Little, $500.00

Aug. 31. Draws salary of $500.00 for the month, check made payable to John Smith. H.G. Little gives his 30-day note for $500.00. Cash Sales, $2,104.00. John Pollard pays $64.50; Robert Black pays $272.50; Henry Kelly pays $43.35; William Dickson pays $81.50; Macy & Co. pays $95.00. George Cornwell pays $134.00.

ASSIGNMENT

(1) Summarize the petty cash disbursements, enter in the Cash Journal, and issue a check to replenish the petty cash fund. Spalding & Co. pays $84.00; Selden Hawley pays $102.50. Pays White & Co. $263.75; pays Fulton Supply Co. $350.00; pays Brown Durrell Co. $1,362.25.

(2) Summarize all books of original entry and post.

(3) Prepare a trial balance of the general ledger. See that the sum of the subsidiary ledger balances equals the balance of the controlling accounts.

(4) Prepare a work sheet, taking the following adjustments into consideration:

> ### Adjustments:
>
> (a) The merchandise inventory, August 31 is $8,487.50.
> (b) Accrued delivery expenses amount to $125.00
> (c) Set up a reserve for bad debts of $151.45.
> Set up a reserve for depreciation on Delivery Equipment for $75.00 for August).
> Set up a reserve for Depreciation on Building of $100.00 for Aug.
> (d) Depreciate store fixtures $41.00.
> (e) Accrued store wages are $60.00.
> Accrued interest payable on the mortgage is $125.00 for August.

(5) Journalize and post the adjusting entries.

(6) Journalize and post the closing entries.

(7) Prepare a Balance Sheet in account form (Exhibit A). Prepare schedules for accounts receivable (Schedule 1) and account payable (Schedule 2).

(8) Prepare a statement of Profit and Loss for the month of August (Exhibit B).

(9) Rule and balance the accounts.

3. JOHN SMITH TAKES IN A PARTNER

On September 1, John Smith decides to admit Edward Clark as a partner under the name of Smith & Clark, on the condition that Clark invests $25,000.00 in cash in the business. Clark is to receive a one-fourth interest in the profits and is to bear one-fourth of the losses. Smith's salary is to be $24,000.00 and Clark's salary is to be $15,000.00 per year. Drawings may be made by each partner, but not to exceed the monthly salaries of the partners. At the end of each month the salary of each partner is to be journalized and posted by debiting Salaries of Partners and crediting the Drawing account of each partner.

Sept. 1. Edward Clark invests $25,000.00. Pays Sun Insurance Co. $250.00 for fire insurance premiums covering the merchandise and fixtures for a period of one year.

Sept. 2. H.C. Young pays $250.00 on account. Pays $7.50 out of petty cash for advertising.

Sept. 3. Purchases merchandise from Harper Wholesale Co., on account $3,500.00, terms n/30. Pays the Remington Co. for Billing machine purchased August 16. Pays the Herrick Supply Co. for purchases of August 17.

Sept. 4. Buys $10,000.00 of bonds at par from Shields & Co. Sells on account to H.S. Darby, $100.00 Pays $20.00 out of petty cash for supplies.

Sept. 5. Edward Clark draws $900.00. Pays accrued delivery expense to the General Delivery Co.

Sept. 6. Pays Wilson & Co. for purchases of August 30. Pays $6.25 out of petty cash for repairs to the typewriter. Pays truck driver $125.00. Cash Sales, $3,500.00.

Sept. 8. Pays O.A. Waters $75.00 for building repairs. H.C. Taylor pays $75.00.

Sept. 9. Purchases merchandise from Wilson & Co., on account, $3,500.00, terms 2/10/n/30. Pays Local Times $250.00 for advertising.

Sept. 10. Edward Clark draws $350.00.

Sept. 11. Sells on account to E.W. Russell, $200.00; to H.C. Taylor $52.50. Buys supplies from the Carter Paper Co., cash, $250.00.

Sept. 12. Pays $20.00 out of petty cash for gasoline.

Sept. 13. Pays W.C. Worth $660.00 ($600.00 for the first two weeks of August, and $60.00 for the August accrual). Pays truck driver $125.00. E.W. Russell returns merchandise $50.00.

Sept. 15. Pays Sanford & Co. for purchases of August 29.

Sept. 16. Sells on account to H.C. Young $250.00. Sells on account to George Crane $575.00. Sells on account to G.C. Doyle $600.00. Sells on account to W.S. Lee, $250.00. H.S. Roy pays his account in full. E.C. Griffin pays $125.00 on account.

Sept. 17. Pays Wilson & Co. for September 9 purchase.

Sept. 18. Sells on account to E.C. Griffin $175.00. G.C. Doyle pays his account to September 1. Purchases merchandise on account from Brown & Co., $4,500.00, terms 1/10/60. W.S. Lee merchandise returned $10.00.

Sept. 19. Pays Local Times for advertisement, $225.00.

Sept. 20. Pays Astor Oil Co. $100.00 for gasoline. Pays A.P. Plog $250.00 for building repairs. Pays truck driver $125.00. Cash sales $7,052.50. Sells on account to H.S. Gibbs $100.00. Sells on account to E.J. Kemp $50.00.

Sept. 22. Pays Grimes & Co. for August 22 purchase.

Sept. 23. H.C. Evans pays his account in full.

Sept. 24. Pays Harper Wholesale Co. for purchases of September 3.

Sept. 25. Purchases merchandise on account from Springer & Co., $8,500.00, terms 2/10/n/30. Pays Brown & Co. for purchases of September 18.

Sept. 26. Pays $20.00 out of petty cash for gasoline.

Sept. 27. Cash Sales, $9,975.65.

Sept. 28. H.G. Little pays his note of August 31. Pays wages to W.C. Worth $600.00. H.S. Darby pays balance of his account. George Crane pays August account. W.S. Lee pays August account. H.C. Young pays $413.55 on account. Pays truck driver $125.00. Journalize and post the partners' salaries.

Sept. 30. Purchases merchandise from Lane & Co., on account, $5,253.00, terms 2/10/n/30. Returns merchandise to Lane & Co., $100.00. Cash Sales $2,505.60.

ASSIGNMENT

(1) Take care of the Petty Cash Disbursements.

(2) Pay John Smith's salary for September, $2,000.00.

(3) Summarize all books of original entry and post.

(4) Prepare a trial balance of the general ledger. See that the subsidiaries and controls are in agreement.

(5) Prepare a work sheet, taking the following adjustments into consideration.

> *Adjustments:*
>
> (a) The merchandise inventory, September 30, is $16,250.00.
> (b) Set up a reserve for bad debts of $100.00 for September.
> (c) Depreciate store fixtures of $41.00.
>
> (d) Depreciate delivery equipment $72.50 for September
> (e) The estimated tax liability for the month is $$50.00.
> (f) Defer eleven-twelfths of the fire insurance premium.
>
> (g) Accrued Interest Receivable on bonds is $25.00. Wages accrued are $100.00. Accrued Interest Payable on the mortgage is $225.00. Depreciation on Building is $100.00 for September.

(6) Journalize and post the adjusting entries.

(7) Journalize and post the closing entries.

(8) Prepare a Balance Sheet in account form (Exhibit A). Prepare schedules of Accounts Receivable (Schedule 1) and Accounts Payable (Schedule 2).

(9) Prepare a statement of Profit and Loss for the month of September (Exhibit B).

(10) Rule and balance the accounts.

4. THE PARTNERSHIP INCORPORATES

On Oct. 1, John Smith and Edward Clark decide to incorporate. The corporation laws of the State of New York in which the charter is secured require that there be three incorporators. To fulfill this requirement, James Smith, brother of John Smith, agrees to act as incorporator and to purchase one share of stock at par. The name of the newly formed corporation is to be Smith-Clark, Inc. The charter provides for an authorized capital stock of $125,000.00 consisting of 250 shares of common stock of a par value of $500.00 per share.

Oct. 1. Make necessary General Journal entries to adjust prepaid and accrued accounts. Record the authorization of the Capital Stock in the General Journal. Pay John Smith $661.79 and Edward Clark $342.11 in order to reduce their Net Worth Accounts to even hundreds of dollars, so that the issuance of fractional shares may be avoided.

Subscriptions are received to the Capital Stock as follows:

John Smith	84 shares
Edward Clark	50 shares
James Smith.	1 share
Total Stock Subscribed.	135 shares

This leaves 115 shares of stock for future disposition.

NOTE: Two more books (a) Stock Certificate Book and (b) Capital Stock Ledger are now required. While for convenience these two books are represented at the end of the General Ledger, they are two separate books in actual practice.

The subscriptions are recorded by a Debit to Subscriptions and a credit to Unissued Common Stock. The subscriptions are paid. Stock Certificates are issued and posted in the Capital Stock Ledger. James Smith pays cash for his share and John Smith and Edward Clark turn over their partnership net worth for their subscriptions. The entry for payment from James Smith is made in the cash receipts journal; the liquidation of the partners' subscriptions is made in the general journal, by a debit to each Net Worth account and a credit to subscriptions. Complete explanations must accompany each journal entry.

Since there are no Drawing accounts in the corporation, salaries will be paid to Smith and Clark at the end of each month.

Oct. 2. H.C. Young pays the balance of his account. Pays Local Times $150.00 for advertisement.

Oct. 3. Purchases merchandise from the Harper Wholesale Co., on account, $1,875.00, terms n/30. Pays Springer & Co. for purchases of Sept. 25. Sells on account to H.S. Darby $280.00; to H.C. Young $162.00.

Oct. 4. Sells on account to E.W. Russell $110.00; W.S. Lee $84.75. Russell pays $150.00 on account. Pays A.P. Plog $250.00 for building repairs.

Oct. 5. The corporation receives subscriptions from David Jones for eight shares of stock at $500.00 per share. The subscriptions are paid today.

Oct. 6. Frank Snyder pays his account in full. Sells on account to W.S. Lee $136.70; H.S. Roy $109.50. Pays the truck driver $125.00. Cash sales $4,809.95.

Oct. 8. W.S. Lee returns $25.00 of merchandise. Sells on account to Frank Snyder, $93.75. Pays Astor Oil Co. $125.00 for gasoline. Paid Lane & Co. for invoice of September 24.

Oct. 9. Purchases merchandise from Sanford & Co. on account, $4,950.00, terms n/60. Sells on account to George Crane $102.50. Crane pays $250.00 on account. E.W. Russell returns $11.00 of merchandise.

Oct. 11. Sells on account to H.S. Kirby $105.00; to H.L. Pratt $202.25. Purchases merchandise from Lane & Co. on account $2,500.00, terms, 2/20/n/30.

Oct. 12. Pays A.P. Plog $400.00 for building repairs.

Oct. 13. Buys store supplies from the Carter Paper Co., cash $290.00. Pays Local Times $400.00 for advertisement.

Oct. 15. Sells on account to H.S. Darby $135.00; to H.S. Roy $112.00. Pays wages to W.C. Worth $600.00. Pays truck driver $125.00.

Oct. 16. E.C. Griffin pays his account in full. H.S. Roy returns $10.00 of merchandise.

Oct. 17. Pays A.P. Plog for building repairs $90.00.

Oct. 18. Sells on account to G.C. Doyle $145.35; to Frank Snyder $93.75.

Oct. 19. Pays John Brewer $61.50 for furniture repairs. Pays $29.00 out of petty cash for Supplies. Pays $34.50 out of petty cash for gasoline. Frank Snyder returns $28.75 of merchandise.

Oct. 20. Sells on account to George Crane $100.00. Cash sales, $8,353.50.

Oct. 22. Buys supplies from Walsh & Co., cash $62.00. Pays Daily Times Co. for advertising. Pays $117.50 for delivery truck repairs. Pays truck driver $125.00.

Oct. 23. Pays $17.50 out of petty cash for gasoline.

Oct. 24. Pays $40.00 out of petty cash for merchandise.

Oct. 25. E.J. Kemp pays his account in full.

Oct. 26. Pays $20.00 out of petty cash for advertising.

Oct. 27. H.L. Pratt pays $80.00.

Oct. 29. Sells on account to H.L. Pratt $250.00. Pays wages to W.C. Worth, $600.00. Pays truck driver $125.00.

Oct. 31. Purchases merchandise from Harper Wholesale Co., on account, $8,500.00 terms 2/10/n/60. Smith & Clark draw their salaries. (Charge to Officers' Salaries) Pays Harper Wholesale Co., $1,875.00. Pays Lane & Co. invoice of Oct. 11. Cash Sales, $8,906.07.

ASSIGNMENT

(1) Take care of the petty cash disbursements.

(2) Summarize the books of original entry and post.

(3) Prepare a trial balance of the general ledger. See that the subsidiaries and controls are in agreement.

(4) Prepare a work sheet, taking the following adjustments into consideration:

Adjustments:

(a) The merchandise inventory, Oct. 31, is $19,500.00.

(b) Set up a reserve for bad debts of $100.00.

(c) Depreciate the store fixtures $41.00.

(d) Depreciate the delivery equipment by $72.50.

(e) Depreciate the building by $100.00.

(f) The estimated tax liability for September and October is $150.00.

(g) Charge off one-twelfth of the fire insurance premium of $250.00.

(h) Accrued wages payable are $60.00.

(i) Accrued interest receivable on investments is $50.00.

(5) Journalize and post the adjusting entries.

(6) Journalize and post the closing entries.

(7) Prepare a balance sheet in account form (Exhibit A). Prepare schedules for accounts receivable (Schedule 1) and for account payable (Schedule 2).

(8) Prepare a statement of profit and loss for the month of October (Exhibit B)

(9) Rule and balance the accounts.

EXPLANATION OF PRACTICE SET
ACCOUNTING AND BOOKKEEPING PRINCIPLES

EXPLANATORY NOTE

In presenting the work called for in the Practice Set Material, of this Unit, it has been found advisable to arrange the books in the sequence in which they appear in the text. Following these are the monthly Trial Balances of the General Ledger, and the Work Sheets for the same months, which are succeeded by the exhibits and schedules prepared therefrom.

For ready reference an index follows:

Book No. 1 – General Journal (GJ)
Book No. 2 – General Ledger (GL)
Book No. 3 – Cash Journal which is divided into
Book No. 3a– Cash Receipts Journal (CR) and
Book No. 3b– Cash Disbursements Journal (CD)
Book No. 4 – Sales Journal (SJ) containing Sales Returns & Allowances (SRJ)
Book No. 5 – Purchase Journal (PJ) containing Purchase Returns (PRJ)
Book No. 6 – Petty Cash Journal (PCJ)
Book No. 7 – Accounts Receivable Ledger or Customers' Ledger (CL)
Book No. 8 – Accounts Payable Ledger or Creditors' Ledger (CrL)
Trial Balances of General Ledger for July, August, September and October 198–.
Work Sheets for July, August, September and October 198–.
Exhibits "A" – Balance Sheets for July, August, September and October 198–.
Schedules No. 1 – Accounts Receivable Trial Balances for: August, September and October 198–.
Schedules No. 2 – Accounts Payable Trial Balances for: August, September and October 198–.
Exhibits "B" – Statements of Profit and Loss for July, August, September and October, 198–.

The reason schedules Nos. 1 and 2 follow Exhibits "A", is that they are a detailed analysis of two amounts appearing on the Balance Sheet, namely, Accounts Receivable and Accounts Payable.

Instructions were given in Section 1, of this Unit, to number the General Journal entries consecutively. In actual practice it is customary to first prepare the Journal entry on a "Journal Voucher" form, which is approved by someone in authority. These "Journal Vouchers" are numbered consecutively. The use of numbers in the General Journal eliminates (a) the omission of an entry and (b) the inclusion of unauthorized entries.

In actual practice when posting from a book of original entry, the page number from which the entry is taken is entered in the "Reference" column in the Ledger. At the same time the Ledger page number is entered in the "Reference" column in the book of original entry. This is to facilitate tracing an entry. But, in printing this book it was found impractical to use the actual page numbers of the books in the reference column, therefore, in the Journals "oo" has been substituted for the actual page number. In Ledgers the letters designating the book from which the entry is made has been substituted.

BOOK NO. 1

DATE			F	DEBIT	CREDIT
198–		–1–			
July	1	Cash	∞	$40,000.00	
		John Smith, Proprietorship	∞		$40,000.00
		Investment in the business			
		–2–			
	1	Rent	∞	375.00	
		Cash	∞		375.00
		Rent for the month			
		–3–			
	1	Advertising	∞	25.00	
		Cash	∞		25.00
		Advertising in local paper			
		–4–			
	1	Purchases	∞	1,000.00	
		Brown Wholesale Co.	∞		1,000.00
		Merchandise purchased on account			
		–5–			
	1	Furniture	∞	1,750.00	
		Cash	∞		1,750.00
		Furniture purchased for store			
		–6–			
	2	Furniture	∞	200.00	
		Clark & Co.	∞		200.00
		Additional furniture purchased on account for the store			
		–7–			
	2	Macy & Co.	∞	66.25	
		Sales	∞		66.25
		Merchandise sold on account			
		–8–			
	2	Spalding & Co.	∞	54.00	
		Sales	∞		54.00
		Merchandise sold on account			
		–9–			
	2	Cash	∞	355.25	
		Cash Sales	∞		355.25
		Cash Sales for the day			
		–10–			
	3	Purchases	∞	4,185.00	
		Hamilton Supply Co.	∞		4,185.00
		Merchandise purchased on account			

JOURNAL – July, 198–

DATE			F	DEBIT	CREDIT
		–11–			
July	3	Spalding & Co.	OO	$ 30.00	
		Sales	OO		$ 30.00
		Merchandise sold on account			
		–12–			
	3	John Pollard	OO	64.50	
		Sales	OO		64.50
		Merchandise sold on account			
		–13–			
	3	Sales Returns	OO	16.25	
		Macy & Co.	OO		16.25
		Merchandise returned			
		–14–			
	3	Cash	OO	383.50	
		Cash sales	OO		383.50
		–15–			
	5	Automobile Delivery Truck	OO	3,625.00	
		Cash	OO		3,625.00
		Used Automobile Delivery Truck purchased for cash			
		–16–			
	5	Automobile expense	OO	125.00	
		Cash	OO		125.00
		License for Automobile Delivery Truck			
		–17–			
	5	Automobile expense	OO	15.50	
		Cash	OO		15.50
		Gasoline for truck			
		–18–			
	5	Macy & Co.	OO	85.00	
		Sales	OO		85.00
		Merchandise sold on account			
		–19–			
	5	Brown Wholesale Co.	OO	1,000.00	
		Cash	OO		1,000.00
		Payment for merchandise purchased July 1			
		–20–			
	5	Cash	OO	412.25	
		Cash sales	OO		412.25
		Cash sales for the day			

DATE			F	DEBIT	CREDIT
		-21-			
July	5	Building (store)	∞	14,625.00	
		Cash	∞		14,625.00
		Store building purchased for $6000.00 subject			
		to mortgage of $3000.00 paying balance in			
		cash with rent $75.00 paid on July 1			
		-22-			
	5	Building (store)	∞	375.00	
		Rent	∞		375.00
		Rent of $75.00 paid on July 1 taken by the			
		seller as payment on the building.			
		-23-			
	5	Building (store)	∞	15,000.00	
		Mortgage Payable	∞		15,000.00
		Store building purchased for $6000.00 subject			
		to mortgage of $3000.00			
		-24-			
	6	Cash	∞	135.00	
		Macy & Co.	∞		135.00
		Account paid in full			
		-25-			
	6	William Dickson	∞	51.50	
		Sales	∞		51.50
		Merchandise sold on account			
		-26-			
	6	Clark & Co.	∞	200.00	
		Cash	∞		200.00
		Payment for furniture purchased on July 2			
		-27-			
	6	Hamilton Supply Co.	∞	4,185.00	
		Cash	∞		4,185.00
		Payment for purchases of July 3			
		-28-			
	6	Wages	∞	150.00	
		Cash	∞		150.00
		Wages of clerk for the week			
		-29-			
	6	Cash	∞	289.45	
		Cash Sales	∞		289.45
		Merchandise cash sales			

JOURNAL – July, 198–

DATE			F	DEBIT	CREDIT
		–30–			
July	8	Robert Black	CO	$ 55.00	
		Sales	CO		$ 55.00
		Merchandise cash sales			
		–31–			
	8	Henry Kelly	CO	31.35	
		Sales	CO		31.35
		Merchandise sold on account			
		–32–			
	8	Repairs to Building	CO	355.00	
		Cash	CO		355.00
		Repairs to Store Building			
		–33–			
	8	Purchases	CO	750.00	
		Cash	CO		750.00
		Merchandise purchased for cash			
		–34–			
	9	Advertising	CO	35.00	
		Cash	CO		35.00
		Advertising in local paper			
		–35–			
	9	Macy & Co.	CO	95.00	
		Sales	CO		95.00
		Merchandise sold on account			
		–36–			
	9	George Cornwell	CO	29.45	
		Sales	CO		29.45
		Merchandise sold on account			
		–37–			
	10	Purchases	CO	385.00	
		Fulton Supply Co.	CO		385.00
		Merchandise purchased on account			
		–38–			
	10	Building Repairs	CO	17.50	
		Cash	CO		17.50
		Cash paid for Building Repairs			
		–39–			
	11	Fulton Supply Co.	CO	35.00	
		Purchase returns	CO		35.00
		Merchandise returned			

DATE		F	DEBIT		CREDIT	
	−40−					
July 11	Sales Returns	∞	$	$5.45		
	George Cornwell	∞			฿	$5.45
	Merchandise returned					
	−41−					
11	Cash	∞		15.00		
	Robert Black	∞				15.00
	Payment on account					
	−42−					
12	Selden Hawley	∞		66.00		
	Sales	∞				66.00
	Merchandise sold on account					
	−43−					
12	Furniture and Fixtures	∞		750.00		
	Cash	∞				750.00
	Accounting machine purchased for cash					
	−44−					
13	Cash	∞		1,498.00		
	Cash sales	∞				1,498.00
	Cash sales for the week					
	−45−					
13	Wages	∞		150.00		
	Cash	∞				150.00
	Wages for the week					
	−46−					
15	Advertising	∞		60.00		
	Cash	∞				60.00
	Advertising in local paper					
	−47−					
15	Purchases	∞		313.75		
	White & Co.	∞				313.75
	Merchandise purchased on account					
	−48−					
15	George Cornwell	∞		30.00		
	Sales	∞				30.00
	Merchandise sold on account					
	−49−					
15	Henry Kelly	∞		15.00		
	Sales	∞				15.00
	Merchandise sold on account					

JOURNAL – July, 198–

DATE		F	DEBIT	CREDIT
	–50–			
July 16	White & Co.	OO	$ 50.00	
	Purchase Returns	OO		$ 50.00
	Merchandise returned			
	–51–			
16	Robert Black	OO	30.00	
	Sales	OO		30.00
	Merchandise sold on account			
	–52–			
16	Henry Kelly	OO	22.00	
	Sales	OO		22.00
	Merchandise sold on account			
	–53–			
17	Purchases	OO	469.00	
	Cash	OO		469.00
	Merchandise purchased for cash			
	–54–			
18	George Cornwell	OO	35.00	
	Sales	OO		35.00
	Merchandise sold on account			
	–55–			
18	Selden Hawley	OO	36.50	
	Sales	OO		36.50
	Merchandise sold on account			
	–56–			
18	Automobile expense	OO	31.00	
	Cash	OO		31.00
	Repairs to delivery truck			
	–57–			
19	Purchases	OO	270.00	
	Cash	OO		270.00
	Merchandise purchased for cash			
	–58–			
20	Donations	OO	50.00	
	Cash	OO		50.00
	Donation to Red Cross			
	–59–			
20	Cash	OO	15.00	
	George Cornwell	OO		15.00
	Payment on account			

DATE		F	DEBIT	CREDIT
	-60-			
July 20	Purchases	CO	$ 436.00	
	Brown Durrell Co.	CO		$ 436.00
	Merchandise purchased on account			
	-61-			
20	Cash	CO	1,576.20	
	Cash sales	CO		1,576.20
	Cash sales for the week			
	-62-			
20	Wages	CO	150.00	
	Cash	CO		150.00
	Wages for the week			
	-63-			
22	William Dickson	CO	30.00	
	Sales	CO		30.00
	Merchandise sold on account			
	-64-			
22	Henry Kelly	CO	15.00	
	Sales	CO		15.00
	Merchandise sold on account			
	-65-			
22	Purchases	CO	415.60	
	Cash	CO		415.60
	Merchandise purchased for cash			
	-66-			
23	Automobile expense	CO	10.00	
	Cash	CO		10.00
	Paid for Truck repairs			
	-67-			
24	Purchases	CO	991.50	
	Brown Durrell Co.	CO		991.50
	Merchandise purchased on account			
	-68-			
25	Brown Durrell Co.	CO	65.25	
	Purchase returns	CO		65.25
	Merchandise returned			
	-69-			
25	Cash	CO	25.00	
	Henry Kelly	CO		25.00
	Payment on account			

JOURNAL – July, 198–

DATE		F	DEBIT	CREDIT
	–70–			
July 26	Robert black	CO	$ 202.50	
	Sales	CO		$ 202.50
	Merchandise sold on account			
	–71–			
26	George Cornwell	CO	60.00	
	Sales	CO		60.00
	Merchandise sold on account			
	–72–			
27	Cash	CO	1,691.00	
	Cash sales	CO		1,691.00
	Cash sales for the week			
	–73–			
27	Wages	CO	150.00	
	Cash	CO		150.00
	Wages for the week			
	–74–			
29	Cash	CO	15.00	
	Henry Kelly	CO		15.00
	Payment on account			
	–75–			
31	Cash	CO	489.50	
	Cash sales	CO		489.50
	Cash sales for July 29–31			
	–76–			
31	Inventory (merchandise)	CO	3,436.50	
	Purchases	CO		3,436.50
	Inventory 7/31/8–			
	–77–			
31	Bad Debts	CO	50.00	
	Reserve for Bad Debts	CO		50.00
	–78–			
31	Interest on Mortgage	CO	62.50	
	Accrued Interest Payable	CO		62.50
	–79–			
31	Depreciation on Delivery Equipment	CO	75.00	
	Reserve for Depreciation on Delivery Equipment	CO		75.00
	–80–			
31	Depreciation on Furniture & Fixtures	CO	50.00	
	Reserve for Depreciation on Fur. & Fix.	CO		50.00

DATE		F	DEBIT	CREDIT
	−81−			
July 31	Depreciation on Buildings	∞	$ 100.00	
	Reserve for Depreciation on Buildings	∞		$ 100.00
	−82−			
31	Wages Accrued	∞	75.00	
	Wages Payable	∞		75.00
	−83−			
31	Sales (Regular)	∞	1,104.05	
	Sales (Cash)	∞	6,695.15	
	Profit & Loss	∞		7,799.20
	To close sales for the period to P. & L.			
	−84−			
31	Profit & Loss	∞	21.70	
	Sales returns	∞		21.70
	To close Sales Returns to P. & L.			
	−85−			
31	Purchase Returns	∞	150.25	
	Profit & Loss	∞		150.25
	To close purchase returns to P. & L.			
	−86−			
31	Profit & Loss	∞	1,461.50	
	Wages	∞		675.00
	Advertising	∞		120.00
	Automobile Expense	∞		181.50
	Repairs to Building	∞		372.50
	Donations	∞		50.00
	Interest on Mortgage	∞		62.50
	Expense accounts transferred to P. & L.			
	−87−			
31	Profit & Loss	∞	5,779.35	
	Purchases	∞		5,779.35
	To close purchases to P. & L.			
	−88−			
31	Profit & Loss	∞	50.00	
	Bad Debts	∞		50.00
	−89−			
31	Profit & Loss	∞	225.00	
	Depreciation on Delivery Equipment	∞		75.00
	Depreciation on Furniture & Fixtures	∞		50.00
	Depreciation on Buildings	∞		100.00
	−90−			
31	Profit & Loss	∞	411.90	
	John Smith − Proprietorship	∞		411.90
	Net Profit transferred			

GENERAL JOURNAL AUGUST, 198–

DATE		F	DEBIT	CREDIT
	—91—			
Aug. 1	Wages Payable	∞	$ 75.00	
	Wages Accrued	∞		75.00
	To reverse entry of 7/31			
	—92—			
1	Accrued Interest on Mortgage	∞	62.50	
	Interest on Mortgage	∞		62.50
	—93—			
1	Accounts Receivable Controlling Account	∞	877.35	
	John Pollard	∞		64.50
	Robert Black	∞		272.50
	Henry Kelly	∞		43.35
	William Dickson	∞		81.50
	Macy & Co.	∞		95.00
	George Cornwell	∞		134.00
	Spalding & Co.	∞		84.00
	Selden Hawley	∞		102.50
	To transfer the above accounts from General Ledger to Accounts Receivable Ledger			
	—94—			
1	White & Co.	∞	263.75	
	Fulton Supply Co.	∞	350.00	
	Brown Durrell Co.	∞	1,362.25	
	Accounts Payable Controlling Account	∞		1,976.00
	To transfer the above accounts from General Ledger to Accounts Payable Ledger			
	—95—			
31	Notes Receivable	∞	500.00	
	Accounts Receivable	∞		500.00
	H.C. Little's note for 30 days			
	—96—			
31	Purchases	∞	3,436.50	
	Merchandise inventory	∞		3,436.50
	Inventory 8/1 trans. to Purchases			
	—97—			
31	Merchandise Inventory	∞	8,487.50	
	Purchases	∞		8,487.50
	Inventory 8/31			
	—98—			
31	Delivery expenses (accrued)	∞	125.00	
	Accrued expenses payable	∞		125.00
	—99—			
31	Bad Debts	∞	151.45	
	Reserve for Bad Debts	∞		151.45.

DATE		F	DEBIT	CREDIT
	-100-			
Aug. 31	Depreciation on Furn. and Fixtures	∞	$ 41.00	
	Reserve for Depreciation on Fur. & Fix.	∞		$ 41.00
	-101-			
31	Wages Accrued	∞	60.00	
	Wages Payable	∞		60.00
	-102-			
31	Interest Accrued on Mortgage	∞	125.00	
	Accrued Interest on Mortgage Payable	∞		125.00
	-103-			
31	Depreciation on Delivery Equipment	∞	75.00	
	Reserve for Depreciation on Del'y Equip.	∞		75.00
	-104-			
31	Depreciation on Buildings	∞	100.00	
	Reserve for Depreciation on Buildings	∞		100.00
	-105-			
31	John Smith, Proprietorship Account	∞	500.00	
	John Smith, Personal Account	∞		500.00
	Transfer of account			
	-106-			
31	Sales (Regular)	∞	4,239.15	
	Sales (Cash)	∞	11,010.10	
	Profit & Loss	∞		15,249.25
	To close sales for period to Profit & Loss			
	-107-			
31	Profit & Loss	∞	102.50	
	Sales Returns	∞		102.50
	To close Sales Returns for period to P.&L.			
	-108-			
31	Profit & Loss	∞	11,389.00	
	Purchases	∞		11,389.00
	To close purchases for period to P. & L.			
	-109-			
31	Purchase Returns	∞	50.00	
	Profit & Loss	∞		50.00
	To close Purchase Returns for the period to Profit & Loss			
	-110-			
31	Purchase Discount	∞	231.00	
	Profit & Loss	∞		231.00
	Discount transferred to Profit & Loss			

GENERAL JOURNAL AUGUST, 198—

DATE		F	DEBIT	CREDIT
	—111—			
Aug. 31	Profit & Loss	CO	1,947.75	
	Wages	CO		985.00
	Advertising	CO		243.75
	Repairs to Building	CO		70.00
	Interest Accrued on Mortgage	CO		62.50
	Store Supplies	CO		206.50
	Delivery Expenses	CO		367.50
	Repairs to Store Fixtures	CO		12.50
	Expenses transferred to Profit & Loss			
	—112—			
31	Profit & Loss	CO	367.45	
	Bad Debts	CO		151.45
	Depreciation on Furniture & Fixtures	CO		41.00
	Depreciation on Delivery Equipment	CO		75.00
	Depreciation on Buildings	CO		100.00
	To charge Profit & Loss with Depreciation			
	—113—			
31	Profit & Loss	CO	1,723.55	
	John Smith, proprietorship	CO		1,723.55
	Net Profit for the period			

Sept. 1   John Smith has this day admitted Edward Clark
as a partner under the firm name of Smith &
Clark, and has entered into the following
agreement: a copy of which has been filed in
the office of the County Clerk of New York
County, in the City of New York, State of New
York.

Edward Clark is to invest $25,000.00 in cash
in the business. Clark is to receive a one-
fourth interest in the profits and is to bear
one-fourth of the losses. John Smith's salary is to be $24,000.00 and Edward Clark's
salary is to be $15,000.00 per year. Drawings
may be made by each partner, but not to exceed
the monthly salaries of the partners. At the
end of each month, the salary of each partner
is to be Journalized and posted by debiting
salaries of partners and crediting the Drawing Account of each partner.

See entry in Cash Journal.

DATE		F	DEBIT	CREDIT

-114-

Sept 1	Wages Payable	CO	$ 60.00	
	Wages Accrued	CO		$ 60.00
	To reverse entry of 8/31			

-115-

1	Accrued Interest on Mortgage Payable	CO	125.00	
	Interest Accrued on Mortgage	CO		125.00
	To reverse entry of 8/31			

-116-

1	Accrued Expense Payable	CO	125.00	
	Delivery Expenses Accrued	CO		125.00
	To reverse entry of 8/31			

-117-

30	Partner's Salaries	CO	3,250.00	
	John Smith, Personal Account	CO		2,000.00
	Edward Clark, Personal Account	CO		1,250.00
	Partner's Salaries for the month of Sept.			

-118-

30	Merchandise Inventory	CO	16,250.00	
	Purchases	CO		16,250.00
	Inventory, September 30			

-119-

| 30 | Bad Debts | CO | 100.00 | |
| | Reserve for Bad Debts | CO | | 100.00 |

-120-

30	Depreciation on Furniture & Fixtures	CO	$ 41.00	
	Reserve for Depreciation on Furn. & Fix	CO		$ 41.00
	1% of balance, $820.00			

-121-

30	Depreciation on Delivery Equipment	CO	72.50	
	Reserve for Depreciation of Del. Equip.	CO		72.50
	2% of the cost			

-122-

30	Taxes (Accrued)	CO	50.00	
	Accrued Taxes Payable	CO		50.00
	Estimated tax liability for the period			

-123-

30	Prepaid Insurance	CO	229.15	
	Insurance (Expense)	CO		229.15
	Eleven-twelfths of the insurance premium deferred			

GENERAL JOURNAL, SEPTEMBER 198–

DATE		F	DEBIT	CREDIT
	—124—			
Sept 30	Accrued Interest Receivable	OO	25.00	
	Accrued Interest on Bonds	OO		25.00
	Accrued interest on bonds purchased			
	—125—			
30	Wages Accrued	OO	100.00	
	Wages Payable	OO		100.00
	—126—			
30	Interest Accrued on Mortgage	OO	225.00	
	Accrued interest on Mortgage Payable	OO		225.00
	—127—			
30	Depreciation on Building	OO	100.00	
	Reserve for Depreciation on Building	OO		100.00
	—128—			
30	Purchases	OO	8,487.50	
	Merchandise Inventory	OO		8,487.50
	Inventory 9/1 transferred to Purchases			
	—129—			
30	Sales (Regular)	OO	2,352.50	
	Sales (Cash)	OO	23,033.75	
	Profit & Loss	OO		25,386.25
	To close sales for the period to P. & L.			
	—130—			
30	Profit & Loss	OO	60.00	
	Sales Returns	OO		60.00
	to close Sales Returns for the period to P&L			
	—131—			
30	Profit & Loss	OO	17,490.50	
	Purchases	OO		17,490.50
	To close Purchases for the period to P. & L.			
	—132—			
30	Purchase Returns	OO	100.00	
	Profit & Loss	OO		100.00
	To close Purchase Returns for the period to Profit & Loss			
	—133—			
30	Purchase Discount	OO	165.80	
	Interest on Bonds	OO	25.00	
	Profit & Loss	OO		190.80
	Account transferred to Profit & Loss			

DATE		F	DEBIT	CREDIT
	-134-			
Sept 30	Profit & Loss	∞	6,444.60	
	Wages	∞		1,300.00
	Advertising	∞		482.50
	Automobile Expense	∞		140.00
	Repairs to Building	∞		325.00
	Repairs to Fixtures	∞		6.25
	Interest accrued on Mortgage	∞		100.00
	Store Supplies	∞		270.00
	Delivery Expense	∞		500.00
	Insurance premiums	∞		20.85
	Taxes	∞		50.00
	Partners' Salaries	∞		3,250.00
	Expenses transferred to Profit & Loss			
	-135-			
30	Profit & Loss	∞	313.50	
	Bad Debts	∞		100.00
	Depreciation on Furniture & Fixtures	∞		41.00
	Depreciation on Delivery Equipment	∞		72.50
	Depreciation on Building	∞		100.00
	Depreciation transferred to Profit & Loss			
	-136-			
30	Profit & Loss	∞	1,368.45	
	John Smith, Capital account	∞		1,026.34
	Edward Clark, Capital account	∞		342.11
	Distribution of Net Profit transferred from Profit & Loss to Partners' Capital account.			
	-137-			
Oct. 1	Interest on Bonds	∞	$ 25.00	
	Accrued Interest Receivable	∞		$ 25.00
	To reverse entry of 9/30			
	-138-			
1	Accrued Taxes Payable	∞	50.00	
	Taxes (Accrued)	∞		50.00
	To reverse entry of 9/30			
	-139-			
1	Wages Payable	∞	100.00	
	Wages Accrued	∞		100.00
	To reverse entry of 9/30			
	-140-			
1	Accrued Interest on Mortgage Payable	∞	225.00	
	Interest accrued on Mortgage	∞		225.00
	To reverse entry of 9/30			

GENERAL JOURNAL — OCTOBER, 198—

DATE			F	DEBIT	CREDIT
		—141—			
Oct.	1	Insurance (Expense)	∞	229.15	
		Prepaid Insurance	∞		229.15
		To reverse entry of 9/30			
		—142—			
	1	Smith-Clark, Inc. was this day organized under the laws of the State of New York, with an authorized issue of $125,000.00 capital stock, consisting of 250 shares of common stock of a par value of $500.00 per share.			
		Common Stock Unissued	∞	125,000.00	
		Common Stock Authorized	∞		125,000.00
		—143—			
	1	Subscriptions Common Stock	∞	67,500.00	
		Unissued Common Stock	∞		67,500.00
		John Smith, 84 shares, Certif. No. 1			
		Edward Clark, 50 shares, Certif. No. 2			
		James Smith, 1 share , Certif. No. 3			
		135 shares			
		—144—			
	1	John Smith, Capital Account	∞	42,000.00	
		Subscriptions, Common Stock	∞		42,000.00
		To liquidate Net Worth in partnership account for 84 shares of Capital Stock of Smith-Clark, Inc.			
		—145—			
	1	Edward Clark, Capital Account	∞	25,000.00	
		Subscriptions, common stock	∞		25,000.00
		To liquidate Net Worth in Partnership Account for 50 shares of Capital Stock of Smith-Clark, Inc.			
		—146—			
	5	Subscriptions, Common Stock	∞	4,000.00	
		Unissued Common Stock	∞		4,000.00
		Sale of 8 shares of common stock to David Jones, Certif. No. 4.			

DATE		F	DEBIT	CREDIT
	−147−			
Oct. 31	Purchases	∞	16,250.00	
	Merchandise Inventory	∞		16,250.00
	Inventory 10/1 transferred to Purchases			
	−148−			
31	Merchandise Inventory	∞	19,500.00	
	Purchases	∞		19,500.00
	Inventory 10/31			
	−149−			
31	Provision for Bad Debts	∞	100.00	
	Reserve for Bad Debts	∞		100.00
	−150−			
31	Depreciation on Furniture and Fixtures	∞	41.00	
	Reserve for Depreciation on Fur. & Fix.	∞		41.00
	−151−			
31	Depreciation on Delivery Equipment	∞	72.50	
	Reserve for Depreciation on Del'y Equip.	∞		72.50
	−152−			
31	Depreciation on Building	∞	100.00	
	Reserve for Depreciation on Building	∞		100.00
	−153−			
31	Taxes (Accrued)	∞	150.00	
	Accrued Taxes Payable	∞		150.00
	Estimated tax liability for a period of two months			
	−154−			
31	Prepaid Insurance	∞	208.35	
	Insurance (Expense)	∞		208.35
	Ten-twelfths of insurance premiums deferred			
	−155−			
31	Wages Accrued	∞	60.00	
	Wages Payable	∞		60.00
	−156−			
31	Interest Accrued on Mortgage	∞	287.50	
	Accrued Interest on Mortgage Payable	∞		287.50
	−157−			
31	Accrued Interest Receivable	∞	50.00	
	Accrued Interest on Bonds	∞		50.00
	Accrued Interest on Investment			

GENERAL JOURNAL – OCTOBER, 198–

DATE		F	DEBIT	CREDIT
	–158–			
Oct. 31	Sales (Regular)	OO	2,222.55	
	Sales (Cash)	OO	22,069.52	
	Profit & Loss	OO		24,292.07
	To close Sales for the period to Profit & Loss			
	–159–			
31	Profit & Loss	OO	74.75	
	Sales Returns	OO		74.75
	To close Sales Returns for the period to Profit & Loss			
	–160–			
31	Profit & Loss	OO	7,578.30	
	Wages	OO		1,160.00
	Advertising	OO		695.00
	Automobile Expense	OO		176.50
	Repairs	OO		919.00
	Building $ 740.00			
	Store Fixtures 61.50			
	Delivery Truck 117.50			
	Accrued Interest	OO		62.50
	Store Supplies	OO		381.00
	Delivery Expense	OO		500.00
	Insurance	OO		20.80
	Taxes	OO		100.00
	Officers' Salaries	OO		3,250.00
	Bad Debts	OO		100.00
	Depreciation on Furniture & Fixtures	OO		41.00
	Depreciation on Delivery Equipment	OO		72.50
	Depreciation on Building	OO		100.00
	Expenses transferred to Profit & Loss			
	–161–			
31	Purchase Discount	OO	$ 323.06	
	Interest on Bonds	OO	25.00	
	Profit & Loss	OO		$ 348.06
	Accounts transferred to Profit & Loss			
	–162–			
31	Profit and Loss	OO	14,615.00	
	Purchases	OO		14,615.00
	To close purchases for the period to Profit and Loss			
	–163–			
31	Profit and Loss	OO	2,372.08	
	Surplus	OO		2,372.08
	Net Profit transferred to Surplus Account			

General Ledger (GL)

BOOK NO. 2

CASH IN BANK

198–				198–			
July	1	GJ	$ 40,000.00	July	1	GJ	$ 375.00
	2	GJ	355.25		1	GJ	25.00
	3	GJ	383.50		1	GJ	1,750.00
	5	GJ	412.25		5	GJ	3,625.00
	6	GJ	135.00		5	GJ	125.00
	6	GJ	289.45		5	GJ	15.50
	11	GJ	15.00		5	GJ	1,000.00
	13	GJ	1,498.00		5	GJ	14,625.00
	20	GJ	15.00		6	GJ	200.00
	20	GJ	1,576.20		6	GJ	4,185.00
	25	GJ	25.00		6	GJ	150.00
	27	GJ	1,691.00		8	GJ	355.00
	29	GJ	15.00		8	GJ	750.00
	31	GJ	489.50		9	GJ	35.00
					10	GJ	17.50
					12	GJ	750.00
					13	GJ	150.00
					15	GJ	60.00
					17	GJ	469.00
					18	GJ	31.00
					19	GJ	270.00
					20	GJ	50.00
					20	GJ	150.00
					22	GJ	415.60
					23	GJ	10.00
					27	GJ	150.00
				Balance			17,161.55
			46,900.15				46,900.15
Aug.	1 Balance		17,161.55	Aug. 31	Summary	CD	18,145.25
	31 Summary	CR	12,452.45		Balance		11,468.75
			29,614.00				29,614.00
Sept	1 Balance		11,468.75	Sept 30	Summary	CD	31,857.95
	30 Summary	CR	51,005.80		Balance		30,616.60
			62,474.55				62,474.55
Oct.	1 Balance		30,616.60	Oct. 31	Summary	CD	25,870.34
	31 Summary	CR	27,799.52		Balance		32,545.78
			$58,416.12				$58,416.12
Nov.	1 Balance		$ 32,545.78				

PETTY CASH

Aug. 13		CD	$ 250.00	Balance			
Oct.	1 Balance		$ 250.00				

JOHN POLLARD

198–					198–				
July 3		GJ	$	64.50		Balance		$	64.50
				64.50					64.50
Aug. 1 Balance			$	64.50	Aug. 1 by transfer		GJ	$	64.50

ROBERT BLACK

July 8		GJ	$	55.00	July 11		GJ	$	15.00
16		GJ		30.00		Balance			272.50
26		GJ		202.50					
			$	287.50				$	287.50
Aug. 1 Balance			$	272.50	Aug. 1 by transfer		GJ	$	272.50

HENRY KELLY

July 8		GJ	$	31.35	July 25		GJ	$	25.00
15		GJ		15.00	29		GJ		15.00
16		GJ		22.00		Balance			43.35
22		GJ		15.00					
				83.35					83.35
Aug. 1 Balance			$	43.35	Aug. 1 by transfer		GJ	$	43.35

WILLIAM DICKSON

July 6		GJ	$	51.50		Balance		$	81.50
22		GJ		30.00					
				81.50					81.50
Aug. 1 Balance			$	81.50	Aug. 1 by transfer		GJ	$	81.50

MACY & CO.

July 2		GJ	$	66.25	July 3		GJ	$	16.25
5		GJ		85.00	6		GJ		135.00
9		GJ		95.00		Balance			95.00
				246.25					246.25
Aug. 1 Balance			$	95.00	Aug. 1 by transfer		GJ	$	95.00

GEORGE CORNWELL

198–				198–			
July 9	GJ	$	29.45	July 11	GJ	$	5.45
15	GJ		30.00	20	GJ		15.00
18	GJ		35.00	Balance			134.00
26	GJ		60.00				
			154.45				154.45
Aug. 1 Balance		$	134.00	Aug. 1 by transfer	GJ	$	134.00

SPALDING & CO.

July 2	GJ	$	54.00	Balance		$	84.00
3			30.00				
		$	84.00			$	84.00
Aug. 1 Balance		$	84.00	Aug. 1 by transfer	GJ	$	84.00

SELDEN HAWLEY

July 12	GJ	$	66.00	Balance		$	102.50
18			36.50				
			102.50				102.50
Aug. 1 Balance		$	102.50	Aug. 1 by transfer	GJ	$	102.50

MERCHANDISE INVENTORY

July 31	GJ	$ 3,436.50	Aug. 31	GJ	$ 3,436.50
Aug. 31	GJ	8,487.50	Balance		8,487.50
		11,927.00			11,927.00
Sept. 1 Balance		8,487.50	Sept 30	GJ	8,487.50
30	GJ	16,250.00	Balance		16,250.00
		24,737.50			24,737.50
Oct. 1 Balance		16,250.00	Oct. 31	GJ	16,250.00
31	GJ	19,500.00	Balance		19,500.00
		$35,750.00			$35,750.00
Nov. 1 Balance		$19,500.00			

INVESTMENTS

Sept 4 Bonds at par	CD	$10,000.00	Balance	$10,000.00
Oct. 1 Balance		$10,000.00		

PREPAID INSURANCE

198–					198–				
Sept 30		GJ	$	229.15		Balance		$	229.15
Oct. 1 Balance				229.15			GJ		229.15
31		GJ		208.35		Balance			208.35
			$	437.50				$	437.50
Nov. 1 Balance			$	208.35					

ACCOUNTS RECEIVABLE (CONTROLLING ACCOUNT)

Aug. 1		GJ	$	877.35	Aug. 31		CR	$	1,442.35
31		SJ		4,239.15	31		SJ		102.50
					31		GJ		500.00
						Balance			3,071.65
				5,116.50					5,116.50
Sept 1 Balance				3,071.65	Sept 30		SRJ		60.00
30		SJ		2,352.60	30		CR		2,472.05
						Balance			2,892.10
				5,424.15					5,424.15
Oct. 1 Balance				2,892.10	Oct. 31		SRJ		74.75
31		SJ		2,222.55	31		CR		1,230.00
						Balance			3,809.90
			$	5,114.65				$	5,114.65
Nov. 1 Balance				3,809.90					

NOTES RECEIVABLE

Aug. 31 A.M. Broadus	GJ	$	500.00	Sept 28		CR	$	500.00

ACCRUED INTEREST RECEIVABLE

Sept. 30 Accrued on Bonds	GJ	$	25.00		Balance		$	25.00
Oct. 1 Balance			25.00	Oct. 1		GJ		25.00
31	GJ		50.00		Balance			50.00
		$	75.00				$	75.00
Nov. 1 Balance		$	50.00					

FURNITURE AND FIXTURES

198–				198–		
July	1 Furniture	GJ	$ 1,750.00		Balance	$ 2,700.00
	2 Furniture	GJ	200.00			
	12 Accounting machine	GJ	750.00			
			2,700.00			2,700.00
Aug.	1 Balance		2,700.00		Balance	4,100.00
	16 Typewriter	CD	375.00			
	23 Table office	CD	150.00			
	16 Billing machine	PJ	875.00			
			$ 4,100.00			$ 4,100.00
Sept.	1 Balance		$ 4,100.00			

AUTOMOBILE DELIVERY TRUCK

July	5	GJ	$ 3,625.00		Balance	$ 3,625.00
Aug.	1 Balance		$ 3,625.00			

BUILDING

July	5	GJ	14,625.00		Balance	30,000.00
	5	GJ	375.00			
	5	GJ	15,000.00			
			30,000.00			30,000.00
Aug.	1 Balance		30,000.00			

RENT

July	1	GJ	$ 375.00	July	5	GJ	$ 375.00

WAGES

198–					198–					
July 6		GJ	$	150.00	July 31	Profit & Loss	GJ	$	675.00
13		GJ		150.00					
20		GJ		150.00					
27		GJ		150.00					
31	accrued	GJ		75.00					
				675.00					675.00
Aug. 31		CD		1,000.00	Aug. 1		GJ		75.00
31	accrued	GJ		60.00	31	Profit & Loss	GJ		985.00
				1,060.00					1,060.00
Sept 30		CD		1,260.00	Sept 1		GJ		60.00
30	accrued	GJ		100.00	30	Profit & Loss	GJ		1,300.00
				1,360.00					1,360.00
Oct. 31		CD		1,200.00	Oct. 1	accrued	GJ		100.00
31	accrued	GJ		60.00	31	Profit & Loss	GJ		1,160.00
				$1,260.00					$1,260.00

ADVERTISING

July 1	GJ	$	25.00	July 31	Profit & Loss	GJ	$	120.00
9	GJ		35.00					
15	GJ		60.00					
		$	120.00				$	120.00
Aug. 31	CD		243.75	Aug. 31	Profit & Loss	GJ		243.75
Sept 30	CD		482.50	Sept 30	Profit & Loss	GJ		482.50
Oct. 31	CD	$	695.00	Oct. 31	Profit & Loss	GJ	$	695.00

AUTOMOBILE EXPENSE

198–					198–				
July	5 License	GJ	$	125.00	July 31 Profit & Loss	GJ	$	181.50
	5 Gasoline	GJ		15.50				
	18 Repair Truck	GJ		31.00				
	23 Repair Truck	GJ		10.00				
				181.50				181.50
Sept 20 Gasoline		CD		100.00	Sept 30 Profit & Loss	GJ		140.00
	30	CD		40.00				
				140.00				140.00
Oct. 8		CD		125.00	Oct. 31 Profit & Loss	GJ		176.50
	29	CD		51.50				
			$	176.50			$	176.50

REPAIRS TO BUILDING

July 8		GJ	$	355.00	July 31 Profit & Loss	GJ	$	372.50
	10	GJ		17.50				
				372.50				372.50
Aug. 5		CD		40.00	Aug. 31 Profit & Loss	GJ		70.00
	14	CD		30.00				
				70.00				70.00
Sept 8		CD		75.00	Sept.30 Profit & Loss	GJ		325.00
	20	CD		250.00				
				325.00				325.00
Oct. 4		CD		250.00	Oct. 31 Profit & Loss	GJ		740.00
	12	CD		400.00				
	17	CD		90.00				
			$	740.00			$	740.00

DONATIONS

July 20 Red Cross	GJ	$	50.00	July 31 Profit & Loss	GJ	$	50.00

INTEREST

198–				198–			
July 31 Accrued on Mtge	GJ	$	62.50	July 31 Profit & Loss	GJ	$	62.50
Aug. 31 Accrued on Mtge	GJ		125.00	Aug. 1 accrued	GJ		62.50
				31 Profit & Loss	GJ		62.50
			125.00				125.00
Sept 30 Accrued on Mtge	GJ		225.00	Sept 1 accrued	GJ		125.00
				30 Profit & Loss	GJ		100.00
			225.00				225.00
Oct. 31 Accrued on Mtge	GJ		287.50	Oct. 1 accrued	GJ		225.00
				31 Profit & Loss	GJ		62.50
		$	287.50			$	287.50

STORE SUPPLIES

Aug. 1	CD	$	125.00	Aug. 31 Profit & Loss	GJ	$	206.50
9	CD		50.00				
31	CD		31.50				
			206.50				206.50
Sept 30	CD		270.00	Sept 30 Profit & Loss	GJ		270.00
Oct. 31	CD	$	381.00	Oct. 31 Profit & Loss	GJ	$	381.00

DELIVERY EXPENSE

Aug. 7	CD	$	85.00	Aug. 31 Profit & Loss	GJ	$	367.50
21	CD		150.00				
31	CD		7.50				
31 accrued	GJ		125.00				
		$	367.50			$	367.50
Sept. 30	CD		625.00	Sept 1 accrued	GJ		125.00
				30 Profit & Loss	GJ		500.00
			625.00				625.00
Oct. 31	CD	$	500.00	Oct. 31 Profit & Loss	GJ	$	500.00

REPAIRS TO STORE FIXTURES

198–				198–			
Aug. 31		CD	$ 12.50	Aug. 31 Profit & Loss		GJ	$ 12.50
Sept 30		CD	6.25	Sept 30 Profit & Loss		GJ	6.25
Oct. 19		CD	$ 61.50	Oct. 31 Profit & Loss		GJ	$ 61.50

REPAIRS TO DELIVERY TRUCK

Oct. 22		CD	$ 117.50	Oct. 31 Profit & Loss		GJ	$ 117.50

INSURANCE (FIRE)

Sept 1 Premium		CD	$ 250.00	Sept 30		GJ	$ 229.15
				30 Profit & Loss		GJ	20.85
			250.00				250.00
Oct. 1		GJ	229.15	Oct. 31 Profit & Loss		GJ	208.35
				31 Profit & Loss		GJ	20.80
			$ 229.15				$ 229.15

TAXES

Sept 30 accrued		GJ	$ 50.00	Sept 30 Profit & Loss		GJ	$ 50.00
Oct. 31 accrued		GJ	150.00	Oct. 1		GJ	50.00
				31 Profit & Loss		GJ	100.00
			$ 150.00				$ 150.00

PARTNERS' SALARIES

Sept 30 John Smith		GJ	2,000.00	Sept. 30 Profit & Loss		GJ	3,250.00
30 Edward Clark		GJ	1,250.00				
			3,250.00				3,250.00
Oct. 31 Officers' Salaries				Oct. 31 Profit & Loss		GJ	3,250.00
John Smith		CD	2,000.00				
Edward Clark		CD	1,250.00				
			3,250.00				3,250.00

BAD DEBTS

198–				198–			
July 31		GJ	50.00	July 31	Profit & Loss	GJ	50.00
Aug. 31		GJ	151.45	Aug. 31	Profit & Loss	GJ	151.45
Sept. 30		GJ	100.00	Sept 30	Profit & Loss	GJ	100.00
Oct. 31		GJ	100.00	Oct. 31	Profit & Loss	GJ	100.00

DEPRECIATION ON DELIVERY EQUIPMENT

July 31		GJ	75.00	July 31	Profit & Loss	GJ	75.00
Aug. 31		GJ	75.00	Aug. 31	Profit & Loss	GJ	75.00
Sept 30		GJ	72.50	Sept 30	Profit & Loss	GJ	72.50
Oct. 31		GJ	72.50	Oct. 31	Profit & Loss	GJ	72.50

DEPRECIATION ON FURNITURE AND FIXTURES

July 31		GJ	50.00	July 31	Profit & Loss	GJ	50.00
Aug. 31		GJ	41.00	Aug. 31	Profit & Loss	GJ	41.00
Sept. 30		GJ	41.00	Sept 30	Profit & Loss	GJ	41.00
Oct. 31		GJ	41.00	Oct. 31	Profit & Loss	GJ	41.00

DEPRECIATION ON BUILDINGS

July 31		GJ	100.00	July 31	Profit & Loss	GJ	100.00
Aug. 31		GJ	100.00	Aug. 31	Profit & Loss	GJ	100.00
Sept. 30		GJ	100.00	Sept 30	Profit & Loss	GJ	100.00
Oct. 31		GJ	100.00	Oct. 31	Profit & Loss	GJ	100.00

HAMILTON SUPPLY CO.

198–				198–		
July 6		GJ	4,185.00	July 3	GJ	4,185.00

WHITE & CO.

July 16		GJ	50.00	July 15	GJ	313.75
	Balance		263.75			
			313.75			313.75
Aug. 1 to transfer		GJ	263.75	Aug. 1 Balance		263.75

FULTON SUPPLY CO.

July 11		GJ	35.00	July 10	GJ	385.00
	Balance		350.00			
			385.00			385.00
Aug. 1 to transfer		GJ	350.00	Aug. 1 Balance		350.00

BROWN WHOLESALE CO.

July 5		GJ	1,000.00	July 1	GJ	1,000.00

CLARK & CO.

July 6		GJ	200.00	July 2	GJ	200.00

BROWN DURRELL CO.

July 25		GJ	65.25	July 20	GJ	436.00
	Balance		1,362.25	24		991.50
			1,427.50			1,427.50
Aug. 1 to transfer		GJ	1,362.25	Aug. 1 Balance		1,362.25

ACCOUNTS PAYABLE CONTROLLING ACCOUNT

198–				198–				
Aug. 31		CD	15,276.00	Aug. 1		GJ	1,976.00
31		PRJ	50.00	31		PJ	16,390.00
	Balance		3,915.00	31		PJ	875.00
			19,241.00				19,241.00
Sept 30		CD	15,415.00	Sept 1	Balance		3,915.00
30		PRJ	100.00	30		PJ	25,253.00
	Balance		13,653.00				
			29,168.00				29,168.00
Oct. 31		CD	18,028.00	Oct. 1	Balance		13,653.00
	Balance		13,450.00	31		PJ	17,825.00
			31,478.00				31,478.00
				Nov. 1	Balance		13,450.00

MORTGAGE PAYABLE

	Balance	15,000.00	July 5		GJ	15,000.00
			Aug. 1	Balance		15,000.00

WAGES PAYABLE

Aug. 1		GJ	75.00	July 31 accrued		GJ	75.00
	Balance		60.00	Aug. 31 accrued		GJ	60.00
			135.00				135.00
Sept 1		GJ	60.00	Sept 1 Balance			60.00
	Balance		100.00	30		GJ	100.00
			160.00				160.00
Oct. 1		GJ	100.00	Oct. 1 Balance			100.00
	Balance		60.00	31		GJ	60.00
			160.00				160.00
				Nov. 1 Balance			60.00

ACCRUED INTEREST PAYABLE

198–					198–				
Aug. 1		GJ	62.50		July 31	Accrued on Mtge.	GJ	62.50
	Balance		125.00		Aug. 31	Accrued on Mtge.	GJ	125.00
			187.50					187.50
Sept 1		GJ	125.00		Sept 1	Balance		125.00
30	Balance		225.00		30	Accrued on Mtge.	GJ	225.00
			350.00					350.00
Oct. 1		GJ	225.00		Oct. 1	Balance		225.00
	Balance		287.50		31		GJ	287.50
			512.50					512.50
					Nov. 1	Balance		287.50

ACCRUED EXPENSES PAYABLE

198–					198–				
	Balance		125.00		Aug. 31	(Delivery)	GJ	125.00
Sept. 1		GJ	125.00		Sept. 1	Balance		125.00

ACCRUED TAXES PAYABLE

198–					198–				
Oct. 1		GJ	50.00		Sept 30		GJ	50.00
	Balance		150.00		Oct. 31		GJ	150.00
			200.00					200.00
					Nov. 1	Balance		150.00

RESERVE FOR BAD DEBTS

198–				198–				
	Balance	201.45		July 31		GJ	50.00
				Aug. 31		GJ	151.45
		201.45					201.45
	Balance	301.45		Sept 1	Balance		201.45
				30		GJ	100.00
		301.45					301.45
	Balance	401.45		Oct. 1	Balance		301.45
				31		GJ	100.00
		401.45					401.45
				Nov. 1	Balance		401.45

RESERVE FOR DEPRECIATION ON DELIVERY EQUIPMENT

198–					198–				
Balance			150.00		July 31			GJ	75.00
					Aug. 31			GJ	75.00
			150.00						150.00
Balance			222.50		Sept 1	Balance			150.00
						30		GJ	72.50
			222.50						222.50
Balance			295.00		Oct. 1	Balance			222.50
						31		GJ	72.50
			295.00						295.00
					Nov. 1	Balance			295.00

RESERVE FOR DEPRECIATION ON FURNITURE & FIXTURES

Balance			91.00		July 31			GJ	50.00
					Aug. 31			GJ	41.00
			91.00						91.00
Balance			132.00		Sept. 1	Balance			91.00
						30		GJ	41.00
			132.00						132.00
Balance			173.00		Oct. 1	Balance			132.00
						31		GJ	41.00
			173.00						173.00
					Nov. 1	Balance			173.00

RESERVE FOR DEPRECIATION ON BUILDINGS

Balance			200.00		July 31			GJ	100.00
					Aug. 31			GJ	100.00
			200.00						200.00
Balance			300.00		Sept 1	Balance			200.00
						30		GJ	100.00
			300.00						300.00
Balance			400.00		Oct. 1	Balance			300.00
						31		GJ	100.00
			400.00						400.00
					Nov. 1	Balance			400.00

SALES

198–					198–				
July 31			GJ	$1,104.05	July	2		GJ	$ 66.25
						2		GJ	54.00
						3		GJ	30.00
						3		GJ	64.50
						5		GJ	85.00
						6		GJ	51.50
						8		GJ	55.00
						8		GJ	31.35
						9		GJ	95.00
						9		GJ	29.45
						12		GJ	66.00
						15		GJ	30.00
						15		GJ	15.00
						16		GJ	30.00
						16		GJ	22.00
						18		GJ	35.00
						18		GJ	36.50
						22		GJ	30.00
						22		GJ	15.00
						26		GJ	202.50
						26		GJ	60.00
				1,104.05					1,104.05
Aug. 31	Profit & Loss		GJ	4,239.15	Aug. 31			SJ	4,239.15
Sept 30	Profit & Loss		GJ	2,352.50	Sept 30			SJ	2,352.50
Oct. 31	Profit & Loss		GJ	2,222.55	Oct. 31			SJ	2,222.55

SALES RETURNS AND ALLOWANCES

July	3		GJ	$ 16.25	July 31	Profit & Loss		GJ	$ 21.70
	11		GJ	5.45					
				21.70					21.70
Aug. 31			SRJ	102.50	Aug. 31	Profit & Loss		GJ	102.50
Sept 30			SRJ	60.00	Sept 30	Profit & Loss		GJ	60.00
Oct. 31			SRJ	$ 74.75	Oct. 31	Profit & Loss		GJ	$ 74.75

CASH SALES

198–				198–			
July 31	Profit & Loss	GJ	$6,695.15	July 2		GJ	$ 355.25
				3		GJ	383.50
				5		GJ	412.25
				6		GJ	289.45
				13		GJ	1,498.00
				20		GJ	1,576.20
				27		GJ	1,691.00
				31		GJ	489.50
			6,695.15				6,695.15
Aug. 31	Profit & Loss	GJ	11,010.10	Aug. 31		CR	11,010.10
Sept 30	Profit & Loss	GJ	23,033.75	Sept 30		CR	23,033.75
Oct. 31	Profit & Loss	GJ	22,069.52	Oct 31		CR	22,069.52

PURCHASES

July 1		GJ	1,000.00	July 31	Inventory	GJ	$ 3,436.50
3		GJ	4,185.00	31	Profit & Loss	GJ	5,779.35
8		GJ	750.00				
10		GJ	385.00				
15		GJ	313.75				
17		GJ	469.00				
19		GJ	270.00				
20		GJ	436.00				
22		GJ	415.60				
24		GJ	991.50				
			9,215.85				9,215.85
Aug. 31		PJ	16,390.00	Aug. 31	Inventory	GJ	8,437.50
31		CD	50.00	31	Profit and Loss	GJ	11,389.00
31		GJ	3,436.50				
			19,876.50				19,876.50
Sept 30		PJ	25,253.00	Sept 30	Inventory	GJ	16,250.00
30		GJ	8,487.50	30	Profit & Loss	GJ	17,490.50
			33,740.50				33,740.50
Oct. 29		CD	40.00	Oct. 31		GJ	19,500.00
31		PJ	17,825.00	31		GJ	14,615.00
31		GJ	16,250.00				
			34,115.00				34,115.00

PURCHASES (RETURNED)

198–					198–				
July 31	Profit & Loss	GJ	$	150.25	July 11		GJ	$	35.00
					16		GJ		50.00
					25		GJ		65.25
				150.25					150.25
Aug. 31	Profit & Loss	GJ		50.00	Aug. 3		PRJ		50.00
Sept 30	Profit & Loss	GJ	$	100.00	Sept 30		PRJ	$	100.00

PURCHASE DISCOUNT

Aug. 31	Profit & Loss	GJ	$	231.00	Aug. 31		CD	$	231.00
Sept 30	Profit & Loss	GJ		165.80	Sept 30		CD		165.80
Oct. 31	Profit & Loss	GJ	$	323.06	Oct. 31		CD	$	323.06

INTEREST ON BONDS

Sept 30	Profit & Loss	GJ	$	25.00	Sept 30	accrued	GJ	$	25.00
Oct. 1		GJ		25.00					
31	Profit & Loss	GJ		25.00	Oct. 31	accrued	GJ		50.00
			$	50.00				$	50.00

PROFIT & LOSS

July 31	Bad Debts	GJ	$	50.00	July 31	Sales, regular	GJ	1,104.05
31	Dep. on Dely Equip.	GJ		75.00	31	Sales, cash	GJ	6,695.15
31	Dep. on Fur. & Fix.	GJ		50.00	31	Purchase ret.	GJ	150.25
31	Dep. on Building	GJ		100.00				
31	Wages	GJ		675.00				
31	Advertising	GJ		120.00				
31	Auto. expense	GJ		181.50				
31	Repairs to bldg.	GJ		372.50				
31	Donations	GJ		50.00				
31	Interest on mtge.	GJ		62.50				
31	Sales returns	GJ		21.70				
31	Purchases	GJ		5,779.35				
31	John Smith, Proprietorship a/c	GJ		411.90				
			$7,949.45					$7,949.45

PROFIT & LOSS (continued)

198–					198–				
Aug.	31	Sales Returns	GJ	$ 102.50	Aug.	31	Sales, regular	GJ	4,239.15
	31	Purchases	GJ	11,389.00		31	Sales, cash	GJ	11,010.10
	31	Wages	GJ	985.00		31	Purchase returns	GJ	50.00
	31	Advertising	GJ	243.75		31	Purchase discount	GJ	231.00
	31	Repairs to Bldg.	GJ	70.00					
	31	Int. accd. on mtge	GJ	62.50					
	31	Store supplies	GJ	206.50					
	31	Delivery expense	GJ	367.50					
	31	Rep. to Store fix.	GJ	12.50					
	31	Bad Debts	GJ	151.45					
	31	Dep. on Fur.&Fix.	GJ	41.00					
	31	Dep. on Dely Equip	GJ	75.00					
	31	Dep. on Building	GJ	100.00					
	31	John Smith, Proprietorship	GJ	1,723.55					
				15,530.25					15,530.25
Sept	30	Sales Returns	GJ	$ 60.00	Sept	30	Sales, regular	GJ	2,352.50
	30	Purchases	GJ	17,490.50		30	Sales, cash	GJ	23,033.75
	30	Wages	GJ	1,300.00		30	Purchase Returns	GJ	100.00
	30	Advertising	GJ	482.50		30	Purchase discount	GJ	165.80
	30	Auto. expense	GJ	140.00		30	Interest on bonds	GJ	25.00
	30	Repairs to bldg.	GJ	325.00					
	30	Rep. to Furn&Fix.	GJ	6.25					
	30	Int. accd. on mtge	GJ	100.00					
	30	Store supplies	GJ	270.00					
	30	Dely expense	GJ	500.00					
	30	Ins premium	GJ	20.85					
	30	Taxes	GJ	50.00					
	30	part. salaries	GJ	3,250.00					
	30	Prov. for Bad Debts	GJ	100.00					
	30	" dep. on F.&F.	GJ	41.00					
	30	" " Dely Equip	GJ	72.50					
	30	" " Building	GJ	100.00					
	30	John Smith, Capital account	GJ	1,026.34					
	30	Edward Clark, Capital account	GJ	342.11					
				$25,677.05					$25,677.05
Oct.	31	Sales Returns	GJ	$ 74.75	Oct.	31	Sales, regular	GJ	2,222.55
	31	Purchases	GJ	14,615.00		31	Sales, cash	GJ	22,069.52
	31	Wages	GJ	1,160.00		31	Purchase discount	GJ	323.06
	31	Advertising	GJ	695.00		31	Interest on bonds	GJ	25.00
	31	Auto. Expense	GJ	176.50					
	31	Repairs							
		bldg. 740.00	GJ						
		F.&F. 61.50	GJ						
		Dely tk 117.50	GJ	919.00					
		Forward		$17,640.25			Forward		$24,640.13

PROFIT & LOSS (continued)

	Forward		$17,640.25	Forward		$24,640.13
Oct. 31 Interest accrued	GJ	62.50				
31 Store supplies	GJ	381.00				
31 Dely Expense	GJ	500.00				
31 Insurance	GJ	20.80				
31 Taxes	GJ	100.00				
31 Officers' sal.	GJ	3,250.00				
31 Prov. Bad Debts	GJ	100.00				
31 Dep. on Fur.&Fix.	GJ	41.00				
31 Dep. on Del. Equip.	GJ	72.50				
31 Dep. on Building	GJ	100.00				
31 To surplus		2,372.08				
		$24,640.13				$24,640.13

JOHN SMITH, PERSONAL ACCOUNT

Aug. 31 Salary	CD	$ 500.00	Aug. 31	GJ		500.00
Sept 30 Salary	CD	2,000.00	Sept 30	GJ		2,000.00

JOHN SMITH, PROPRIETORSHIP

Balance		40,411.90	July 1	GJ	40,000.00	
			31	GJ	411.90	
		40,411.90			40,411.90	
Aug. 31 Personal	GJ	500.00	Aug. 1 Balance		40,411.90	
Balance		41,635.45	31 Profit & Loss	GJ	1,723.55	
		42,135.45			42,135.45	
Sept 30 Balance		42,661.79	Sept 1 Balance		41,635.45	
			30 Profit & Loss	GJ	1,026.34	
		42,661.79			42,661.79	
Oct. 1	CD	661.79	Oct. 1 Balance		42,661.79	
1	GJ	42,000.00				
		42,661.79			42,661.79	

EDWARD CLARK, PERSONAL ACCOUNT

Sept 5	CD	$ 900.00	Sept 30	GJ	1,250.00	
10	CD	350.00	30		1,250.00	
		1,250.00				

EDWARD CLARK, PROPRIETORSHIP

198–				198–			
Sept 30 Balance			25,342.11	Sept 1		CR	25,000.00
				30		GJ	342.11
			25,342.11				25,342.11
Oct. 1		CD	342.11	Oct. 1 Balance			25,342.11
1		GJ	25,000.00				
			25,342.11				25,342.11

SURPLUS

Balance	$ 2,372.08	Oct. 31 Profit & Loss	GJ	$ 2,372.08
		Balance		$ 2,372.08

SUBSCRIPTIONS TO COMMON STOCK

Oct. 1		GJ	$ 67,500.00	Oct. 1		GJ	$ 42,000.00
5		GJ	4,000.00	1		GJ	25,000.00
				1		CR	500.00
				5		CR	4,000.00
			$ 71,500.00				$ 71,500.00

COMMON STOCK UNISSUED

Oct. 1		GJ	125,000.00	Oct. 1		GJ	$ 67,500.00
				5		GJ	4,000.00
				Balance			53,500.00
			125,000.00				125,000.00
Balance			53,500.00				

COMMON STOCK AUTHORIZED

				Oct. 1		GJ	125,000.00

Stock Certificate Book

STUB (posting from this stub is made to Capital Stock Ledger)	CERTIFICATE (torn out of the book and issued to the stockholder)
Certificate No. 1 for 84 shares Issued to John Smith Dated: Oct. 1, 198–	No. 1 (Common Stock) SMITH-CLARK, INC. This certifies that John Smith is the owner of eighty-four (84) shares of the Capital Stock of Smith-Clark, Inc. Par value $100.00 per share. Date: October 1, 198– (Signatures of authorized officers goes here)
Certificate No. 2 for 50 shares Issued to Edward Clark Dated: Oct. 1, 198–	No. 2 (Common Stock) SMITH-CLARK, INC. This certifies that Edward Clark is the owner of fifty (50) shares of the Capital Stock of Smith-Clark, Inc. Par value $100.00 per share. Date: October 1, 198– (Signatures of authorized officers goes here)
Certificate No. 3 for 1 shares Issued to James Smith Dated: Oct. 1, 198–	No. 3 James Smith One (1) shares Date: October 1, 198–
Certificate No. 4 for 8 shares Issued to David Jones Dated: Oct. 5, 198–	No. 4 David Jones Eight (8) shares Date: October 5, 198–

Capital Stock Ledger

OR STOCKHOLDERS LEDGER

JOHN SMITH

	198– Oct. 1	Common Stock Certif. No. 1	84 Shares

EDWARD CLARK

	198– Oct. 1	Common Stock Certif. No. 2	50 Shares

JAMES SMITH

	198– Oct. 1	Common Stock Certif. No. 3	1 Share

DAVID JONES

	198– Oct. 5	Common Stock Certif. No. 4	8 Shares

Cash Journal

CONTAINING CASH RECEIPTS (CR) AND CASH DISBURSEMENTS (CD)

BOOK NO. 3

CASH RECEIPTS – AUGUST, 198–

DATE	EXPLANATION	AMOUNT Dr.	DIS. Dr.	LF	ACC. REC. Cr.	CASH SALES Cr.	GLF	SUNDRIES Cr.
Aug. 1	Cash Bal. from G.L. (✓)	$17,161.55						
3	Cash Sales	1,511.70				1,511.70		
10	Cash Sales	2,727.40				2,727.40		
16	H.C. Young on a/c	250.00		∞	250.00			
17	Cash Sales	2,361.50				2,361.50		
19	H.S. Darby on a/c	75.00		∞	75.00			
19	E.W. Russel on a/c	60.00		∞	60.00			
21	G.C. Doyle on a/c	55.00		∞	55.00			
24	Cash Sales	2,305.50				2,305.50		
28	E.W. Russel on a/c	125.00		∞	125.00			
31	Cash Sales	2,104.00				2,104.00		
31	John Pollard	64.50		∞	64.50			
31	Robert Black	272.50		∞	272.50			
31	Henry Kelly	43.35		∞	43.35			
31	William Dickson	81.50		∞	81.50			
31	Macy & Co.	95.00		∞	95.00			
31	Geo. Cornwell	134.00		∞	134.00			
31	Spalding & Co.	84.00		∞	84.00			
31	Selden Hawley	102.50		∞	102.50			
31	Totals (G. L.)	12,452.45	–0–		1,442.35	11,010.10		–0–
Aug. 1	Balance (✓)	17,161.55			(G.L.)	(G.L.)		
	Total (G. L.)	29,614.00						

CASH DISBURSEMENTS – AUGUST, 198–

DATE	EXPLANATION	AMOUNT Cr.	DIS. Cr.	WAGES Dr.	ADV. Dr.	LF	ACC. PAY. Dr.	GLF	SUNDRIES Dr.
Aug. 1	Advertising in local Times	10.00			10.00				
1	Carter Paper Co., Store Supplies	125.00						00	125.00
5	A.L. Jones, Rep. to Store Bldg.	40.00						00	40.00
6	Pierce & Co.	2,450.00	50.00			00	2,500.00		
7	General Dely Co., Delivery Exp.	85.00						00	85.00
8	Whitney & Co.	931.00	19.00			00	950.00		
8	Hicks & Co.	1,470.00	30.00			00	1,500.00		
9	Cash Advertising in local Times	50.00			50.00				
9	Cash, Edwards Co., Supplies	50.00						00	50.00
13	Petty Cash	250.00						00	250.00
14	Robinson & Co.	2,940.00	60.00			00	3,000.00		
14	R.K. Frost, Repairs to Bldg.	30.00						00	30.00
14	W.C. Worth	500.00		500.00					
16	Underwood Co., Typewriter	375.00						00	375.00
17	Cash Advertising in local Times	75.00			75.00				
21	General Delivery Co., Dely Service	150.00						00	150.00
21	Western Wholesale Co.	3,528.00	72.00			00	3,600.00		
23	Hartley Co., table for office	150.00						00	150.00
26	Harper Wholesale Co.	1,750.00				00	1,750.00		
29	Cash Advertising in local Times	90.00			90.00				
29	W.C. Worth, wages for two weeks	500.00		500.00					
31	John Smith, month salary	500.00						00	500.00
31	Petty Cash	120.25							
	Advertising				18.75				
	Delivery Expense							00	7.50
	Purchases Made							00	50.00
	Supplies							00	31.50
	Repairs to Store Fixtures							00	12.50
31	White & Co.	263.75				00	263.75		
31	Fulton Supply Co.	350.00				00	350.00		
31	Brown-Durrell Co.	1,362.25				00	1,362.25		
31	Total (G.L.)	18,145.25	231.00	1,000.00	243.75		15,276.00		1,856.50
			(G.L.)	(G.L.)	(G.L.)		(G.L.)		(G.L.)
31	Balance (G.L.)	11,468.75							
	Total (G.L.)	29,614.00							

NOTE: To show how "Cash Disbursements" can be further expanded, assuming that we want to save time in posting, the "Delivery Expense" and the "Supplies" columns have been added in September.

CASH RECEIPTS – SEPTEMBER, 198–

DATE	EXPLANATION	AMOUNT Dr	DISC. Dr.	LF	ACC. REC. Cr.	CASH SALES Cr.	GLF	SUNDRIES Cr.
Sept 1	Balance (✓)	$11,468.75						
1	E. Clark, Capital Investment	25,000.00					∞	25,000.00
2	H.C. Young on a/c	250.00		∞	250.00			
6	Cash Sales	3,500.00				3,500.00		
8	H.C. Taylor	75.00		∞	75.00			
16	H.S. Roy	256.50		∞	256.50			
16	E.C. Griffin on a/c	125.00		∞	125.00			
18	G.C. Doyle	277.50		∞	277.50			
20	Cash Sales	7,052.50				7,052.50		
23	H.C. Evans	166.50		∞	166.50			
27	Cash Sales	9,975.65				9,975.65		
28	Notes Receivable (H.G. Little)	500.00					∞	500.00
28	H.S. Darby	150.00		∞	150.00			
28	Geo. Crane	518.00		∞	518.00			
28	W.S. Lee	240.00		∞	240.00			
28	H.C. Young	413.55		∞	413.55			
30	Cash Sales	2,505.60				2,505.60		
30	TOTALS (G.L.)	51,005.80	–0–		2,472.05	23,033.75		25,500.00
Sept 1	Balance (✓)	11,468.75			(G.L.)	(G. L.)		(G. L.)
	Total (G.L.)	62,474.55						

CASH DISBURSEMENTS – SEPTEMBER, 198–

DATE	EXPLANATION	AMOUNT Cr.	DIS. Cr.	WAGES Dr.	ADV. Dr.	DEL'Y Dr.	SUPPL. Dr.	LF	ACC. PAY. Dr.	GLF	SUNDRIES Dr.
Sept 1	Sun Ins. Co., fire insurance premiums on mdse & fixtures	250.00								00	250.00
3	Remington Co.	875.00						00	875.00		
3	Herrick Supply Co.	343.00	7.00					00	350.00		
4	Shields & Co. bonds at par	10,000.00								00	10,000.00
5	Edward Clark, Personal	900.00								00	900.00
5	General Del'y Co., Accd Exp.	125.00				125.00					
6	Wilson & Co.	1,960.00	40.00					00	2,000.00		
6	Truck driver, Delivery Exp.	125.00				125.00					
8	A. Waters, Bldg. Repairs	75.00								00	75.00
9	Local Times Advertising	250.00			250.00						
10	Edward Clark, Personal	350.00								00	350.00
11	Carter Paper Co., Supplies	250.00					250.00				
13	W.C. Worth, 2 wks. accd. wages	660.00		660.00							
13	Truck driver, Delivery Exp.	125.00				125.00					
15	Sanford & Co.	500.00						00	500.00		
17	Wilson & Co.	3,430.00	70.00					00	3,500.00		
19	Local Times, Advertising	225.00			225.00						
20	Astor Oil Co., gasoline	100.00								00	100.00
20	A.L. Plog, bldg. repairs	250.00								00	250.00
20	Truck Driver	125.00				125.00					
22	Grimes & Co.	186.20	3.80					00	190.00		
24	Harper Wholesale Co.	3,500.00						00	3,500.00		
25	Brown & Co.	4,455.00	45.00					00	4,500.00		
28	W.C. Worth	600.00		600.00							
28	Truck Driver	125.00				125.00					
30	Petty Cash	73.75									
	Advertising				7.50						
	Supplies						20.00				
	Repairs to Store Fixtures									00	6.25
	Auto Expenses									00	40.00
30	John Smith, Sept. Salary	2,000.00								00	2,000.00
30	TOTALS (G.L.)	31,857.95	165.80	1,260.00	482.50	625.00	270.00		15,415.00		13,971.25
30	Balance (G.L.)	30,616.60	(GL)	(GL)	(GL)	(GL)	(GL)		(GL)		(GL)
	Total (G.L.)	62,474.55									

CASH RECEIPTS, OCTOBER 198–

DATE	EXPLANATION	AMOUNT Dr.	DIS. Dr.	LF	ACC. REC. Cr.	CASH SALES Cr.	GLF	SUNDRIES Cr.
Oct. 1	Balance (✓)	$30,616.60						
1	James Smith Sub. to Common Stock	500.00					∞	500.00
2	H.C. Young	250.00		∞	250.00			
4	E.W. Russel on a/c	150.00		∞	150.00			
5	David Jones Sub. to Common Stock	4,000.00					∞	4,000.00
6	Frank Snyder	90.00		∞	90.00			
6	Cash Sales	4,809.95				4,809.95		
9	Geo. Crane on a/c	250.00		∞	250.00			
16	E.C. Griffin	225.00		∞	225.00			
20	Cash Sales	9,353.50				8,353.50		
25	E.J. Kemp	185.00		∞	185.00			
27	H.L. Pratt	80.00		∞	80.00			
31	Cash Sales	8,906.07				8,906.07		
Oct. 31	TOTALS (G.L.)	27,799.52	–0–		1,230.00	22,069.52		4,500.00
Oct. 1	Balance (✓)	30,616.60			(G.L.)	(G.L.)		(G.L.)
	Total (G.L.)	58,416.12						
Nov. 1	Balance	32,545.78						

CASH DISBURSEMENTS OCTOBER 198—

DATE	EXPLANATION	AMOUNT CR.	DIS. CR.	WAGES DR.	ADV. DR.	DEL'Y DR.	SUPPL. DR.	LF	ACC. PAY. DR.	GLF	SUNDRIES DR.
Oct. 1	John Smith, Capital a/c	661.79								00	661.79
1	Edward Clark, Capital a/c	342.11								00	342.11
2	Local Times, Advertising	150.00			150.00						
3	Springer & Co.	8,330.00	170.00					00	8,500.00		
4	A.P. Plog, rep. to bldg.	250.00								00	250.00
6	Truck Driver	125.00				125.00					
8	Astor Oil Co., auto exp., gasoline	125.00								00	125.00
8	Lane & Co.	5,049.94	103.06					00	5,153.00		
12	A.P. Plog, bldg. repairs	400.00								00	400.00
13	Carter Paper Co., store sup.	290.00					290.00				
13	Local Times Advertising	400.00			400.00						
15	W.C. Worth	600.00		600.00							
15	Truck Driver	125.00				125.00					
17	A.P. Plog, bldg. repairs	90.00								00	90.00
19	John Brewer, Furn. repairs	61.50								00	61.50
22	Walsh & Co., supplies	62.00					62.00				
22	Daily Times Advertising	125.00			125.00						
22	Delivery truck repairs	117.50								00	117.50
22	Truck driver	125.00				125.00					
29	W.C. Worth	600.00		600.00							
29	Truck Driver	125.00				125.00					
31	John Smith, Oct. Salary	2,000.00								00	2,000.00
31	Edward Clark, Oct. Salary	1,250.00								00	1,250.00
31	Harper Wholesale Co.	1,875.00						00	1,875.00		
	Lane & Co.	2,450.00						00	2,500.00		
	Petty Cash	140.50									
	Advertising				20.00					00	
	Supplies						29.00			00	
31	Auto. Expense										51.50
31	Merchandise										40.00
	TOTALS (G.L.)	25,870.34	323.06	1,200.00	695.00	500.00	381.00		18,028.00		5,389.40
31	Balance (G.L.)	32,545.78	(GL)	(GL)	(GL)	(GL)	(GL)		(GL)		(GL)
	Total (G.L.)	58,416.12									

Sales Journal (SJ)

CONTAINING ALSO SALES RETURNS AND ALLOWANCES (SRJ)

BOOK NO. 4

SALES JOURNAL – AUGUST, 198–

DATE	ACCOUNTS RECEIVABLE (DR.)	F	SALES (CR.)
Aug. 3	H. C. Young	C.L.	250.00
3	H. S. Darby	"	125.00
3	E. W. Russell	"	36.00
3	H. C. Taylor	"	75.00
5	W. S. Lee	"	165.00
5	E. W. Russell	"	91.50
5	H. S. Roy	"	120.00
6	E. C. Griffin	"	175.00
6	G. C. Doyle	"	85.00
7	H. C. Evans	"	80.00
7	H. S. Roy	"	30.00
8	Frank Snyder	"	90.00
9	E. W. Russell	"	60.00
9	W. S. Lee	"	85.00
10	George Crane	"	498.00
13	George Crane	"	20.00
14	E. W. Russell	"	80.00
14	H. S. Kirby	"	43.75
15	H. C. Young	"	663.55
15	H. L. Pratt	"	50.00
15	H. S. Kirby	"	66.35
16	H. L. Pratt	"	30.00
16	H. S. Gibbs	"	20.00
21	L. J. Kemp	"	185.00
21	E. W. Russell	"	50.00
22	H. C. Evans	"	86.50
22	H. S. Roy	"	36.50
23	H. S. Roy	"	15.00
23	E. W. Russell	"	27.00
24	E. W. Russell	"	70.00
24	G. C. Doyle	"	200.00
27	G. C. Doyle	"	75.00
27	H. S. Roy	"	55.00
30	H. G. Little	"	500.00
		TOTAL	4,239.15

SUMMARY AUG. 31
(Dr.) Accounts Receivable (G.L.) 4,239.15
(Cr.)   Sales   (G.L.)   4,239.15

SALES JOURNAL – SEPTEMBER, 198–

DATE	ACCOUNTS RECEIVABLE (DR.)	F	SALES (CR.)
Sept 4	H. S. Darby	C.L.	100.00
11	E. W. Russell	"	200.00
11	H. C. Taylor	"	52.50
16	W. S. Lee	"	250.00
16	H. C. Young	"	250.00
16	George Crane	"	575.00
16	E. C. Doyle	"	600.00
17	E. C. Griffin	"	175.00
20	H. S. Gibbs	"	100.00
20	E. J. Kemp	"	50.00
		TOTAL	2,352.50

SUMMARY SEPT., 30

(Dr.) Accounts Receivable (G.L.) 2,352.50
(Cr.)   Sales   (G.L.)   2,352.50

DATE	ACCOUNTS RECEIVABLE (DR.)	F	SALES (CR.)
Oct. 3	H. S. Darby	C.L.	280.00
3	H. C. Young	"	162.00
4	E. W. Russell	"	110.00
4	W. S. Lee	"	84.75
6	W. S. Lee	"	136.70
6	H. S. Roy	"	109.50
8	Frank Snyder	"	93.75
9	George Crane	"	102.50
11	H. S. Kirby	"	105.00
11	H. L. Pratt	"	202.25
15	H. S. Darby	"	135.00
15	H. S. Roy	"	112.00
18	G. C. Doyle	"	145.35
18	Frank Snyder	"	93.75
20	George Crane	"	100.00
29	H. L. Pratt	"	250.00
		TOTAL	2,222.55

SUMMARY OCT., 31

(Dr.) Accounts Receivable (G.L.) 2,222.55
(Cr.)   Sales   2,222.55

SALES RETURNS AND ALLOWANCES JOURNAL, 198–

DATE	ACCOUNTS RECEIVABLE (CR.)	F.	SALES RET. (DR.)
Aug. 7	H. S. Roy	C.L.	15.00
12	W. S. Lee	"	10.00
22	E. J. Kemp	"	50.00
26	G. C. Doyle	"	27.50
		TOTAL	102.50

SUMMARY:

(Dr.)	Sales Returns and Allowances	(G.L.)	102.50	
(Cr.)	Accounts Receivable	(G.L.)		102.50

DATE	ACCOUNTS RECEIVABLE (CR.)	F.	SALES RET. (DR.)
Sept 13	E. W. Russell	C.L.	50.00
18	W. S. Lee	"	10.00
		TOTAL	60.00

SUMMARY:

(Dr.)	Sales Returns and Allowances	(G.L.)	60.00	
(Cr.)	Accounts Receivable	(G.L.)		60.00

DATE	ACCOUNTS RECEIVABLE (CR.)	F.	SALES RET. (DR.)
Oct. 8	W. S. Lee	C.L.	25.00
9	E. W. Russell	"	11.00
16	H. S. Roy	"	10.00
19	Frank Snyder	"	28.75
		TOTAL	74.75

SUMMARY:

(Dr.)	Sales Returns and Allowances	(G.L.)	74.75	
(Cr.)	Accounts Receivable	(G.L.)		74.75

Purchase Journal (PJ)

INCLUDING ALSO PURCHASE RETURNS (PRJ)

BOOK NO. 5

PURCHASE JOURNAL – 198–

DATE		ACCOUNTS PAYABLE (CR.)	TERMS	F.	PUR. (DR.)	SUND. (DR.)
Aug.	1	Whitney & Co.	2/10/n/30	Cr.L	1,000.00	
	1	Hicks & Co.	2/10/n/30	"	1,500.00	
	6	Robinson & Co.	2/10/n/60	"	3,000.00	
	6	Pierce & Co.	2/10/n/30	"	2,500.00	
	8	Harper Wholesale Co.	n/30	"	1,750.00	
	14	Western Wholesale Co.	2/10/n/30	"	3,600.00	
	16	Remington Co. Billing Machine	n/30	"		875.00
	17	Herrick Supply Co.	2/20/n/60	"	350.00	
	22	Grimes & Co.	2/30/n/60	"	190.00	
	29	Sanford & Co.	n/30	"	500.00	
	30	Wilson & Co.	2/10/n/30	"	2,000.00	
			TOTAL		16,390.00	875.00

SUMMARY:

(Dr.) Purchases   (GL) 16,390.00
(Dr.) Furniture & Fixtures (GL) 875.00
(Cr.)   Accounts Payable (GL)   17,265.00

Sept	3	Harper Wholesale Co.	n/30	Cr.L	3,500.00
	9	Wilson & Co.	2/10/n/30	"	3,500.00
	18	Brown & Co.	1/10/n/60	"	4,500.00
	25	Springer & Co.	2/10/n/30	"	8,500.00
	30	Lane & Co.	2/10/n/30	"	5,253.00
			TOTAL		25,253.00

SUMMARY:

(Dr.) Purchases   (GL) 25,253.00
(Cr.)   Accounts Payable (GL)   25,253.00

Oct.	3	Harper Wholesale Co.	n/30	Cr.L	1,875.00
	9	Sanford & Co.	n/60	"	4,950.00
	11	Lane & Co.	2/20/n/30	"	2,500.00
	31	Harper Wholesale Co.	2/10/n/60	"	8,500.00
			TOTAL		17,825.00

SUMMARY:

(Dr.) Purchases   (GL) 17,825.00
(Cr.)   Accounts Payable (GL)   17,825.00

PURCHASE RETURNS JOURNAL

DATE		F.	PUR. RET. (CR.)
Aug. 3	Whitney & Co.	CrL	50.00
		TOTAL	50.00

SUMMARY, AUG. 31.
(Dr.) Accounts Payable   (G.L.)   50.00
(Cr.)   Purchase Returns (G.L.)   50.00

Sept 30	Lane & Co.	CrL	100.00
		TOTAL	100.00

SUMMARY, SEPT. 30.
(Dr.) Accounts Payable   (G.L.)   100.00
(Cr.)   Purchase Returns (G.L.)   100.00

Petty Cash Journal (PCJ)

BOOK NO. 6

PETTY CASH 198–

DATE 198–	RECPTS Amt	DISB. Amt	DEL. Exp.	PUR. Mdse	SUPP.	ADV.	REP. TO STORE FIX	AUTO Exp.
Aug.								
13 Cash	250.00							
14 Supplies		5.00			5.00			
14 Advertising		10.00				10.00		
15 Spec. Del. of H.C. Young's order of 8/15		7.50	7.50					
15 Purchases (mdse)		10.00		10.00				
19 Supplies		15.00			15.00			
19 Repairs to Store Fixtures		5.00					5.00	
19 Purchases (mdse)		25.00		25.00				
20 Repairs to Store Fixtures		7.50					7.50	
22 Supplies		11.50			11.50			
23 Advertising		8.75				8.75		
27 Purchases (Mdse)		15.00		15.00				
31 TOTALS TO C.D.		120.25	7.50	50.00	31.50	18.75	12.50	
BALANCE		129.75						
	250.00	250.00						
BALANCE	129.75							
CHECK	120.25							
Sept.								
1 Cash Balance	250.00							
2 Advertising		7.50				7.50		
4 Supplies		20.00			20.00			
6 Repairs		6.25					6.25	
12 Gasoline (auto expense)		20.00						20.00
26 Gasoline (auto expense)		20.00						20.00
30 TOTALS TO C.D.		73.75			20.00	7.50	6.25	40.00
BALANCE		176.25						
	250.00	250.00						
BALANCE	176.25							
CHECK	73.75							
Oct.								
1 Cash Balance	250.00							
19 Supplies		29.00			29.00			
19 Gasoline		34.50						34.50
22 Gasoline		17.00						17.00
24 Merchandise		40.00		40.00				
26 Advertising		20.00				20.00		
31 TOTALS TO C.D.		140.50		40.00	29.00	20.00		51.50
BALANCE		109.50						
	250.00	250.00						
BALANCE	109.50							
CHECK	140.50							
Nov.								
1 Cash Balance	250.00							

Accounts Receivable Ledger

OR CUSTOMERS' LEDGER (CL)

BOOK NO. 7

JOHN POLLARD

198– Aug.	1	Bal. from GL	64.50	198– Aug. 31		(CR)	64.50

ROBERT BLACK

198– Aug.	1	Bal. from GL	272.50	198– Aug. 31		(CR)	272.50

HENRY KELLY

198– Aug.	1	Bal. from GL	43.35	198– Aug. 31		(CR)	43.35

WILLIAM DICKSON

198– Aug.	1	Bal. from GL	81.50	198– Aug. 31		(CR)	1.50

MACY & CO.

198– Aug.	1	Bal. from GL	95.00	198– Aug. 31		(CR)	95.00

GEORGE CORNWELL

198– Aug.	1	Bal. from GL	134.00	198– Aug. 31		(CR)	134.00

SPALDING & CO.

198– Aug.	1	Bal. from GL	84.00	198– Aug. 31		(CR)	84.00

SELDEN HAWLEY

198– Aug.	1	Bal. from GL	102.50	198– Aug. 31		(CR)	102.50

H.C. YOUNG

198–				198–			
Aug. 3		(SJ)	250.00	Aug. 16		(CR)	250.00
15		(SJ)	663.55		Balance		663.55
			913.55				913.55
Sept 1	Balance		663.55	Sept 2		(CR)	250.00
16		(SJ)	250.00	28		(CR)	413.55
					Balance		250.00
			913.55				913.55
Oct. 1	Balance		250.00	Oct. 2		(CR)	250.00
3		(SJ)	162.00		Balance		162.00
			412.00				412.00
Nov. 1	Balance		162.00				

H. S. DARBY

198–				198–			
Aug. 3		(SJ)	125.00	Aug. 19		(CR)	75.00
					Balance		50.00
			125.00				125.00
Sept 1	Balance		50.00	Sept 28		(CR)	150.00
4		(SJ)	100.00				
			150.00				150.00
Oct. 3		(SJ)	280.00				
15		(SJ)	135.00		Balance		415.00
			415.00				415.00
Nov. 1	Balance		415.00				

E.W. RUSSELL

198–				198–			
Aug. 3		(SJ)	36.00	Aug. 19		(CR)	60.00
5		(SJ)	91.50	28		(CR)	125.00
9		(SJ)	60.00		Balance		229.50
14		(SJ)	80.00				
21		(SJ)	50.00				
23		(SJ)	27.00				
24		(SJ)	70.00				
			414.50				414.50
Sept 1	Balance		229.50	Sept 13		(SRJ)	50.00
11		(SJ)	200.00		Balance		379.50
			429.50				429.50
Oct. 1	Balance		379.50	Oct. 4		(CR)	150.00
4		(SJ)	110.00	9		(SRJ)	11.00
					Balance		328.50
			489.50				489.50
Nov. 1	Balance		328.50				

H.C. TAYLOR

198–				198–			
Aug. 3		(SJ)	75.00		Balance		75.00
Sept 1	Balance		75.00	Sept 8		(CR)	75.00
11	Net 30	(SJ)	52.50		Balance		52.50
			127.50				127.50
Oct. 1	Balance		52.50				

W.S. LEE

198–				198–			
Aug. 5		(SJ)	165.00	Aug. 12		(SRJ)	10.00
9		(SJ)	85.00		Balance		240.00
			250.00				250.00
Sept 1	Balance		240.00	Sept. 18		(SRJ)	10.00
16		(SJ)	250.00	28		(CR)	240.00
					Balance		240.00
			490.00				490.00
Oct. 1	Balance		240.00	Oct. 8		(SRJ)	25.00
4		(SJ)	84.75		Balance		436.45
4		(SJ)	136.70				
			461.45				461.45
Nov. 1	Balance		436.45				

H.S. ROY

198–					198–				
Aug.	5		(SJ)	120.00	Aug.	7		(SRJ)	15.00
	7		(SJ)	30.00			Balance		241.50
	22		(SJ)	36.50					
	23		(SJ)	15.00					
	27		(SJ)	55.00					
				256.50					256.50
Sept	1	Balance		241.50	Sept	16		(CR)	256.50
					Oct	1	Balance		15.00
Oct.	6		(SJ)	109.50	Oct.	16		(SRJ)	10.00
	15		(SJ)	112.00			Balance		196.50
				221.50					221.50
Nov.	1	Balance		196.50					

E.C. GRIFFIN

198–					198–				
Aug.	6		(SJ)	175.00			Balance		175.00
Sept	1	Balance		175.00	Sept	16		(CR)	125.00
	17		(SJ)	175.00			Balance		225.00
				350.00					350.00
Oct.	1	Balance		225.00	Oct.	16		(CR)	225.00

G.C. DOYLE

198–					198–				
Aug.	6		(SJ)	85.00	Aug.	21		(CR)	55.00
	24		(SJ)	200.00		26		(SJ)	27.50
	27		(SJ)	75.00			Balance		277.50
				360.00					360.00
Sept	1	Balance		277.50	Sept	18		(CR)	277.50
	16		(SJ)	600.00			Balance		600.00
				877.50					877.50
Oct.	1	Balance		600.00			Balance		745.35
	18		(SJ)	145.35					
				745.35					745.35
Nov.	1	Balance		745.35					

H.C. EVANS

198–					198–				
Aug.	7		(SJ)	80.00			Balance		166.50
	22		(SJ)	86.50					
				166.50					166.50
Sept	1	Balance		166.50	Sept 23			(CR)	166.50

FRANK SNYDER

198–					198–				
Aug.	8		(SJ)	90.00			Balance		90.00
Sept	1	Balance		90.00	Oct.	6		(CR)	90.00
Oct.	8		(SJ)	93.75		19		(SRJ)	28.75
	18		(SJ)	93.75			Balance		158.75
				277.50					277.50
Nov.	1	Balance		158.75					

GEORGE CRANE

198–					198–				
Aug.	10		(SJ)	498.00			Balance		518.00
	13		(SJ)	20.00					
				518.00					518.00
Sept	1	Balance		518.00	Sept 28			(CR)	518.00
	16		(SJ)	575.00			Balance		575.00
				1,093.00					1,093.00
Oct.	1	Balance		575.00	Oct.	9		(CR)	250.00
	9		(SJ)	102.50			Balance		527.50
	20		(SJ)	100.00					
				777.50					777.50
Nov.	1	Balance		527.50					

H S. KIRBY

198–					198–			
Aug.	14		(SJ)	43.75		Balance		110.10
	15		(SJ)	66.35				
				110.10				110.10
Sept.	1	Balance		110.10		Balance		215.10
Oct.	11		(SJ)	105.00				
				215.10				215.10
Nov.	1	Balance		215.10				

H.S. PRATT

198–				198–			
Aug. 15		(SJ)	50.00		Balance		80.00
16		(SJ)	30.00				
			80.00				80.00
Sept 1	Balance		80.00	Oct. 27		(CR)	80.00
Oct. 11		(SJ)	202.25		Balance		452.25
29		(SJ)	250.00				
			532.25				532.25
Nov. 1	Balance		452.25				

H.S. GIBBS

198–				198–			
Aug. 16		(SJ)	20.00		Balance		20.00
Sept 1	Balance		20.00		Balance		120.00
20		(SJ)	100.00				
			120.00				120.00
Oct. 1	Balance		120.00				

E.J. KEMP

198–				198–			
Aug. 21		(SJ)	185.00	Aug. 22		(SRJ)	50.00
					Balance		135.00
			185.00				185.00
Sept 1	Balance		135.00		Balance		185.00
11		(SJ)	50.00				
			185.00				185.00
Oct. 1	Balance		185.00	Oct. 25		(CR)	185.00

H.G. LITTLE

198–				198–		
Aug. 30		(SJ)	500.00	Aug. 31	Notes Receivable (GJ)	500.00

Accounts Payable Ledger

OR CREDITORS' LEDGER (CRL)

BOOK NO. 8

WHITE & CO.

198–				198–				
Aug. 31		(CD)	263.75	Aug. 1		Balance from GL		263.75

FULTON SUPPLY CO.

198–				198–				
Aug. 31		(CD)	350.00	Aug. 1		Bal. from GL		350.00

BROWN–DURRELL CO.

198–				198–				
Aug. 31		(CD)	1,362.25	Aug. 1		Bal. from GL		362.25

PIERCE & CO.

198–				198–				
Aug. 6		(CD)	2,500.00	Aug. 6	2/10/n/30		(PJ)	2,500.00

WHITNEY & CO.

198–				198–				
Aug. 3		(PJ)	50.00	Aug. 1	2/10/n/30		(PJ)	1,000.00
8		(CD)	950.00					
			1,000.00					1,000.00

HICKS & CO.

198–				198–				
Aug. 8		(CD)	1,500.00	Aug. 1	2/10/n/30		(PJ)	1,500.00

ROBINSON & CO.

198–				198–				
Aug. 14		(CD)	3,000.00	Aug. 6	2/10/n/60		(PJ)	3,000.00

WESTERN WHOLESALE CO.

198–				198–				
Aug. 21		(CD)	3,600.00	Aug. 14	2/10/n/30		(PJ)	3,600.00

HARPER WHOLESALE CO.

198–				198–				
Aug. 26		(CD)	1,750.00	Aug. 8	n/30		(PJ)	1,750.00
Sept 24		(CD)	3,500.00	Sept 3	n/30		(PJ)	3,500.00
Oct. 31		(CD)	1,875.00	Oct. 3	n/30		(PJ)	1,875.00
	Balance		8,500.00	31	2/10/n/60		(PJ)	8,500.00
			10,375.00					10,375.00
				Nov. 1	Balance			8,500.00

HERRICK SUPPLY CO.

198–				198–				
	Balance		350.00	Aug. 17	2/20/n/60		(PJ)	350.00
Sept 3		(CD)	350.00	Sept 1	Balance			350.00

WILSON & CO

198–				198–				
	Balance		2,000.00	Aug. 30	2/10/n/30		(PJ)	2,000.00
Sept 6		(CD)	2,000.00	Sept 1	Balance			2,000.00
17		(CD)	3,500.00	9	2/10/n/30		(PJ)	3,500.00
			5,500.00					5,500.00

GRIMES & CO.

198–				198–				
	Balance		190.00	Aug. 22	2/30/n/60		(PJ)	190.00
Sept 22		(CD)	190.00	Sept 1	Balance			190.00

SANFORD & CO.

				198–				
	Balance		500.00	Aug. 29	n/30		(PJ)	500.00
Sept 15		(CD)	500.00	Sept 1	Balance			500.00
	Balance		4,950.00	Oct. 9	n/60		(PJ)	4,950.00
				Nov. 1	Balance			4,950.00

REMINGTON CO.

198–				198–			
	Balance		875.00	Aug. 16	n/30	(PJ)	875.00
Sept 3		(CD)	875.00	Sept 1	Balance		875.00

BROWN & CO.

198–				198–			
Sept 25		(CD)	4,500.00	Sept. 18	1/10/n/60	(PJ)	4,500.00

LANE & CO.

198–				198–			
Sept 30		(PRJ)	100.00	Sept 30	2/10/n/30	(PJ)	5,253.00
	Balance		5,153.00				
			5,253.00				5,253.00
Oct 8		(CD)	5,153.00	Oct. 1	Balance		5,153.00
31		(CD)	2,500.00	11	2/20/n/30	(PJ)	2,500.00
			7,653.00				7,653.00

SPRINGER & CO.

198–				198–			
	Balance		8,500.00	Sept. 25	2/10/n/30	(PJ)	8,500.00
Oct. 3		(CD)	8,500.00	Oct. 1	Balance		8,500.00

Trial Balance of General Ledger

JULY, AUG., SEPT. & OCT., 198—

TRIAL BALANCE AS OF JULY 31st, 198—

L.F.			
OO	Cash	$ 17,161.55	
OO	John Pollard	64.50	
OO	Robert Black	272.50	
OO	Henry Kelly	43.35	
OO	William Dickson	81.50	
OO	Macy & Co.	95.00	
OO	George Cornwall	134.00	
OO	Spalding & Co.	84.00	
OO	Selden Hawley	102.50	
OO	Wages	600.00	
OO	Advertising	120.00	
OO	Automobile Expense	181.50	
OO	Furniture & Fixtures	2,700.00	
OO	Automobile Delivery Truck	3,625.00	
OO	Repairs to Building	372.50	
OO	Donations	50.00	
OO	Building	30,000.00	
OO	White & Co.		263.75
OO	Fulton Supply Co.		350.00
OO	Brown—Durrell Co.		1,362.25
OO	Mortgage Payable		15,000.00
OO	Sales		1,104.05
OO	Sales Returns and Allowances	21.70	
OO	Sales Cash		6,695.15
OO	Purchases	9,215.85	
OO	Purchases Returned		150.25
OO	John Smith, Proprietorship		40,000.00
		$64,925.45	$64,925.45

GENERAL LEDGER TRIAL BALANCE OF AUGUST 31st, 198–

L.F.

OO	Cash in Bank	$11,468.75	
OO	Cash in Office (Petty)	250.00	
OO	Merchandise Inventory	3,436.50	
OO	Accounts Receivable	3,071.65	
OO	Notes Receivable	500.00	
OO	Furniture and Fixtures	4,100.00	
OO	Automobile Delivery Truck	3,625.00	
OO	Wages	925.00	
OO	Advertising	243.75	
CO	Repairs to Building	70.00	
OO	Interest Accrued		62.50
OO	Store Supplies	206.50	
OO	Delivery Expense	242.50	
CO	Repairs to Store Fixtures	12.50	
OO	Building	30,000.00	
OO	Accounts Payable		3,915.00
CO	Mortgage Payable		15,000.00
CO	Reserve for Bad Debts		50.00
OO	Reserve for Depreciation on Delivery Equipment		75.00
CO	Reserve for Depreciation on Furniture & Fixtures		50.00
CO	Reserve for Depreciation on Buildings		100.00
OO	Sales, Regular		4,239.15
OO	Sales Returned Allowances	102.50	
CO	Sales Cash		11,010.10
OO	Purchases	16,440.00	
CO	Purchases Returns		50.00
OO	Purchases Discount		231.00
CO	John Smith, Personal Account	500.00	
CO	John Smith, Proprietorship		40,411.90
	TOTALS	75,194.65	75,194.65

GENERAL LEDGER TRIAL BALANCE OF SEPTEMBER 30, 198—

L.F.

CO	Cash in Bank	30,616.60	
CO	Cash In Office (Petty)	250.00	
CO	Merchandise Inventory	8,487.50	
CO	Investment Bonds	10,000.00	
CO	Accounts Receivable	2,892.10	
CO	Furniture and Fixtures	4,100.00	
CO	Building	30,000.00	
CO	Wages	1,200.00	
CO	Advertising	482.50	
OO	Auto Expense	140.00	
OO	Repairs to Building	325.00	
CO	Interest		125.00
CO	Store Supplies	270.00	
CO	Delivery Expense	500.00	
CO	Repairs to Store Fixtures	6.25	
OO	Insurance	250.00	
OO	Partners' Salaries	3,250.00	
CO	Accounts Payable		13,653.00
OO	Mortgage Payable		15,000.00
OO	Reserve for Bad Debts		201.45
OO	Reserve for Depreciation on Delivery Equipment		150.00
OO	Reserve for Depreciation on Furniture and Fixtures		91.00
OO	Reserve for Depreciation on Buildings		200.00
CO	Sales, Regular		2,352.50
OO	Sales Returns and Allowances	60.00	
CO	Sales, Cash		23,033.75
OO	Purchases	25,253.00	
OO	Purchase Returns		100.00
CO	Purchase Discounts		165.80
OO	John Smith, Capital Account		41.635.45
OO	Edward Clark, Capital Account		25,000.00
OO	Automobile Delivery Truck	3,625.00	
	TOTALS	121,707.95	121,707.95

GENERAL LEDGER TRIAL BALANCE OF OCTOBER 31, 198–

L.F.

OO	Cash in Bank	32,545.78	
OO	Petty Cash	250.00	
OO	Merchandise Inventory	16,250.00	
OO	Investments (Bonds)	10,000.00	
OO	Accounts Receivable	3,809.90	
OO	Furniture and Fixtures	4,100.00	
OO	Automobile Delivery Truck	3,625.00	
OO	Building	30,000.00	
OO	Wages	1,100.00	
OO	Advertising	695.00	
OO	Auto Expense	176.50	
OO	Repairs to Building	740.00	
OO	Accrued Interest		225.00
OO	Store Supplies	381.00	
OO	Delivery Expense	500.00	
OO	Repairs to Store Fixtures	61.50	
OO	Repairs to Delivery Truck	117.50	
OO	Insurance	229.15	
OO	Taxes Accrued		50.00
OO	Officers' Salaries	3,250.00	
OO	Accounts Payable		13,450.00
OO	Mortgage Payable		15,000.00
OO	Reserve for Bad Debts		301.45
OO	Reserve for Depreciation on Delivery Equipment		222.50
OO	Reserve for Depreciation on Furniture & Fixtures		132.00
OO	Reserve for Depreciation on Building		300.00
OO	Sales, Regular		2,222.55
OO	Sales Returns	74.75	
OO	Sales, Cash		22,069.52
OO	Purchases	17,865.00	
OO	Purchases Discount		323.06
OO	Interest on Bonds	25.00	
OO	Common Stock Unissued	53,500.00	
OO	Common Stock Authorized		125,000.00
	TOTALS	179,296.08	179,296.08

Work Sheets
FOR
JULY – JOHN SMITH
AUGUST – JOHN SMITH
SEPTEMBER – SMITH & CLARK
OCTOBER – SMITH–CLARK, INC.

JOHN SMITH WORK SHEET

	TRIAL BALANCE		ADJUSTMENTS	
	Dr.	Cr.	Dr.	Cr.
(1) Cash $	17,161.55			
(2) John Pollard	64.50			
(3) Robert Black	272.50			
(4) Henry Kelly	43.35			
(5) William Dickson	81.50			
(6) Macy & Co.	95.00			
(7) George Cornwell	134.00			
(8) Spalding & Co.	84.00			
(9) Selden Hawley	102.50			
(10) Wages	600.00		75.00	
(11) Advertising	120.00			
(12) Automobile Expense	181.50			
(13) Furniture & Fixtures	2,700.00			
(14) Auto Delivery Truck	3,625.00			
(15) Repairs to Building	372.50			
(16) Donations	50.00			
(17) Building	30,000.00			
(18) White & Co.		263.75		
(19) Fulton Supply Co.		350.00		
(20) Brown–Durrell Co.		1,362.25		
(21) Mortgage Payable		15,000.00		
(22) Sales, Regular		1,104.05		
(23) Sales, Cash		6,695.15		
(24) Sales Returns	21.70			
(25) Purchases	9,215.85			3,436.50
(26) Purchase Returns		150.25		
(27) Proprietorship, John Smith		40,000.00		
(28) Wages Payable				75.00
(29) Inventory			3,436.50	
(30) Interest on Mortgage			62.50	
(31) Interest on Mortgage Payable				62.50
(32) Bad Debts			50.00	
(33) Reserve for Bad Debts				50.00
(34) Deprec. for Del'y Equipment			75.00	
(35) Res. for Deprec. of Del'y Equip.				75.00
(36) Deprec. on Furniture & Fixtures			50.00	
(37) Res. for Deprec. on Fur. & Fix.				50.00
(38) Depreciation on Buildings			100.00	
(39) Reserve for Deprec. on Buildings				100.00
TOTALS	$64,925.45	$64,925.45	$3,849.00	$3,849.00

AS AT JULY 31st, 198–

	ADJUSTED TRIAL BALANCE		PROFIT and LOSS		BALANCE SHEET	
	Dr.	**Cr.**	**Dr.**	**Cr.**	**Dr.**	**Cr.**
(1)	17,161.55				17,161.55	
(2)	64.50				64.50	
(3)	272.50				272.50	
(4)	43.35				43.35	
(5)	81.50				81.50	
(6)	95.00				95.00	
(7)	134.00				134.00	
(8)	84.00				84.00	
(9)	102.50				102.50	
(10)	675.00			675.00		
(11)	120.00			120.00		
(12)	181.50			181.50		
(13)	2,700.00				2,700.00	
(14)	3.625.00				3,625.00	
(15)	372.50			372.50		
(16)	50.00			50.00		
(17)	30,000.00				30,000.00	
(18)		263.75				263.75
(19)		350.00				350.00
(20)		1,362.25				1,362.25
(21)		15,000.00				15,000.00
(22)		1,104.05	1,104.05			
(23)		6,695.15	6,695.15			
(24)	21.70			21.70		
(25)	5,779.35			5,779.35		
(26)		150.25	150.25			
(27)		40,000.00		411.90		40,411.90
(28)		75.00				75.00
(29)	3,436.50				3,436.50	
(30)	62.50			62.50		
(31)		62.50				62.50
(32)	50.00			50.00		
(33)		50.00				50.00
(34)	75.00			75.00		
(35)		75.00				75.00
(36)	50.00			50.00		
(37)		50.00				50.00
(38)	100.00			100.00		
(39)		100.00				100.00
	65,337.95	65,337.95	7,949.45	7,949.45	57,800.40	57,800.40

JOHN SMITH – WORK SHEET

	TRIAL BALANCE		ADJUSTMENTS	
	Dr.	Cr.	Dr.	Cr.
(1) Cash in Bank	11,468.75			
(2) Cash in Office (Petty)	250.00			
(3) Merchandise Inventory	3,436.50		8,487.50	3,436.50
(4) Accounts Receivable	3,071.65			
(5) Notes Receivable	500.00			
(6) Furniture & Fixtures	4,100.00			
(7) Auto Delivery Truck	3,625.00			
(8) Wages	925.00		60.00	
(9) Advertising	243.75			
(10) Repairs to Building	70.00			
(11) Interest Accrued		62.50	125.00	
(12) Store Supplies	206.50			
(13) Delivery Expense	242.50		125.00	
(14) Repairs to Store Fixtures	12.50			
(15) Buildings	30,000.00			
(16) Accounts Payable		3,915.00		
(17) Mortgage Payable		15,000.00		
(18) Reserve for Bad Debts		50.00		151.45
(19) Res. for Deprec. Delivery Equip		75.00		75.00
(20) Res. for Deprec. Furn. & Fix.		50.00		41.00
(21) Res. Deprec. Buildings		100.00		100.00
(22) Sales, Regular		4,239.15		
(23) Sales Returns	102.50			
(24) Sales, Cash		11,010.10		
(25) Purchases	16,440.00		3,436.50	8.487.50
(26) Purchase Returns		50.00		
(27) Purchase Discounts		231.00		
(28) John Smith, Personal	500.00			500.00
(29) John Smith, Proprietorship		40,411.90	500.00	
(30) Accrued Expense Payable				125.00
(31) Bad Debts			151.45	
(32) Deprec. of Furn. & Fix.			41.00	
(33) Wages Payable				60.00
(34) Accrued Interest Payable				125.00
(35) Deprec. of Delivery Equipment			75.00	
(36) Deprec. of Buildings			100.00	
TOTALS	75,194.65	75,194.65	13,101.45	13,101.45

AS AT AUGUST 31st, 198–

	ADJUSTED TRIAL BALANCE		PROFIT AND LOSS		BALANCE SHEET	
	Dr.	Cr.	Dr.	Cr.	Dr.	Cr.
(1)	11,468.75				11,468.75	
(2)	250.00				250.00	
(3)	8,487.50				8,487.50	
(4)	3,071.65				3,071.65	
(5)	500.00				500.00	
(6)	4,100.00				4,100.00	
(7)	3,625.00				3,625.00	
(8)	985.00			985.00		
(9)	243.75			243.75		
(10)	70.00			70.00		
(11)	62.50			62.50		
(12)	206.50			206.50		
(13)	367.50			367.50		
(14)	12.50			12.50		
(15)	30,000.00				30,000.00	
(16)		3,915.00				3,915.00
(17)		15,000.00				15,000.00
(18)		201.45				201.45
(19)		150.00				150.00
(20)		91.00				91.00
(21)		200.00				200.00
(22)		4,239.15	4,239.15			
(23)	102.50			102.50		
(24)		11,010.10	11,010.10			
(25)	11,389.00			11,389.00		
(26)		50.00	50.00			
(27)		231.00	231.00			
(28)						
(29)		39,911.90		1,723.55		41,635.45
(30)		125.00				125.00
(31)	151.45			151.45		
(32)	41.00			41.00		
(33)		60.00				60.00
(34)		125.00				125.00
(35)	75.00			75.00		
(36)	100.00			100.00		
	75,309.60	75,309.60	15,530.25	15,530.25	61,502.90	61,502.90

	TRIAL BALANCE		ADJUSTMENTS	
	Dr.	Cr.	Dr.	Cr.
(1) Cash in Bank	30,616.60			
(2) Cash in Office (Petty)	250.00			
(3) Merchandise Inventory	8,487.50		16,250.00	8,487.50
(4) Investments, Bonds	10,000.00			
(5) Accounts Receivable	2,892.10			
(6) Furniture & Fixtures	4,100.00			
(7) Building	30,000.00			
(8) Wages	1,200.00		100.00	
(9) Advertising	482.50			
(10) Auto Expense	140.00			
(11) Repairs to Building	325.00			
(12) Interest		125.00	225.00	
(13) Store Supplies	270.00			
(14) Delivery Expense	500.00			
(15) Repairs to Store Fixtures	6.25			
(16) Insurance	250.00			229.15
(17) Partners' Salaries	3,250.00			
(18) Accounts Payable		13,653.00		
(19) Mortgage Payable		15,000.00		
(20) Reserve for Bad Debts		201.45		100.00
(21) Res. for Deprec. of Del. Equip.		150.00		72.50
(22) Res. for Deprec. of Fur. & Fix.		91.00		41.00
(23) Res. for Deprec. of Buildings		200.00		100.00
(24) Sales, Regular		2,352.60		
(25) Sales Returns	60.00			
(26) Sales, Cash		23,033.75		
(27) Purchases	25,253.00		8,487.50	16,250.00
(28) Purchase Returns		100.00		
(29) Purchase Discounts		165.80		
(30) John Smith, Personal				
(31) Edward Clark, Personal				
(32) John Smith, Capital		41,635.45		
(33) Edward Clark, Capital		25,000.00		
(34) Auto Delivery Truck	3,625.00			
(35) Bad Debts			100.00	
(36) Deprec. on Fur. & Fix.			41.00	
(37) Deprec. on Del. Equip.			72.50	
(38) Taxes Accrued			50.00	
(39) Accrued Taxes Payable				50.00
(40) Prepaid Insurance			229.15	
(41) Accrued Interest Receivable			25.00	
(42) Accrued Interest on Bonds				25.00
(43) Wages Payable				100.00
(44) Accrued Interest Payable				225.00
(45) Deprec. on Buildings			100.00	
TOTALS	121,707.95	121,707.95	25,680.15	25,680.15

CLARK AS AT SEPTEMBER 30th, 198—

	ADJUSTED TRIAL BALANCE		PROFIT AND LOSS		BALANCE SHEET	
	Dr.	Cr.	Dr.	Cr.	Dr.	Cr.
(1)	30,616.60				30,616.60	
(2)	250.00				250.00	
(3)	16,250.00				16,250.00	
(4)	10,000.00				10,000.00	
(5)	2,892.10				2,892.10	
(6)	4,100.00				4,100.00	
(7)	30,000.00				30,000.00	
(8)	1,300.00			1,300.00		
(9)	482.50			482.50		
(10)	140.00			140.00		
(11)	325.00			325.00		
(12)	100.00			100.00		
(13)	270.00			270.00		
(14)	500.00			500.00		
(15)	6.25			6.25		
(16)	20.85			20.85		
(17)	3,250.00			3,250.00		
(18)		13,653.00				13,653.00
(19)		15,000.00				15,000.00
(20)		301.45				301.45
(21)		222.50				222.50
(22)		132.00				132.00
(23)		300.00				300.00
(24)		2,352.50	2,352.50			
(25)	60.00			60.00		
(26)		23,033.75	23,033.75			
(27)	17,490.50			17,490.50		
(28)		100.00	100.00			
(29)		165.80	165.80			
(30)						
(31)						
(32)		41,635.45		1,026.34		42,661.79
(33)		25,000.00		342.11		25,342.11
(34)	3,625.00				3,625.00	
(35)	100.00			100.00		
(36)	41.00			41.00		
(37)	72.50			72.50		
(38)	50.00			50.00		
(39)		50.00				50.00
(40)	229.15				229.15	
(41)	25.00				25.00	
(42)		25.00	25.00			
(43)		100.00				100.00
(44)		225.00				225.00
(45)	100.00			100.00		
	122,296.45	122,196.45	25,677.05	25,677.05	97,987.85	97,987.85

WORK SHEET OF SMITH-CLARK,

	TRIAL BALANCE		ADJUSTMENTS	
	Dr.	Cr.	Dr.	Cr.
(1) Cash in Bank	32,545.78			
(2) Petty Cash	250.00			
(3) Merchandise Inventory	16,250.00		19,500.00	16,250.00
(4) Investments, Bonds	10,000.00			
(5) Accounts Receivable	3,809.90			
(6) Furniture & Fixtures	4,100.00			
(7) Auto Delivery Truck	3,625.00			
(8) Building	30,000.00			
(9) Wages	1,100.00		60.00	
(10) Advertising	695.00			
(11) Auto Expense	176.50			
(12) Repairs to Building	740.00			
(13) Accrued Interest		225.00	287.50	
(14) Store Supplies	381.00			
(15) Delivery Expense	500.00			
(16) Repairs to Store Fixtures	61.50			
(17) Repairs to Delivery Truck	117.50			
(18) Insurance	229.15			208.35
(19) Taxes Accrued		50.00	150.00	
(20) Officers' Salaries	3,250.00			
(21) Accounts Payable		13,450.00		
(22) Mortgage Payable		15,000.00		
(23) Reserve for Bad Debts		301.45		100.00
(24) Res. for Deprec. on Equipment		222.50		72.50
(25) Res. for Deprec. on Fur. & Fix.		132.00		41.00
(26) Res. for Deprec. on Building		300.00		100.00
(27) Sales, Regular		2,222.55		
(28) Sales Returns	74.75			
(29) Sales, Cash		22,069.52		
(30) Purchases	17,865.00		16,250.00	19,500.00
(31) Purchases, Discount		323.06		
(32) Interest on Bonds	25.00			50.00
(33) Common Stock Unissued	53,500.00			
(34) Common Stock		125,000.00		
(35) Bad Debts			100.00	
(36) Deprec. on Fur. & Fix.			41.00	
(37) Deprec. on Delivery Equip.			72.50	
(38) Deprec. on Building			100.00	
(39) Accrued Taxes Payable				150.00
(40) Prepaid Insurance			208.35	
(41) Wages Payable				60.00
(42) Accrued Interest on Mtg. Pay.				287.50
(43) Accrued Interest Receivable			50.00	
(44) Surplus				
TOTALS	179,296.08	179,296.08	36,819.35	36,819.35

- INC. AS OF OCTOBER 31st, 198—

	ADJUSTED TRIAL BALANCE		PROFIT AND LOSS		BALANCE SHEET	
	Dr.	Cr.	Dr.	Cr.	Dr.	Cr.
(1)	32,545.78				32,545.78	
(2)	250.00				250.00	
(3)	19,500.00				19,500.00	
(4)	10,000.00				10,000.00	
(5)	3,809.90				3,809.90	
(6)	4,100.00				4,100.00	
(7)	3,625.00				3,625.00	
(8)	30,000.00				30,000.00	
(9)	1,160.00			1,160.00		
(10)	695.00			695.00		
(11)	176.50			176.50		
(12)	740.00			740.00		
(13)	62.50			62.50		
(14)	381.00			381.00		
(15)	500.00			500.00		
(16)	61.50			61.50		
(17)	117.50			117.50		
(18)	20.80			20.80		
(19)	100.00			100.00		
(20)	3,250.00			3,250.00		
(21)		13,450.00				13,450.00
(22)		15,000.00				15,000.00
(23)		401.45				401.45
(24)		295.00				295.00
(25)		173.00				173.00
(26)		400.00				400.00
(27)		2,222.55	2,222.55			
(28)	74.75			74.75		
(29)		22,069.52	22,069.52			
(30)	14,615.00			14,615.00		
(31)		323.06	323.06			
(32)		25.00	25.00			
(33)	53,500.00				53,500.00	
(34)		125,000.00				125,000.00
(35)	100.00			100.00		
(36)	41.00			41.00		
(37)	72.50			72.50		
(38)	100.00			100.00		
(39)		150.00				150.00
(40)	208.35				208.35	
(41)		60.00				60.00
(42)		287.50				287.50
(43)	50.00				50.00	
(44)				2,372.08		2,372.08
	179,857.08	179,857.08	24,640.13	24,640.13	157,589.03	157,589.03

EXHIBIT "A"

Balance Sheets

FOR JULY, AUG., SEPT. & OCT., 198–

BALANCE SHEET AS OF JULY 31st, 198–

ASSETS			LIABILITIES	
Cash		17,161.55	Trade Accounts Payable	1,976.00
Inventory (Mdse)		3,436.50	Wages Payable	75.00
Accounts Receivable	877.35		Interest on Mortgage Payable	62.50
Less Res. Bad Debts	50.00	827.35	Mortgage Payable	15,000.00
Furniture & Fixtures	2,700.00		John Smith, Proprietorship	40,411.90
Less Res. Deprec.	50.00	2,650.00		
Auto Delivery Truck	3,625.00			
Less Res. Deprec.	75.00	3,550.00		
Building	30,000.00			
Less Res. Deprec.	100.00	29,900.00		
TOTAL		**57,525.40**	**TOTAL**	**57,525.40**

BALANCE SHEET AS OF JULY 31st, 198–

ASSETS			LIABILITIES	
Cash in Bank		$11,468.75	Trade Accounts Payable	3,915.00
Cash in Office (Petty)		250.00	Wages Payable	60.00
Accounts Receivable	3,071.65		Accrued Interest Payable	125.00
Less Res. Bad Debts	201.45	2,870.20	Accrued Expenses Payable	125.00
Notes Receivable		500.00	Mortgage Payable	15,000.00
Inventory (Mdse)		8,487.50	John Smith, Prop., Aug. 1 40,411.90	
Furniture & Fixtures	4,100.00		Less Drawings 500.00	
Less Res. Depreciation	91.00	4,009.00	39,911.90	
Auto Delivery Truck	3,625.00		Net Profit for Period 1,723.55	41,635.45
Less Res. Depreciation	150.00	3,475.00		
Building	30,000.00			
Less Res. Depreciation	200.00	29,800.00		
TOTAL		**60,860.45**	**TOTAL**	**60,860.45**

BALANCE SHEET AS OF SEPTEMBER 30, 198—

ASSETS

Cash in Bank	30,616.60	
Cash in Office (Petty)	250.00	$30,866.60
Accounts Receivable	2,892.10	
Less Reserve for Bad Debts	301.45	2,590.65
Accrued Interest Receivable		25.00
Inventory (Merchandise)		16,250.00
Investments (Bonds)		10,000.00
Furniture & Fixtures	4,100.00	
Less Res. for Depreciation	132.00	3,968.00
Auto Delivery Truck	3,625.00	
Less Res. for Depreciation	222.50	3,402.50
Building	30,000.00	
Less Res. Depreciation	300.00	29,700.00
Prepaid Insurance		229.15
TOTAL		97,031.90

LIABILITIES

Accounts Payable		13,653.00
Accrued Expenses Payable		50.00
Taxes		100.00
Wages		
Accrued Interest Payable		225.00
Mortgage Payable		15,000.00

CAPITAL

John Smith, 9/1/8—	41,635.45	
½ Net Profit, Sept.	1,026.34	
Net Worth, 9/30/8—		42,661.79
Edward Clark, 9/1/8—	25,000.00	
½ Net Profit, Sept.	342.11	
Net Worth, 9/30/8—		25,342.11
TOTAL		97,031.90

BALANCE SHEET AS OF OCTOBER 31, 198—

ASSETS

CURRENT ASSETS		
Cash in Bank	32,545.78	
Cash in Office (Petty)	250.00	$32,795.78
Accounts Receivable	3,809.90	
Less Reserve for Bad Debts	401.45	3,408.45
Accrued Interest Receivable		50.00
Inventory (Merchandise)		19,500.00
Investments (Bonds)		10,000.00
TOTAL CURRENT ASSETS		65,754.23
FIXED ASSETS		
Building	30,000.00	
Less Res. for Deprec.	400.00	29,600.00
Furniture & Fixtures	4,100.00	
Less Res. for Deprec.	173.00	3,927.00
Auto Delivery Truck	3,625.00	
Less Res. for Deprec.	295.00	3,330.00
TOTAL FIXED ASSETS		36,857.00
DEFERRED ASSETS		
Prepaid Insurance		208.35
TOTAL		102,819.58

LIABILITIES & CAPITAL

CURRENT LIABILITIES		
Accounts Payable		13,450.00
Accrued Expenses Payable		
Interest	287.50	
Taxes	150.00	
Wages	60.00	497.50
TOTAL CURRENT LIABILITIES		13,947.50
FIXED LIABILITIES		
Mortgage Payable		15,000.00
TOTAL LIABILITIES		28,947.50

CAPITAL

Capital Stock (common)		
Authorized 250 shares		
par value of $500 each	$125,000.00	
Less unissued 107 shares	53,500.00	
143 shares issued and outstanding		71,500.00
Surplus		2,372.08
TOTAL CAPITAL AND SURPLUS		73,872.08
TOTAL		102,819.58

SCHEDULE NO. 1

Accounts Receivable Trial Balances

FOR AUG., SEPT. & OCT., 198–

ACCOUNTS RECEIVABLE TRIAL BALANCE
AUGUST 31, 198–

L.F.

CO	H. C. Young	663.55
CO	H. S. Darby	50.00
CO	E. W. Russel	229.50
CO	H. C. Taylor	75.00
CO	W. S. Lee	240.00
CO	H. S. Roy	241.50
CO	E. C. Griffin	175.00
CO	G. C. Doyle	277.50
CO	H. C. Evans	166.50
CO	Frank Snyder	90.00
CO	George Crane	518.00
CO	H. S. Kirby	110.10
CO	H. L. Pratt	80.00
CO	H. S. Gibbs	20.00
CO	E. J. Kemp	135.00
	TOTAL	3,071.65

ACCOUNTS RECEIVABLE TRIAL BALANCE
SEPTEMBER 30, 198–

CO	H. C. Young	250.00
CO	E. W. Russell	379.50
CO	H. C. Taylor	52.50
CO	W. S. Lee	240.00
CO	H. S. Roy	(15.00)
CO	E. C. Griffin	225.00
CO	C. C. Doyle	600.00
CO	Frank Snyder	90.00
CO	George Crane	575.00
CO	H. S. Kirby	110.10
CO	H. L. Pratt	80.00
CO	H. S. Gibbs	120.00
CO	E. J. Kemp	185.00
	TOTAL	2,892.10

ACCOUNTS RECEIVABLE TRIAL BALANCE
OCTOBER 31, 198–

L.F.

CO	H. C. Young	162.00
OO	H. S. Darby	415.00
OO	E. W. Russell	328.50
CO	H. C. Taylor	52.50
CO	W. S. Lee	436.45
CO	H. S. Roy	196.50
OO	G. C. Doyle	745.35
CO	Frank Snyder	158.75
OO	George Crane	527.50
CO	H. S. Kirby	215.10
OO	H. L. Pratt	452.25
CO	H. S. Gibbs	120.00
	TOTAL	3,809.90

SCHEDULE NO. 2

Accounts Payable Trial Balances

FOR AUG., SEPT. & OCT., 198–

ACCOUNTS PAYABLE TRIAL BALANCE
AUGUST 31, 198–

L.F.

OO	Herrick Supply Co.	350.00
OO	Wilson & Co.	2,000.00
CO	Grimes & Co.	190.00
CO	Sanford & Co.	500.00
CO	Remington Co.	875.00
	TOTAL	3,915.00

ACCOUNTS PAYABLE TRIAL BALANCE
SEPTEMBER 30, 198–

L.F.

CO	Lane & Co.	5,153.00
OO	Springer & Co.	8,500.00
	TOTAL	13,653.00

ACCOUNTS PAYABLE TRIAL BALANCE
OCTOBER 31, 198–

L.F.

OO	Harper Wholesale Co.	8,500.00
OO	Sanford & Co.	4,950.00
	TOTAL	13,450.00

EXHIBIT "B"

Statements of Profit and Loss

FOR JULY, AUG., SEPT. & OCT., 198–

STATEMENT OF PROFIT AND LOSS FOR MONTH ENDED

JULY 31, 198–

Gross Sales Regular	1.104.05	
Gross Sales Cash	6,695.15	
	7,799.20	
Less Returns	21.70	
NET SALES		7,777.50

COST OF GOODS SOLD

Purchases	9,215.85	
Less Returns	150.25	
	9,065.60	
Less Closing Inventory 7/31	3,436.50	
Cost of Goods Sold		5,629.10
GROSS TRADING PROFIT		2,148.40

OPERATING EXPENSES

Wages	675.00	
Advertising	120.00	
Automobile Expense	181.50	
Repairs to Building	372.50	
Donations	50.00	
Depreciation on Delivery Equipment	75.00	
Depreciation on Furniture & Fixtures	50.00	
Depreciation on Buildings	100.00	1,624.00
OPERATING PROFIT		524.40

DEDUCTIONS FROM INCOME

Interest on Mortgage	62.50	
Bad Debts	50.00	112.50
NET PROFIT		411.90

STATEMENT OF PROFIT AND LOSS FOR MONTH ENDED
AUGUST 31, 198-

Gross Sales Regular		4,239.15	
Gross Sales Cash		11,010.10	
		15,249.25	
Less Returns		102.50	
NET SALES			15,146.75

COST OF GOODS SOLD

Opening Inventory, August 1		$3,436.50	
Purchases	16,440.00		
Less Purchase Returns	50.00	16,390.00	
		19,826.50	
Closing Inventory, August 31		8,487.50	
Cost of Goods Sold			11,339.00
GROSS TRADING PROFIT			3,807.75

OPERATING EXPENSES

Wages	985.00	
Advertising	243.75	
Repairs to Building	70.00	
Repairs to Store Fixtures	12.50	
Store Supplies	206.50	
Delivery Expense	367.50	
Depreciation on Delivery Equipment	75.00	
Depreciation on Furniture & Fixtures	41.00	
Depreciation on Buildings	100.00	2,101.25
OPERATING PROFIT		1,706.50

OTHER INCOME

Purchase Discount		231.00
TOTAL INCOME		1,937.50

DEDUCTIONS FROM INCOME

Interest Cost	62.50	
Bad Debts	151.45	213.95
NET PROFIT		1,723.55

STATEMENT OF PROFIT AND LOSS FOR MONTH ENDED
SEPTEMBER 30, 198—

Gross Sales Regular		$2,352.50	
Gross Sales Cash		23,033.75	
		25,386.25	
Less Returns		60.00	
NET SALES			25,326.25

COST OF GOODS SOLD

Opening Inventory, September 1		8,487.50	
Purchases	25,253.00		
Less Purchase Returns	100.00	25,153.00	
		33,640.50	
Closing Inventory, September 30		16,250.00	
Cost of Goods Sold			17,390.50
GROSS TRADING PROFIT			7,935.75

OPERATING EXPENSES

Wages	1,300.00	
Advertising	482.50	
Auto Expense	140.00	
Repairs to Building	325.00	
Repairs to Store Fixtures	6.25	
Salaries — Partners	3,250.00	
Store Supplies	270.00	
Delivery Expense	500.00	
Insurance Premiums	20.85	
Taxes	50.00	
Depreciation on Delivery Equipment	72.50	
Depreciation on Furniture & Fixtures	41.00	
Depreciation on Buildings	100.00	6,558.10
OPERATING PROFIT		1,377.65

OTHER INCOME

Purchase Discount	165.80	
Interest on Bonds	25.00	190.80
TOTAL INCOME		1,568.45

DEDUCTIONS FROM INCOME

Interest Cost	100.00	
Provision for Bad Debts	100.00	200.00
		1,368.45

STATEMENT OF PROFIT AND LOSS FOR MONTH ENDED
OCTOBER 31, 198–

Gross Sales Regular	$2,222.55	
Gross Sales Cash	22,069.52	
	24,292.07	
Less Returns	74.75	
NET SALES		$24,217.32

COST OF GOODS SOLD

Opening Inventory, October 1	16,250.00	
Purchases	17,865.00	
	34,115.00	
Closing Inventory, October 31	19,500.00	
Cost of Goods Sold		14,615.00
GROSS TRADING PROFIT		9,602.32

OPERATING EXPENSES

Wages	1,160.00	
Advertising	695.00	
Auto Expense	176.50	
Repairs to Building	740.00	
Repairs to Store Fixtures	61.50	
Repairs to Delivery Truck	117.50	
Store Supplies	381.00	
Delivery Expenses	500.00	
Insurance Premiums	20.80	
Taxes	100.00	
Officers' Salaries	3,250.00	
Depreciation on Delivery Equipment	72.50	
Depreciation on Furniture & Fixtures	41.00	
Depreciation on Buildings	100.00	7,415.80
OPERATING PROFIT		2,186.52

OTHER INCOME

Purchase Discount	323.06	
Interest on Bonds	25.00	348.06
TOTAL INCOME		2,534.58

DEDUCTIONS FROM INCOME

Interest Cost	62.50	
Bad Debts	100.00	162.50
NET PROFIT		$2,372.08

ACCOUNTING AND BOOKKEEPING DEFINITIONS

ABATEMENT. A deduction or allowance, as, a discount given for prompt payment.

ACCOUNT. A detailed statement of items affecting property or claims, listed respectively as Debits or Credits, and showing excess of Debits or Credits in form of a balance. Sufficient explanatory matter should be given to set forth the complete history of the account. There need not be both Debits and Credits, nor more than one of either of these. If Debits and Credits, or both are made frequently, the account is active. Items held in suspense awaiting future classification or allocation may be charged or credited to an adjustment account. When desirable to keep a separate accounting for specific shipments of goods, it is known as an Adventure Account. If more than one party is interested in such shipment, it is a joint venture account.

Asset Accounts record value owned.

Book Accounts are kept in books, and show in formal manner the details regarding transactions between parties. To be of legal effect the entries must be original, not transferred or posted.

Capital Accounts show the amounts invested in an enterprise either net, as in case of the Capital Accounts of proprietors, partners, and stockholders shown on the liability side of Balance Sheets; or gross, as in case of the Asset Accounts which show both owned and borrowed Capital invested.

Cash Accounts set forth receipts and disbursements of cash as well as balance on hand at beginning and end of period.

Clearing Accounts are employed to collect items preliminary to their allocation to a more detailed classification of the accounts, or preliminary to the determination of the accounts to which such items properly belong.

Contingent Accounts are those which list liabilities or assets dependent for their validity upon some event which may or may not occur.

Contra Accounts are those which offset each other.

Controlling Accounts are those which summarize and afford an independent check upon detailed accounts of a given class which are usually kept in a subordinate ledger. The controlling accounts are kept in the General Ledger. The balance of the controlling account equals the aggregate of the balances of the detailed accounts when all postings affecting these accounts are completed.

Current Accounts are open or running accounts not balanced or stated.

Deficiency Accounts supplement statements of affairs of an insolvent enterprise, showing what items comprise the deficiency of assets subject to lien for payment of unsecured creditors.

Depreciation Accounts are expense accounts which are charged periodically with the amounts credited to the respective Depreciation Reserve Accounts.

Depreciation Reserve Accounts are credited periodically with the amounts charged to contra depreciation expense accounts. Depreciation Reserve Accounts are valuation accounts because they supplement or evaluate the asset accounts for the ultimate replacement of which they are intended.

Discount Accounts are: accounts which are either charged with discounts allowed to customers or credited with discounts secured from creditors; or accounts which are charged with amounts paid to have Notes Discounted; or accounts which are carried unamortized differences between par of Bonds sold and the amounts realized at time of sale, such amounts realized being less than the par of the Bonds.

Dividend Accounts are credited with amounts declared payable as dividends by boards of directors. These accounts are charged for amounts disbursed in payment, the charge being made either at time checks are sent out and for full amount of dividend, or for the amounts of the individual checks as they are returned for payment.

Impersonal Accounts record expenses and revenues, assets and liabilities, but do not make reference to persons in their titles.

Income Accounts show sources and amounts of operating revenues, expenses incurred for operations, sources and amounts of non-operating revenues, fixed charges, net income and disposition thereof.

Investment Accounts record property owned but not used for operating purposes.

Liability Accounts record value owed.

Merchandise Accounts are charged with cost of buying goods and crediting with sales, thus exhibiting Gross Profit when opening and closing inventories are taken into consideration.

Nominal Accounts are those which, during the accounting period, record changes which affect proprietorship favorably or unfavorably.

Open Accounts are those not balanced or closed.

Personal Accounts are those with individuals, usually customers and creditors.

Profit and Loss Account is an account into which all earnings and expenses are closed.

Real Accounts record Assets and Liabilities.

Revenue Accounts are equivalent to nominal accounts, showing income and expense.

Sales Accounts are rendered by agents to principals in explanation of consigned goods sold.

Sinking Fund Accounts record periodic installments paid into sinking funds and interest accretions added thereto.

Surplus Accounts record accretions to capital from profits.

ACCOUNTING. The science of accounts, their construction, classification and interpretation.

ACCRUE. Accumulation of wealth or liabilities based on passage of time.

ACCRUED EXPENSE. A liability representing expense that has accrued but is not yet due and payable. It is in reality postpaid expense, and therefore the opposite of prepaid expense, which is an asset.

ACCRUED INCOME. Income that has accrued but is not yet due. It is in reality postpaid income, and therefore the opposite of prepaid income, which is a liability.

AGENT. One possessing authority to act for another to a more or less limited extent.

ALLOCATION. Determination of the proper distribution of a given sum among a series of accounts.

AMORTIZATION. Extinction of a debt by systematic application of installments to a sinking fund, or reduction of premiums or discount incurred on sale or purchase of bonds by application of the effective interest rate.

ANNUITY. A sum of money payable periodically in installments.

APPRECIATION. Increase in value of assets.

ASSET. Wealth owned. Assets may be classified in various ways. From the point of view of ease of liquidation they are Quick or Fixed in varying degrees.

AUDIT. Verification of the accuracy of account books by examination of supporting vouchers, making tests of postings and computations and determining whether all entries are made according to correct accounting principles making sure that there are no omissions.

BALANCE. The excess of the sum of the items on one side of an account over the sum of the items on the other side.

BALANCE SHEET. A schedule of Assets and Liabilities so classified and arranged as to enable an intelligent study to be made of the important financial ratios existing between different classes of assets, between different classes of liabilities and between assets and liabilities; also to enable one to observe the origin of the equity existing in the assets and to determine to whom it belongs.

BOND. A bond is a written promise under seal to pay a certain sum of money at a specified time. Bonds bear interest at a fixed rate, usually payable semiannually. Bonds may be sold either above or below par, in which case the coupon rate of interest differs from the effective rate when the bonds are sold below par and higher when bonds are sold above par.

BURDEN. Elements of production cost which, not being directly allocable to output, must be distributed on more or less arbitrary basis.

CAPITAL. In accounting, capital is excess of assets over liabilities of a given enterprise.

Fixed Capital consists of wealth in form of land, buildings, machinery, furniture and fixtures, etc.

Floating Capital is capital which can be readily converted into cash.

Nominal Capital is the authorized capital stock of a corporation.

Paid-Up Capital is the amount of capital stock issued and fully paid.

Working Capital is the excess of current assets over current liabilities.

CASH. All forms of exchange media which by custom are received in settlement of debts.

CHARGES. Items debited in accounts.

CHECK OR CHECQUE. See Draft.

COLLATERAL SECURITY. Personal property transferred by the owner to another to secure the carrying out of an obligation.

CONSIGNEE. An agent who receives shipments of goods from his principal to be sold on commission basis, title to goods remaining in the principal or consignor.

CONSIGNMENT. A shipment of goods to another and held by him for account of the principal or consignor.

CONSIGNOR. One who ships goods to an agent or factor who holds them for account of the principal or consignor.

CONSOLIDATION. Unification or affiliation of enterprises engaged in competitive or supplementary undertakings.

CONTINGENT. That which depends upon some happening or occurence; doubtful, conditional.

CORPORATION. An artificial person created by law to carry out a certain purpose or purposes.

COST. Cost is the outlay, usually measured in terms of money, necessary to buy or to produce a commodity. The two elements of Cost are Prime Cost and Overhead or Burden. Prime Cost is the outlay on direct labor and raw materials necessary to produce a commodity. Burden includes all elements of Cost other than direct labor and raw materials.

COST ACCOUNTING. Determination, by means ot applying accounting principles, of the elements of Cost entering into the production of a commodity or service.

CREDITOR. One who gives credit in business matters; one to whom money is due.

DEBT. An obligation to pay money or that which one owes to another.

DEBTOR. One who owes money.

DEFERRED ASSET OR CHARGE. See Prepaid Expense.

DEFERRED CREDIT & INCOME OR LIABILITY. See Prepaid Income.

DEFICIENCY. Insufficiency of assets to discharge debts or other obligations.

DEPRECIATION. Decline in value of assets resulting from one or more of the following:

1. Wear and tear.
2. Tenure of holding.

3. Permanency or steadiness of industry.
4. Exhaustion of raw materials.
5. Obsolescence.
6. Accidents.
7. Fluctuations in trade.
8. Inadequacy.

DISBURSEMENTS. Cash payments.

DISCOUNT. Deduction from a listed or named figure, usually computed on a percentage basis.

DIVIDEND. Division of profits among stockholders on a pro rata basis.

DRAFT. A draft or bill of exchange is defined by Uniform Negotiable Instrument Law as, "an unconditional order in writing addressed by one person to another, signed by the person giving it, requiring the person to whom it is addressed to pay on demand or at a fixed or determinable future time a certain sum in money to order or to bearer."

DRAWEE. The person against whom a draft is drawn and who becomes primarily liable upon acceptance.

DRAWER. The maker of a draft or bill of exchange.

ENTRY. Written description of a business transaction or adjustment made in books of accounts.

ESTATE. A right of ownership in property.

FIXED ASSETS. Those assets which are not readily convertible into cash and in the usual routine of business are not so converted.

FRANCHISE. A privilege or liberty given by the Government to certain individuals.

GOOD WILL. Present right to receive expected future superprofits, superprofits being the amount by which future profits are expected to exceed all economic expenditure incident to its production.

IMPREST SYSTEM. Plan used to account for petty cash disbursements whereby the cashier is at intervals reimbursed for the amount disbursed by him through a check drawn to Cash and charged to the accounts against which such disbursements were made.

INCOME. A flow of benefits from wealth over a period of time.

INTEREST. Expense or income resulting from use of wealth over a period of time.

INVENTORY. An itemized list of goods giving amounts and prices.

INVOICE. A statement issued by a seller of goods to the purchaser giving details regarding quantities, prices and terms of payment.

JOURNAL. The book of original entry in double entry bookkeeping.

Cash Journal is a combination cash book and journal, containing columns for both cash and non-cash transactions.

Purchases Journal records purchases made and the names of persons credited therefor.

Sales Journal records sales and the names of persons charged therefor.

LEDGER. A ledger is the book in which transactions are classified according to function. When subordinate ledgers are used, the General Ledger becomes a digest of details kept in subordinate ledgers, as well as the record of all usual ledger accounts.

Accounts Receivable Ledger contains a record of all transactions affecting trade debtors.

Accounts Payable Ledger contains a record of all transactions affecting trade creditors.

LIABILITY. A debt.

Capital Liabilities are those which are incurred in the acquisition of permanent assets, and which are usually in form on bonded indebtedness having a maturity date removed more than a year.

Contingent Liability are those which may or may not become definite obligations, depending upon some event.

Current Liability are those which will fall due within a period of a year.

Deferred Liability are income received but not yet due; see Prepaid Income.

Fixed Liability are those in form of bonds or long term notes.

NOTES PAYABLE. The sum of all notes and acceptances upon which a concern is primarily liable as maker, endorser or acceptor.

NOTES RECEIVABLE. The sum of all notes and acceptances upon which others are liable to the holding concern.

NOTES RECEIVABLE DISCOUNTED. Contingent Liability for all notes receivable discounted at bank but not yet liquidated by the makers.

OVERDRAFT. A debit balance in a deposit account which should normally have a credit balance.

POSTING. Transferring items from journals to ledgers, and making the necessary cross-references in folio columns.

PREMIUM ON BONDS. Amount above par at which bonds are bought or sold.

PREPAID EXPENSE. An asset representing expenditures for services not yet rendered. Also known as Deferred Charge or Deferred Asset.

PREPAID INCOME. Income received for services not yet rendered. It is therefore a liability. Also known as Deferred Credit or Deferred Liability.

PROFIT. Increase in net worth resulting from business operations.

PROPRIETORSHIP. Equity in assets over and above liability.

QUICK ASSETS. Assets that can ordinarily be readily converted into cash without involving heavy loss.

RESERVE. A segregation of surplus, or a retention of revenues equivalent to losses in asset values. In the former case it is a reserve of surplus, in the latter case, a valuation reserve.

RESERVE FUND. An amount set aside in form of cash or investments for general or special purposes.

REVENUE. Income from all sources.

SINKING FUND. An amount set aside in form of cash or investments for the purpose of liquidating some liability.

STATEMENT. To set forth in systematic form all data with reference to some phase of a business undertaking. To present essential details, subordinate schedules are frequently appended. A statement of Assets and Liabilities.

Balance Sheets set forth the status of a business as of a given date.
Consolidated Balance Sheets set forth the status of affiliated businesses as of a given time.

Consolidated Income Statements set forth the results of operations of affiliated enterprises over a period.

Income Statements set forth the result of operations over a period.

Statement of Affairs set forth the status of an insolvent business as of a given time, the arrangement being such as to show both book value of assets, what they are expected to realize and gross liabilities, how they are expected to rank.

STOCK. Share issued by a corporation, evidenced by formal certificates representing ownership therein. The total amount of such shares is known as the Capital Stock of the corporation.

Common Stock is that upon which dividends are paid only after dividend requirements on preferred stock and interest requirements on bonds are met.

Donated Stock is stock of a corporation which has been given back to be sold at a discount, usually to afford working capital in cases where the stock was originally issued in payment for fixed assets.

Guaranteed Stock is that which is guaranteed as to principal or interest or both by some other corporation or corporations.

Inactive Stock is that which is seldom traded on the exchange.

Preferred Stock is that which has prior rights over common stock either as to dividends or assets or both. Various provisions are found relative to the voting power, as for example, the preferred stock may be given control of the corporation if dividends thereon remain unpaid for two consecutive years. In case of cumulative preferred stock, unpaid dividends become a lien upon profits of following years.

Treasury Stock is that which has been returned to the treasury of the issuing corporation.

Unissued Stock is the excess of Authorized over Issued Stock.

STOCK BONUSES. Gifts of stock offered to furnish incentive to investors to buy some other security of the issuing company.

STOCK RIGHTS. Privileges extended to stockholders to subscribe to new stock at a price below the market value of outstanding stock.

STOCK SUBSCRIPTIONS. Agreements to purchase the stock of a corporation. They become effective only when ratified by the corporation, unless accepted by a trustee in behalf of the corporation.

SURPLUS. In case of corporations having only par value stock, surplus ordinarily measures excess of net worth or proprietorship over par value of stock outstanding.

Capital Surplus is that derived from extraordinary sources, as sale of stock at premium or sale of fixed assets at a profit.

Surplus from Operations is that derived from undertakings from the carrying out of which the business was established.

TRIAL BALANCE. A list of balances of all General Ledger accounts made to determine the correctness of postings from books of original entry as well as the correctness of the work of determining these balances.

TURNOVER. Rapidity of replacement of capital invested in inventories, accounts receivable, etc.

VOUCHER. Any document which serves as proof of a transaction.

VOUCHER SYSTEM. A scheme of accounting under which distribution of all expenditures is made on vouchers preliminary to their entry in the voucher register.

WORK IN PROCESS. Materials in process of manufacture, partly finished goods including all material, labor and overhead costs incurred on those goods up to the time of taking inventory.

BOOKS OF ACCOUNT

PRACTICE TEST QUESTIONS

1. Does a trial balance of the ledger taken before the books are closed differ from a trial balance taken immediately after the books are closed?

2. If the assets of a business exceed the liabilities, is the business solvent or insolvent?

3. If the cost of merchandise sold exceeds the sales, the result would be a gross profit or loss. Which is correct?

4. Does the Profit and Loss Account show the total proprietary interest (or proprietorship) in the business?

5. Does the exchange of one asset for another of equal value affect the proprietory interest (or proprietorship)?

6. Should the amount of fuel consumed during an accounting period be entered in the Profit and Loss Statement as an expense?

7. Would the use of several books (or journals) of original entry reduce the number of postings to be made at the end of a period?

8. At the close of each period, is the interest income (interest earned) account closed into the Notes Receivable Account?

9. If the proprietor's drawing (personal) account shows a debit balance at the close of a period, would it appear

   (A) in the Balance Sheet (financial statement) as a liability?
   (B) in the Balance Sheet (financial statement) as an asset?
   (C) in the Balance Sheet (financial statement) as a deduction from the Proprietor's Investment (capital) account?
   (D) in the Profit and Loss Statement as an income?
   (E) in the Profit and Loss Statement as an expense?

10. After a ledger has been closed, P. & L. shows a credit balance. What kind of item is this if it is not an operating item?

11. If you find the P. & L. Balance on the debit side, what kind of item is it if it is not in the Trading Account?

12. For paying his bill promptly, William Jones receives an allowance of $10.00. What does he call it?

13. What does the man who makes the allowance call it?

14. Name three common financial expenses:

   (A) _____   (B) _____
            (C) _____

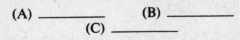

15. Which of the above is brought onto the books through an adjustment entry?

16. Make a type entry for writing off a bad debt.

17. Is Sales Discount in favor of the buyer or of the seller?

18. Make a type entry for closing the three financial expenses.

19. Make a type entry for two common financial incomes.

20. In what account is inventory shown in the Ledger?

21. In what account is initial inventory closed?

22. Is it debited or credited to this account?

23. Through what kind of an entry is final inventory brought onto the books?

24. What two accounts are affected when final inventory is debited?

25. Which account is debited?

26. What account is credited?

27. Which of the two accounts remains open after the books have been closed?

28. Is initial inventory added to or subtracted from Net Purchases?

29. Is final inventory added to or subtracted from Net Purchases?

30. What is the guide to be followed in placing a value on items of merchandise inventory?

31. Does initial inventory increase or decrease cost of sales?

32. Does final inventory increase or decrease cost of sales?

33. Mr. X finds his expired insurance is $20.00. His office supplies used $10.00. Make an adjusting entry.

34. His depreciation on mimeograph, multigraph and other duplicating machines used in preparing advertising material is $40.00. Make an adjusting entry.

35. His depreciation on delivery equipment is $50.00. Make the entry.

36. Gross Trading Margin is $2000. Net Trading Profit is $600. What can you determine?

37. Give the amount.

38. Operating costs total $800. Gross Trading Margin is $1500. What can you determine?

39. Give the amount.

40. Operating Costs total is $1200. Trading Profit is $900. What can you determine?

41. Give the amount.

42. In the Accounts Receivable Ledger it is found that John Jones owes $40. His account is considered worthless and written off. Make the Journal entry, assuming there is an account "Reserve for Bad Debts."

43. James Ryan owes me on a note, $100. I decide it is uncollectible. Make the entry.

44. John Jones and James Ryan have paid their respective obligations, which I had written off. Make one entry for the two settlements, crediting Bad Debt recoveries.

45. In a given entry, Reserve for Depreciation is credited. What kind of entry is it?

46. An automobile account shows a debit of $1400. What value does that show?

47. The "Book Value" of the account is $800. From the facts in Question #54, the value of what account may you determine?

48. If the volume of posting is to be reduced, what three special journals are usually necessary?

49. What two ledgers are used in conjunction with the above?

50. If the Sales Journal has only one money column, to what accounts are the totals posted?

51. If the Cash Receipts Journal has four money columns, to what accounts are the totals of three of them posted?

52. If the Cash Payment Journal has four money columns, to what accounts are the totals of three of them posted?

53. If the General Journal has four money columns, to what accounts are the totals of two of them posted?

54. The following summary entry is on X's books: Accounts Receivable, $2130; Sales, $2130. In what journal is the total sales on account found?

55. To what ledger are the detailed items that make up the sales of $2130 posted?

56. What other ledger is affected for the debit?

57. Do the amounts in the Purchase Journal increase or decrease "cost of goods sold"?

58. How do they affect trading margin?

59. I hold James Duke's three months note for $300, dated May 26, 198—. I discount it the same day at 4%. I receive the proceeds in cash, $297. Make the entry.

60. The note was paid by James Duke at maturity. Make the entry.

61. Name a common form of Contingent Liability.

62. What journal feature is a requirement when subsidiary ledgers are used?

63. When subsidiary ledgers are used what kind of account is required in the main ledger which is not necessary where there are no subsidiary ledgers?

64. What account title is given to this account for accounts owing us?

65. What must be the relationship between the subsidiary ledger and its control account?

66. By what method may this be determined?

67. What two accounts involving subsidiary ledgers appear in the trial balances and in the balance sheet?

68. Name the two most universal control accounts for which subsidiary ledgers are provided.

69. In case a subsidiary ledger is broken up into a number of divisions, what is the most com-

mon basis for the divisions?

70. On what other basis are subdivisions sometimes made?

71. What kind of entries other than current entries made at the beginning of a period, are usually included in the trial balance?

72. After adjustments are made, into what sections of the Working Sheet are all items extended?

73. In a given period, the net sales are $20,000. The cost of sales is 80%, operating expenses, 17%. Give the amount of:

    (A) cost of sales   (B) operating expenses
              (C) trading profit.

74. What is the gross income?

75. What is the percentage to net sales?

76. Assume that a given firm's sales average $15,000 per month. What are the annual sales?

77. If there are three partners in a certain business concern, how many capital accounts are kept?

78. A partnership consists of three equal partners; Smith, Jones and Brown. Make the entry for distributing the profits of $3,000, assuming that they are closed direct into the partners' capital accounts.

79. What is the governing body in a corporation?

80. In what ledger are accounts with individual stockholders kept?

81. What is it's main ledger control account?

82. Corporation X is organized with assets of $20,000, liabilities of $3,000 and capital stock of $15,000. What can you determine?

83. What is the amount?

84. Corporation Z is organized with assets of $10,000, liabilities of $1,000 and surplus of $1,500. What can you determine?

85. Give the amount.

86. In corporation X, the net income for a given year is $2,000. Make the entry for closing out the Profit & Loss Account.

Answer Key

1. Yes
2. Solvent
3. Gross Loss
4. No
5. No
6. Yes
7. Yes
8. No.
9. (A) No   (B) No
   (C) Yes   (D) No
        (E) No
10. Net profit

11. Net Loss
12. Cash Discount
13. Sales Discount
14. (A) Interest Cost
    (B) Sales Discount
    (C) Provision for Bad Debts
15. Provision for Bad Debts
16. Dr. Reserve for Bad Debts
    Cr. Accounts Receivable
17. Buyer
18. Dr. Profit & Loss
    Cr. Interest Cost

    Cr. Sales Discount
    Cr. Provision for Bad Debts
19. Dr. Interest Earned
    Dr. Purchase Discount
    Cr. Profit & Loss
20. Merchandise Inventory
21. Purchases
22. Dr.
23. Adjustment entry
24. Merchandise inventory
    and purchases
25. Merchandise inventory

26. Purchases
27. Merchandise inventory
28. Added to
29. Subtracted from
30. Market or Cost (whichever is lower)
31. Increase
32. Decrease
33. Dr. Profit & Loss
    Cr. Insurance
    Cr. Expense
34. Dr. Depreciation of Furniture & Fixtures
    Cr. Reserve for Depreciation of Furniture & Fixtures
35. Dr. Depreciation of Delivery Equipment
    Cr. Reserve for Depreciation of Delivery Equipment
36. Operating Expenses
37. $1400
38. Net Trading Profit
39. $700
40. Loss
41. $300
42. Dr. Reserve for Bad Debts $40
    Cr. John Jones—Acc. Receivable $40
    Control, General Ledger
43. Dr. Reserve for Bad Debts $100
    Cr. Notes Receivable (Jas. Ryan) $100
44. Dr. Cash $140
    Cr. Bad Debts recovered $140
45. Adjusting entries
46. Cost value
47. Reserve for Depreciation of Delivery Equipment $600
48. Cash Journal, Sales Journal, Purchase Journal
49. Accounts Receivable Ledger, Accounts Payable Ledger
50. Dr. Accounts Receivable
    Cr. Sales
51. Dr. Cash
    Dr. Discount
    Cr. Accounts Receivable
52. Dr. Accounts Payable
    Cr. Cash
    Cr. Discount
53. Accounts Receivable and Accounts Payable
54. General Journal
55. Accounts Receivable Subsidiary Ledger
56. The General Ledger
57. Increase
58. Decrease
59. Dr. Cash $297
    Dr. Discount $ 3
    Cr. Notes Rec. discounted (James Duke) $300
60. Dr. Notes Receivable discounted $300
    Cr. Notes Receivable $300
61. Endorsement of a customer's note
62. Special columns
63. Controlling account
64. Accounts Receivable Controlling Account
65. They must be in agreement
66. A Trial Balance of Subsidiary Ledger
67. Accounts Receivable and Accounts Payable
68. (A) Accounts Receivable
    (B) Accounts Payable
69. Alphabetical
70. Departmental or Territorial
71. Adjusting entries
72. Profit and Loss or Balance Sheet
73. (A) $16,000   (B) $3,400   (C) $600
74. $4,000
75. 20%
76. $180,000
77. Three
78. P. & L. $3,000
    To Smith —Capital Account—$1,000
    To Jones —Capital Account—$1,000
    To Brown—Capital Account—$1,000
79. The Board of Directors
80. Stockholder's Ledger
81. Capital Stock
82. The amount of surplus
83. $2,000
84. The capital stock issued
85. $7,500
86. P. & L. $2,000
    To Surplus $2,000

JOURNAL ENTRIES

DIRECTIONS: Using the numbers in front of each account title, make the journal entries for the following transactions. Do not write the names of the accounts; simply indicate the number of the account titles to be debited or credited. Always give the number of the account to be debited first; then give the number of the account to be credited. For example: if cash is to be debited and sales is to be credited, write in the answer space 1;35.

For any transaction, a series of journal entries arises. To determine the correct journal entries:

1. Determine the accounts affected.

2. Determine what effect each of these accounts has on the Balance Sheet.

3. An account is debited when:

   (A) it increases an account on the assessed (left) side; or

   (B) it decreases an account on the liability and net worth (right) side.

4. An account is credited when:

   (A) it increases an account on the liability and and net worth (right) side; or

   (B) it decreases an account on the asset (left) side.

5. Note: Since income accounts increase the net worth (right) side they are credited with any increase. Since expenses accounts decrease the net worth (right) side they are debited with any increase.

6. Since (all other things being equal) a greater purchase account will decrease the net worth (right) side any increase in purchases is debited.

EXAMPLES:

(A) We receive $100.00 cash in payment of account from a customer. The accounts involved are: Cash $100.00; Accounts Receivable $100.00. In this case the Cash $100.00 increases the left side of the balance sheet and the Accounts Receivable $100.00 decreases the left side of the balance sheet. Therefore debit Cash and credit Accounts Receivable.

(B) We sell $100.00 merchandise on account. The accounts involved are Sales $100.00; Accounts Receivable $100.00. In this case Accounts Receivable $100.00 represents an increase of the left side and Sales represents an increase of the right side, Net Worth. Therefore debit Accounts Receivable and credit Sales.

(C) We issue $100.00 note to a creditor. The accounts involved are Notes Payable $100.00; Accounts Payable $100.00. In this case Notes Payable represents an increase in a right side account and Accounts Payable represents a decrease in a right side Account. Therefore debit Accounts Payable and credit Notes Payable.

(D) Set up an accrual of wages of $100.00. The accounts involved are Wages $100.00; and Accrued Wages $100.00—the former being an expense account and the latter a liability account, which increases the right side. Therefore, debit Wages and credit Accrued Wages.

JOURNALIZING BY ACCOUNT NUMBERS

DIRECTIONS: Using the numbers in front of each account title, make the journal entries for the following transactions. Do not write the names of the accounts; simply indicate the number of the account titles to be debited or credited. Always give the number of the account to be debited first; then give the number of the account to be credited. For example: if cash is to be debited and sales is to be credited, write in the answer space 1; 35.

NUMBERED LEDGER ACCOUNT TITLES

1. Cash
2. Accounts Receivable
3. Reserve for Bad Debts
4. Notes Receivable
5. Notes Receivable Discounted
6. Inventory
7. Real Estate
8. Reserve for Depreciation (Real Estate)
9. Equipment
10. Reserve for Depreciation (Equipment)
11. Sinking Fund

12. Goodwill
13. Legal Expense
14. Interest Expense
15. Delivery Expense
16. Rent Expense
17. Depreciation Expense
18. Bad Debts
19. Selling Expense
20. Purchases
21. Purchases Returned
22. Purchases Discount
23. Accounts Payable
24. Notes Payable
25. Accrued Expenses

26. Dividends Payable
27. Mortgages Payable
28. Bonds Payable
29. Capital Stock
30. Reserve for Sinking Fund
31. Reserve for Contingence
32. Capital Surplus
33. Earned Surplus
34. Profit and Loss
35. Sales
36. Sales Returns
37. Sales Discount
38. Interest Income
39. Miscellaneous Income

1. Cash sales of $225.00 are made.

2. An invoice for $350.00 for merchandise purchased on account is received.

3. $25.00 of merchandise purchased on account is returned.

4. A new delivery truck is purchased for $1,000.00 in cash and a $2,500.00 note.

5. $5000.00 is borrowed from the bank for 60 days @ 6%.

6. The old delivery truck, which is carried on the books at $1500 and has depreciation recorded to date of $1150, is sold for $275.

7. Rent is paid in the amount of $150.

8. Salesmen are paid $500.

9. A suit against us is won and we pay $150.

10. A customer pays his account in the amount of $380 by a note.

11. The note is discounted at the bank, the proceeds of $376 being credited to our account.

12. A customer returns $25 of merchandise sold to him on account.

13. Semi-annual interest in the amount of $1,000 on the bond is paid to the bond holders.

14. A customer pays a $250 balance, taking 2% discount.

15. Legal fees are paid to our attorneys in the amount of $50.

16. The board of directors orders the annual contribution of $750 set up in the sinking fund reserve.

17. An error is discovered in a previous posting, in that $50 of supplies for the delivery department were incorrectly charged to the selling department.

18. A person paid us $20 rent for the use of our windows.

19. One account owing us $83 is found to be worthless.

20. Accrued wages on December 31 are as follows: selling department $50 and delivery department $40.

21. Bad debts for this year are estimated to be 2% of the $150,000 sales on account.

22. Close out the purchase returns and discounts to purchases.

23. Close out sales returns and discounts to sales.

24. Close out all of the income accounts.

25. Close out the profit and loss account, assuming there is a gross profit.

26. A dividend of $7500 is declared.

27. The dividend is paid in cash.

Answer Key

1. 1; 35	10. 4; 2	19. 3; 2
2. 20; 23	11. 1; 14; 5	20. 15; 19; 25
3. 23; 21	12. 36; 2	21. 18; 3
4. 9; 1; 24	13. 14; 1	22. 21; 22; 20
5. 1; 24	14. 1; 37; 2	23. 35; 36; 37
6. 1; 10; 34; 9	15. 13; 1	24. 35; 38; 39; 34
7. 16; 1	16. 33; 30	25. 34; 33
8. 19; 1	17. 15; 19	26. 33; 26
9. 31; 1	18. 1; 39	27. 26; 1

BALANCE SHEET

Balance sheet sections:

A. Current Assets Section

Consists of those assets which the firm intends to turn into cash in the normal course of business.
Example: Accounts Receivable; Merchandise Inventory. Also valuation accounts of those assets.
Example: Reserve for Bad Debts.

B. Fixed Assets Section

Consists of the Properties and other values of a permanent nature to be continually retained as the fixed investment of the business but which is not the intention of the firm to turn into cash in the normal course of business.
Example: Machinery; Land. Also valuation accounts of those assets.
Example: Depreciation of Machinery.

C. Deferred Charges Section

Consists of those payments for materials or services which should not be charged to the current expenses, but which will eventually be such a charge.
Example: Prepaid Expenses: Organization Expenses.

D. Intangible Assets

Consists of those payments for intangible values such as goodwill, etc.

E. Current Liabilities Section

Consists of those liabilities which will have to be paid within a fixed period of time—usually one year.

F. Deferred Credits Section

Consists of that part of income which has not been earned by the balance sheet date.
Example: Deferred Rent Income.

G. Fixed Liabilities Section

Consists of those liabilities which will have to be paid after a period of time which is more than a year.
Example: Mortgage Payable; Bonds Payable.

H. Net Worth Section

Consists of Capital Accounts in the case of single proprietorship or partnerships or, in case of Corporations, of Capital Stock Accounts, Surplus and divisions of Surplus.

DIRECTIONS: The following listed accounts were taken from the balance sheets of the Middletown Corporation as of December 31, 198—. The sections used in setting up the balance sheet are lettered from A to H. Indicate by letters A to H in which section of the balance sheet each item appeared.

A. Current Asset Section
B. Fixed Asset Section
C. Deferred Charge Section

D. Intangible Assets Section
E. Current Liability Section

F. Deferred Credits Section
G. Fixed Liabilities Section
H. Net Worth Section

1. Accounts Receivable
2. Unissued Common Stock
3. Reserve for Federal Income Tax
4. Accrued Payabies
5. Bonds Payable
6. Cash in Bank
7. Reserve for Depreciation
8. Reserve for Plant Extension
9. Insurance Unexpired
10. Common Stock Authorized
11. Prepaid Advertising
12. Dividends Payable

13. Interest Accrued on Notes Receivable
14. Interest Accrued on Bonds Payable
15. Machinery & Equipment
16. Reserve for Doubtful Accounts
17. Reserve for Real Estate Taxes
18. Sinking Fund Reserve
19. Surplus
20. Rent Collected in Advance
21. Treasury Stock
22. Notes Receivable Discounted
23. Goodwill
24. Accrued Commission Receivable
25. Discount on Bonds
26. Due from Officers and Employees
27. Bonus Payable
28. Trade Acceptance Payable
29. Mortgage Payable
30. Three-Year Notes Payable
31. Customers' Deposits—Due on Demand
32. Deposit on Royalties
33. Deficit
34. Donated Surplus
35. Reserve for Redemption of Preferred Stock
36. Reserves for Contingencies

37. Work in Process Inventory
38. Finished Goods Inventory
39. Office Supplies Inventory
40. Investment in Subsidiary

BALANCE SHEET

Answer Key

1. A	11. C	21. H	31. E
2. H	12. E	22. A	32. C
3. E	13. A	23. D	33. H
4. E	14. E	24. A	34. H
5. G	15. B	25. C	35. H
6. A	16. A	26. A	36. H
7. B	17. E	27. E	37. A
8. H	18. H	28. E	38. A
9. C	19. H	29. G	39. C
10. H	20. F	30. G	40. B

ACCOUNTING PRACTICE QUIZZER

TRUE - FALSE QUESTIONS

DIRECTIONS: Each of the following statements is either True or False. Mark T if the statement is True, and F if the statement is False.

1. Capital is increased by income.

2. Current ratio is the ratio of total current assets to total current liabilities.

3. Cumulative preferred dividends in arrears should be shown as a liability in a balance sheet.

4. Operating profits should be credited to surplus account.

5. Loss and expense are synonymous.

6. Merchandise inventory should be valued at market price.

7. Discount in stock should be written off over the life of the stock.

8. Unrealized profits, which result from mere book entries writing up assets, should most properly be credited to capital surplus.

9. Inventory is considered a current asset.

10. Reserve for depreciation is a liability.

11. Preferred stock is usually non-participating.

12. A corporation does not have the right under the law to declare a dividend unless it has sufficient cash with which to pay it.

13. Bonds payable is considered a current liability.

14. Notes received discounted should be shown in the balance sheet as a subtraction from an asset.

15. Preferred stock cannot be issued in no-par form.

16. The balance sheet should most properly include among the liabilities all declared dividends, payable in cash, provided that notice of the declaration has been made to the stockholders.

17. Bonds payable is not treated as a fixed asset.

18. The excess received on a sale of a bond over its par value is known as premium on bonds.

19. Treasury stock should be shown in the balance sheet as a deduction from capital stock outstanding.

196 | *Bookkeeper-Account Clerk*

20. Extraneous profits should be credited to surplus account.

21. Reserve for Income Taxes is a current liability.

22. Voting power is never granted to preferred stock.

23. In the event that a partnership is incorporated, the assets should be taken over by the corporation at the same values at which they have been carried on the partnership books.

24. It is best to show in a footnote on the balance sheet, the amount of dividends in arrears on all classes of preferred stock.

25. Treasury stock is stock which has not been subscribed for.

26. The reserve for bad debts should be set up by a study of past experience.

27. In such case where the asset values of a corporation are to be adjusted, the adjusting entries should be made on the books of the corporation.

28. Bond discount should be amortized over the life of the bonds.

29. Usury is any interest rate over six per cent.

30. The resulting increase or decrease in net worth, which is realized when asset values are adjusted on partnership books, should be divided among the partners in the profit and loss ratio.

31. Depreciation is caused by income tax regulations.

32. Interest accured on bonds owned should be shown as a current asset.

33. An entirely new set of books should be opened by a partnership business at the time of its incorporation.

34. A perpetual inventory is maintained to avoid the expense of an annual physical inventory.

35. A time draft is a loan which may be called at any time.

36. Stock which has not been issued may be sold at a discount without the imposition of any discount liability on the purchaser.

37. Deferred charges are always assets.

38. Excess provision for depreciation results in an understatement of net income.

39. No discount liability need be imposed on the purchaser when treasury stock is sold to him at a discount.

40. Prepaid insurance, prepaid rent and prepaid taxes are considered as deferred charges.

41. The valuation accounts at the end of a period should be closed against the accounts against which they are valued.

42. All the stock which is owned by a corporation may be shown in its balance sheet as treasury stock.

43. Land is an intangible asset.

44. The increase in value of fixed assets due to unpredictable events, such as shortage caused by economic conditions, is known as appreciation.

45. There is not necessary relation between the par value and the real value of a stock share.

46. A patent is an intangible asset.

47. Obsolescence is the loss in value of fixed assets due to the invention of more modern devices.

48. An individual purchasing no-par value stock cannot be held liable for discount on stock.

49. A post-closing trial balance proves that the closing entries have been correctly made.

50. During construction, interest paid on money borrowed may be capitalized.

51. When no-par stock is recorded, no journal entry can be made to record the authorized issue.

52. Interest prepaid on notes payable is an accrued expense.

53. Special columns are often put into the books of original entry in order to save time in journalizing.

54. When no-par stock is issued, it may be recorded by crediting the capital stock account with the entire proceeds.

55. Merchandise turnover is the ratio of cost of goods sold to average inventory.

56. The reserve for depreciation is a valuation account.

57. Dividends should be paid only out of earnings.

58. The pledging of an asset as security for a loan should be indicated in the balance sheet by a footnote.

59. Interest prepaid on notes receivable is deferred income.

Answer Key

1. T	16. T	31. F	46. T
2. T	17. T	32. T	47. T
3. F	18. T	33. F	48. T
4. T	19. T	34. F	49. F
5. F	20. F	35. F	50. T
6. F	21. T	36. F	51. T
7. F	22. F	37. T	52. F
8. F	23. F	38. T	53. F
9. T	24. F	39. T	54. T
10. F	25. F	40. T	55. T
11. F	26. T	41. F	56. T
12. F	27. F	42. F	57. T
13. F	28. T	43. F	58. T
14. T	29. F	44. T	59. T
15. F	30. T	45. T	

MULTIPLE CHOICE QUIZ - ACCOUNTING PRACTICE

DIRECTIONS: For each of the following questions, circle *the choice which best answers the question or completes the statement.*

1. Of the following taxes, the one which is levied most nearly according to ability to pay is

    (A) an excise tax
    (B) an income tax
    (C) a general property tax
    (D) a sales tax

2. When a check has been lost, the bank on which it is drawn should be notified and instructed to

    (A) stop payment on the check
    (B) issue a duplicate of the check
    (C) charge the account of the drawer for the amount of the check
    (D) certify the check

3. The amounts of transactions recorded in a journal are transferred to general ledger accounts by a process known as

    (A) auditing   (B) balancing
    (C) posting   (D) verifying

4. Sales minus cost of goods sold equals

    (A) net profit   (B) gross sales
    (C) gross profit   (D) net sales

5. The chief disadvantage of single-entry bookkeeping is that it

    (A) is too difficult to operate
    (B) is illegal for income tax purposes
    (C) provides no possibility of determining net profits
    (D) furnishes an incomplete picture of the business

6. The phrase "3%—10 days" on an invoice usually means that

    (A) 3% of the amount must be paid each 10 days
    (B) the purchaser is entitled to only ten days credit

(C) a discount of 3% will be allowed for payment in 10 days

(D) the entire amount must be paid in 10 days or a penalty of 3% of the amount due will be added

7. A firm which voluntarily terminates business, selling its assets and paying its liabilities, is said to be in

(A) receivership   (B) liquidation
(C) depletion   (D) amortization

8. Many business firms provide a petty cash fund from which to pay for small items in order to avoid issuing many small checks. If this fund is replenished periodically to restore it to its original amount, the fund is called

(A) an imprest fund
(B) a debenture fund
(C) an adjustment fund
(D) an expense reserve fund

9. Many business firms maintain a book of original entry in which all bills to be paid are recorded. This book is known as a

(A) purchase returns journal
(B) subsidiary ledger
(C) voucher register
(D) notes payable register

10. A trial balance will *not* indicate that an error has been made in

(A) computing the balance of an account
(B) entering an amount in the wrong account
(C) carrying forward the balance of an account
(D) entering an amount on the wrong side of an account

11. When an asset is depreciated on the straight-line basis, the amount charged off for depreciation

(A) is greater in the earlier years of the asset's life
(B) is greater in the later years of the asset's life
(C) varies each year according to the extent to which the asset is used during the year
(D) is equal each full year of the asset's life

12. The essential nature of an asset is that

(A) it must be tangible
(B) it must be easily converted into cash
(C) it must have value
(D) its cost must be included in the profit and loss statement

13. A controlling account

(A) contains the totals of the accounts used in preparing the balance sheet at the end of the fiscal period
(B) contains the totals of the individual amounts entered in the accounts of a subsidiary ledger during the fiscal period
(C) contains the totals of all entries in the general journal during the fiscal period
(D) contains the totals of the accounts used in preparing the profit and loss statement for the fiscal period

14. A trial balance is a

(A) list of the credit balances in all accounts in a general ledger
(B) list of all general ledger accounts and their balances
(C) list of the asset accounts in a general ledger and their balances
(D) list of the liability accounts in a general ledger and their balances

15. An accounting system which records revenues as soon as they are earned and records liabilities as soon as they are incurred regardless of the date of payment, is said to operate on

(A) an accrual basis
(B) a budgetary basis
(C) an encumbrance basis
(D) a cash basis

16. The term "current assets" usually includes such things as

(A) notes payable
(B) machinery and equipment
(C) furniture and fixtures
(D) accounts receivable

17. An item which is never properly considered a negotiable instrument is

(A) an invoice
(B) a bond
(C) a promissory note
(D) an endorsed check

18. A statement of the assets, liabilities and net worth of a business is called

    (A) a trial balance
    (B) a budget
    (C) a profit and loss statement
    (D) a balance sheet

19. A subsidiary ledger contains accounts which show

    (A) details of contingent liabilities of undetermined amount
    (B) totals of all asset accounts in the general ledger

(C) totals of all liability accounts in the general ledger
(D) details of an account in the general ledger

Answer Key

1. B	6. C	11. D	16. D
2. A	7. B	12. C	17. A
3. C	8. A	13. B	18. D
4. C	9. C	14. B	19. D
5. D	10. B	15. A	

ACCOUNTING TERMS AND PRACTICES

DIRECTIONS: Each of the completion questions in this series consists of an incomplete sentence or idea. Use the appropriate space to write in the correct, missing word or words.

1. Everything a business owns is called _____.

2. Everything a business owes is called _____.

3. The Proprietorship Equation is _____.

4. The statement which shows the state of a business at a certain date is called a _____.

5. The statement which shows the result of the operations over a certain period is called a _____.

6. The principal book of records in which a summary of the accounts is found is called the _____.

7. A book in which daily entries are recorded is called _____.

8. The book in which cash received is recorded is called the _____ book.

9. The book in which cash paid is recorded is called the _____ book.

10. What kind of purchases are entered in the purchase book? _____

11. What kind of sales are entered in the sales book? _____

12. Where are closing entries first recorded? _____

13. Gross Sales minus Sales Returns, and Allowances equals _____.

14. Net Sales minus cost of goods sold equals _____.

15. Gross Profit minus Operating Expenses equals _____.

16. The list of account balances taken from the General Ledger is called a _____.

17. Which asset item on the Balance Sheet at Dec. 31 is also found in the Profit and Loss Statement for year ended Dec. 31? _____

18. Dividends Account is closed to _____.

19. Office Salaries account is closed to _____.

20. The entering of the debit and credit for each transaction in the journal is called _____ ____.

21. The transferring of the debits and credits from the journal to ledger accounts is called _____.

22. "An unconditional promise in writing made by one person to another, signed by the maker, engaging to pay, on demand or at a fixed, or determinable future time, a certain sum in money to order or to bearer" is called a _____.

23. The party signing a note is called the _____.

24. The party to whom the note is made payable is called the _____.

25. "Pay to the order of A Company, without recourse" is called a _____ indorsement.

26. A written order by one person to another person, requiring him to pay a certain sum of money to a third party is called a _____.

27. A written acknowledgment of a debt by a buyer in favor of the seller, for merchandise that the seller had placed in the hands of the buyer is called a _____.

28. When a check bears on its back the words "Accepted X Bank; John Jones, Cashier" it is called a _____.

29. A draft drawn by one bank on another bank in transferring money to parties in another city is called a _____.

30. A temporary partnership for the purpose of carrying out some specific project of a trading nature is known as a _____.

31. The face or nominal value placed on a share of stock, when the value is the same for all shares of a like class, is called the _____.

32. The corporation's net worth divided by the number of shares of outstanding common stock (if the only stock is common stock) is called the _____ of a share.

33. Stock which has once been issued by a corporation and later reacquired by purchase or gift is called _____.

34. Common stock issued as a bonus to investors who purchase preferred stock is called _____.

35. What is the accountant's view of the incorporation of a partnership? _____

36. In mergers, two conditions which may exist are _____ and _____.

37. Purchase Price of a business less Net Worth of the business is called _____.

38. A statement which certifies or verifies the correctness of a transaction is called a _____.

39. The book of original entry in which vouchers and their distribution are recorded is called a _____.

40. Anything which undergoes some process in the factory before becoming a part of the product is called _____.

41. Such items as buttons, thread, etc., in a clothing factory that are essential materials in manufacture, fall under the general classification of _____.

42. That labor which is employed directly in processing the raw materials or in assembling the parts into the finished product is called _____.

43. Labor, such as janitor's duties to keep the factory clean, etc., is called _____.

44. That element of cost of production, which includes all expenses arising from the operation of the factory, which cannot, like material and direct labor, be definitely traced to the product is termed _____.

45. Direct material plus Direct labor equals _____.

46. Cost of production equals _____ plus _____.

47. A continuous record of all materials and supplies as they are received in the storeroom, of all materials and supplies as they are taken out of the storeroom and put into process, and of all manufactured goods taken out of the factory and put in the finishing-stock room is called a _____.

48. The three inventory items in a manufacturing plant are _____, _____ and _____.

49. The stores ledger is controlled by the _____ Account.

50. The cost ledger is controlled by the _____ Account.

51. The system of bookkeeping concerning itself with recording transactions affecting only personal accounts is called _____.

52. Those expenditures which affect the real or capital accounts, and thus increase the net amount of capital invested in the business, are called _____ expenditures.

53. Those expenditures which affect the operating or revenue accounts, and are thus a charge against profits for the period instead of an investment of capital, are called _____ expenditures.

54. Renewals differ from Repairs in that the former _____.

55. Repairs should be charged to what account? _____

56. Renewals should be charged to _____.

57. The two general methods of inventory valuation are _____ and _____.

58. Suburban land bought by a real estate company for the purpose of sub-division falls under _____ assets.

59. Ordinarily, land (increases, decreases) in value. _____

60. As a general principle, buildings should be shown at (cost price, selling price). _____

61. In general, patents should be amortized over a period of _____ years.

62. In general, copyrights should be amortized over a period of _____ years.

63. Five causes of depreciation are _____, _____, _____, _____ and _____.

64. If the current assets are $40,000 and the current liabilities are $20,000, the current ratio is _____.

65. Bonds which have been repurchased by a corporation, but not cancelled, are known as _____.

66. An indorsement which represents the acceptance of a note or a bill by one party who receives no value therefor, for the use or benefit of some other party is called an _____.

67. The mortgage on property, which designates the trustee who represents the bondholders and states all the terms and conditions of the issue and the security for the bonds, is called the _____.

68. An amount accumulated through periodical installments, and invested in interest bearing securities, which together with the interest earned will provide a fund sufficient to liquidate a debt at maturity, is called a _____.

69. When the capital of a going concern is increased simply by inflating the assets, without the justification of earning power, the term applied to the stock of the concern is _____.

70. _____ stock represents the right to issue stock when the full amount authorized has not been issued.

71. The number of times the average amount of stock is sold during the fiscal period is best referred to as _____.

72. The list of the balances, the total of which should equal the balance in the controlling account would most appropriately be called the _____.

73. The formal legal contract, generally under seal, by means of which the seller of goods transfers the title of these goods to the buyer is known as the _____.

74. The rate of turnover is generally computed by dividing the _____ by the _____.

75. Values which have accumulated but which have not yet been entered as, for example, interest accumulated on notes payable, are most generally termed _____.

76. When a part of an expense charge has not been used within the fiscal period, it is referred to as _____.

77. The relation of current assets to current liabilities is known as the _____.

78. A written promise under seal given for the payment of a long-time loan is referred to as a _____.

79. Securities which are pledged to a bank as security for a loan are known as _____.

80. A classified Balance Sheet should most generally show three groups of assets, under the heads of _____, _____, and _____.

Answer Key

1. Assets
2. Liabilities
3. Assets – Liabilities = Net Worth
4. Balance Sheet
5. Profit and Loss Statement
6. General Ledger
7. Journal
8. Cash receipts
9. Cash Disbursements
10. Purchases on Account
11. Sales on Account
12. General Journal
13. Net Sales
14. Gross Profit
15. Net Operating Profit
16. Trial Balance
17. Merchandise Inventory Dec. 31, 1970
18. Surplus
19. Profit and Loss
20. Journalizing
21. Posting
22. Negotiable Promissory Note
23. Maker
24. Payee
25. Qualified
26. Draft
27. Trade Acceptance
28. Certified Check
29. Bank Draft
30. Joint Venture
31. Par Value
32. Book Value
33. Treasury Stock
34. Bonus Stock
35. That the partnership sells its assets and liabilities to the newly formed corporation
36. Merger by consolidation; merger by absorption
37. Goodwill
38. Voucher
39. Voucher register
40. Raw material
41. Manufacturing Supplies
42. Direct Labor
43. Indirect Labor
44. Manufacturing Expense
45. Prime Cost
46. Prime Cost; factory expense
47. Perpetual inventory
48. Raw Materials; Goods-in-Process; Finished Goods
49. Raw materials
50. Goods-in-Process
51. Single-Entry
52. Capital
53. Revenue
54. Tend to extend the serviceable life of the property
55. To some expense account
56. Reserve for Depreciation
57. At cost; cost or market, whichever is lower
58. Current
59. Increases
60. Cost price
61. Seventeen
62. Twenty-eight
63. Expiration of time; deterioration from exposure to to the elements; wear and tear due to use; inadequacy; obsolescence
64. 2 to 1
65. Treasury Bonds
66. Accommodation indorsement
67. Deed of trust
68. Sinking Fund
69. Watered Stock
70. Unissued
71. Turnover
72. Abstract of subsidiary ledger
73. Bill of Sale
74. Cost of sales Average Inventory at cost
75. Accruals
76. Deferred charges to expense
77. Current Ratio
78. Bond
79. Collateral
80. Current assets; fixed assets; deferred charges

PART THREE

*Clerical and
Math Skills Practice*

3

FILING REVIEW

Filing Equipment

The spindle file is a spike, straight or curved, upon which the papers to be preserved are impaled. It is a temporary expedient and not a true filing device, since it does not provide any means of sorting and classifying the material.

Clip files are also temporary expedients, since the clip is merely equipped to hold papers together for a while. Unlike the spindle it does not mutilate papers. The clip file consists of a board with a metal clip at the top. The clip is controlled by a strong spring. When material is placed under the clip, the spring is released, and the clip closes, gripping the papers tightly.

The Shannon file consists of a board at the top of which are two metal rods bent like an inverted "U." The paper to be filed is first placed in a device which punches two neat holes as distant from each other as are the two rods. The rods, which are cut through near the top, may be sprung open by a spring device and the paper can then be slipped onto the lower part of the rods. The upper part is then closed.

The box file is a box, usually metal, which opens from the top and from one side so that a series of alphabetized guides are made easily accessible. Letters and papers are filed behind the appropriate guide.

Flat files are a modification of the box file. They consist of a series of drawers, each one containing a subdivision of the alphabet. Papers are usually pressed down by a wire spring or similar device in each drawer.

Vertical file. In all of the files that have been described, the papers lie flat, and all the papers must be disturbed to get at a single one. This disadvantage is removed by the vertical file, in which the papers are made to stand on edge. Papers are usually placed in manila folders when they are classified in vertical files.

Out-cards, also called out-guides and guide-cards, are heavy, colored cardboards which are filed in place of a file that has been temporarily removed. They give the date that the file was removed and indicate its whereabouts.

Coding refers to the marking which is placed on a letter to show how it is to be filed.

Cross reference card is under one heading in a file and refers the searcher to the permanent file which is located under another heading.

Tickler file is a system of folders or cards, marked from 1 to 31. If any work is to be done on a particular day of the month a note is placed in the appropriate folder and is thus turned up when that day of the month rolls around.

METHODS OF FILING

ALPHABETIC FILING

This is by far the most important method and besides, it is fundamental to the proper operation of all the other methods.

When alphabetic filing is employed, the papers are sorted according to the letters of the alphabet. The following are the most important rules governing alphabetic filing:

1. Consider the surname first, then the given name, then the middle initial, and lastly the title.

Bonomo, Henry J.
Bonomo, Leo
Caudwell, Fred
Charters, John D. (Dr.)

If the surnames are the same, then the given names are considered, and if the given names are the same then the middle name or initial is the deciding factor in filing the name. All material must be arranged in A-Z sequence of letters down to the last letter of the item.

2. Many names are pronounced exactly alike but are spelled differently. They must be filed exactly as spelled.

3. Mac and Mc are filed exactly as they are spelled, Mc coming after Mac.

4. In filing a group of names, all of which have the same surname, two principles must be borne in mind: (A) Nothing comes before something. (B) Initials comes before names beginning with the same letter.

King
King, D
King, Dorothy

5. Hyphenated surnames are indexed as though the hyphen joined the two parts making one.

Lytton-Strachey, John
Lyttonte, Amadeus

6. Foreign names are filed as spelled and prefixes are not considered separately. Likewise, foreign language articles (Le, La, Les, El, etc.) are considered part of the name when they appear: L'Aiglon; Les Miserables.

Da Costa, Carl
D'Agnota, Ugo
Des Verney, Elizabeth
De Takacs, Maria

7. When the same names appear with different addresses, arrange them alphabetically to town or city, considering state only where there is a duplication of town or city names.

American Tobacco Co.   Norfolk, Va.
American Tobacco Co.   Osceola, Fla.

8. Names of firms, corporations and institutions are indexed as written, except where they include the full names of individuals, in which case the surnames are considered first, the Christian names next, the middle initial next, and then the remainder of the title.

Rice, A.
Rice, B., & Co.
Rice, Bernard
Rice and Co.
Rice, Edward and Bros.
Rice, Henry, and Son

9. Names that begin with numbers should be indexed as if spelled out. The numeral is treated as one word.

8th Avenue Bookshop
Fifth Street Church
4th National Bank
7th Avenue Restaurant

10. Abbreviations are alphabetized as though they were spelled out in full.

Indus. Bros. of America
Indus. and Loan Assoc.

11. Hyphenated firm names are treated as separate words.

Oil-O-Matic Heating Company
Oilimatic Heating Company

12. Words which may be spelled either as one word or as two words are treated as one word.

North Pole Expedition
North East Grocery Corporation

13. Compound geographic names are always treated as two words.

West Chester
West Milton
Westinghouse

14. Parts of names which are omitted in indexing and filing are the following: (A) The article *the*, unless, as indicated above, it occurs in a foreign name. (B) Phrases such as *dep't. of, board of*, etc. applied to municipal, state and federal agencies are placed in parentheses after the words they modify and are disregarded, in filing. (C) *and, &, of*, abbreviations such as *Jr., 2nd;* titles or degrees of individuals, except a foreign title with one name and a title forming the first word of a firm name: Bailey and Allen, Jonson, Ben (Jr.), Peabody, C. W. (Prof.), Prince Henry. (D) Apostrophe s ('s) indicating the possessive case.

15. Parts of names which are included in filing are: *Ltd., Inc., Co., Son, Bros., Mfg.,* and *Corp.* When abbreviated, these words are treated as though spelled in full, and as though they were Christian names.

16. Institutions or societies beginning with a Christian name should be filed under the surname with the Christian name following.

Franklin, Benjamin, Hotel

Hopkins, Johns, University

Gibbs, Katharine, School

Sage, Russell, College

Roosevelt, Theodore, High School

GEOGRAPHICAL FILING

When geographical filing is employed, the matter to be filed is grouped first according to states; then according to cities or towns; and last, according to alphabetic arrangement of names of correspondents in each city or town.

This method of filing is used when there is a need to keep material from particular localities in one place. Thus a firm sponsoring a radio program might wish to keep together all letters of criticism from individual states so that the feeling of a state might be the more easily gauged. To facilitate the use of a geographical file, an alphabetic card file is kept, so that letters from a particular correspondent may be located even if the correspondent's address has been forgotten.

NUMERICAL FILING

This method is less popular now than it used to be. Its greatest use is in courts and professional offices where it is desirable to have a quick indication as to when a case was received. Numbers are assigned to cases as they come in. Thus a later case will receive a higher number. An alphabetic card index is kept and by looking up the name of the case, one obtains the number. The cases are filed in numerical order and so it is a simple matter to find one if the number is known.

If letters are to be filed numerically, then a number is assigned to each correspondent with whom the firm does business. Any letter that comes in is placed in the folder assigned to the correspondent. As the firm acquires new correspondents, new numbers are assigned. Unless the clerk knows all the numbers by heart he must consult the card index each time he wants to file or find a letter. This makes the system rather cumbersome. It is useful where two or three cases may be filed under the same name, and it is necessary to make a quick distinction between the cases. If three cases, 167, 1169, 1584 have been filed against one man in a court, it is quickly apparent that cases 1169 and 1584 have been filed later than 167 and when the number is used in referring to each case, the clerk knows immediately which one is meant.

SUBJECT FILING

This method is used in cases where there is much correspondence on many subjects between a small number of people. The main difficulty with the method lies in building up a logical, inclusive, and consistent subject classification and adhering to it strictly. Supervision over the subject of filing is usually placed in the hands of a responsible person who reads each letter and writes on it the subject under which it is to be filed.

PREVIOUS QUESTIONS ON FILING

TEST-TYPE QUIZZES FOR PRACTICE

TEST ONE

DIRECTIONS: For each of the following questions, circle the choice which best answers the questions or completes the statement.

The Answer Key for these test questions will be found at the end of the test.

1. The system of filing most generally used is the
   (A) alphabetic file
   (B) geographic file
   (C) numeric file
   (D) Dewey decimal classification.

2. When filing papers that are to be held together the best procedure to follow is to
   (A) clip the papers together before filing
   (B) staple the papers together before filing
   (C) tear the corners of the papers and hold them together by turning down the torn corners
   (D) pin the papers together.

3. Everyone should know something about filing in order to
   (A) become a file clerk
   (B) write checks
   (C) find information readily
   (D) make out an income tax blank.

4. Indexing information under two or more headings is called
   (A) out-charging
   (B) transferring
   (C) cross-referencing
   (D) sorting.

5. The marking of a letter to show how it is to be filed is called
   (A) sorting
   (C) coding
   (B) filing
   (D) transferring.

6. A good file clerk allows no paper to be removed from the file unless replaced by
   (A) an out-card
   (B) an expansion folder
   (C) a cross-reference card
   (D) a tab folder.

7. If a letter from the Better Printing Co. of Ohio has the word Printing underlined the letter is to be filed by the
   (A) alphabetic method
   (B) numeric method
   (C) subject method
   (D) geographic method.

8. Names in classified telephone directories are first arranged according to
   (A) alphabetic filing   (B) occupation
   (C) location   (D) numerical filing.

9. Confusion regarding the exact location of certain papers missing from files can probably best be avoided by
   (A) using colored tabs
   (B) using the Dewey Decimal System
   (C) making files available to few persons
   (D) consistently using "out" guides.

10. The Dewey Decimal System is most widely used in
    (A) offices in government departments
    (B) libraries
    (C) offices in private industry
    (D) social welfare organizations.

11. Provision for handling a letter from the Brooklyn Home for Children marked "The first of next month" would necessitate that the letter be placed in a
    (A) subject file   (B) follow-up file
    (C) geographic file   (D) numeric file.

12. In a correspondence file miscellaneous folders should be filed
    (A) in front of all other folders in the filing drawer
    (B) behind all other folders in the filing drawer.
    (C) immediately behind the appropriate guide
    (D) following all other folders behind the appropriate guide.

13. When correspondence is to be filed according to both subject matter and the name of the writer, the file clerk should prepare
    (A) a double file
    (B) a tickler
    (C) an index of names and subject matter
    (D) a cross-reference sheet.

14. The box file, the clipboard file and the bellows file are types of
    (A) flat files   (B) vertical files
    (C) visible files   (D) chronological files.

15. A vertical file folder "1/4 cut" means
    (A) four possible "cuts" to the folder
    (B) the folder is cut one-quarter inch from the top
    (C) the folder has one-quarter inch expansion
    (D) the folder has cuts one-quarter inch wide.

16. The term used to describe the best arrangement of tabs to secure maximum visibility in a file is
    (A) numeric   (B) staggered
    (C) alternative   (D) consecutive.

17. A follower is used
    (A) to follow up delinquent accounts
    (B) to follow up correspondence which has been removed from the file
    (C) to bring to mind matters requiring attention on a certain date
    (D) to keep contents of a vertical file in an upright position.

18. In the Variadex system of filing, an additional check is furnished by

    (A) a card index
    (B) the use of color
    (C) a set of monthly guides
    (D) direct name labeling.

19. Of the following firms, the one which does not specialize in filing equipment is
    (A) Amberg   (B) Shaw-Walker
    (C) Monroe   (D) Globe-Wernicke.

20. The most costly system to maintain is subject filing because
    (A) filing and finding are very slow processes when this system is used
    (B) a great number of subjects must be maintained
    (C) the system cannot easily be adapted to new demands
    (D) capable and experienced employees must be employed to select the headings which describe the contents.

21. In filing, a requisition card is
    (A) a card showing where material related to a subject may be located under another title
    (B) a card or form recording material requested to be taken from the files, identifying its location
    (C) a card of a different color from the other cards in the file, flagging a matter needing attention
    (D) a card in an alphabetic file, giving the index to the numbers in a numeric file

22. In a filing system, "primary guides" are known as
    (A) guide cards which separate into special sections, a voluminous number of the same names, as Brown, Jones, Smith, etc.
    (B) guides indicating the places from which correspondence or other material has been removed from the files by request for reference
    (C) guides, the tabs of which appear in "first position" in the file
    (D) guide cards separating from the rest of the material in the file, correspondence or other material of a miscellaneous nature for which no special folder has been provided

23. Generally speaking, the best arrangement of folder tabs, for easy location of material in the files, is

(A) staggered from left to right
(B) zigzagged in alternate positions
(C) staggered from right to left
(D) placed in one center positon, one tab directly behind the other.

24. In filing terminology, coding means
(A) making a preliminary arrangement of names according to caption before bringing them together in final order of arrangement
(B) reading correspondence and determining the proper caption under which it is to be filed
(C) marking a card or paper with symbols or other means of identification to indicate where it is to be placed in the files according to a pre-determined plan
(D) placing a card or paper in the files showing where correspondence may be located under another name or title.

25. A duplex-numeric system of filing is
(A) a decimal system
(B) an arrangement of guides and folders with a definite color scheme to aid in filing and locating material
(C) a system of filing by which classified subjects are divided and subdivided by number for the purpose of expansion
(D) a method of filing names according to sound instead of spelling.

26. Of the following, which statement regarding microfilm is false?
(A) The film requires a small fraction of the space occupied by the original material
(B) Miscellaneous copied data can be easily indexed for rapid reference
(C) There is no necessity to go to a storehouse for consulting old records
(D) It has a legal aspect since the film may stand as evidence in court after the original document has been lost or destroyed.

27. The two-period method of transfer consists of consisting of
(A) constantly removing closed or dead matter from the active files to the transfer files at irregular periods
(B) removing all the contents of the file from the active files to the transfer files and starting a new active file periodically, as once a year
(C) keeping active or current material in one drawer and semi-active material in a sep-

arate drawer, and at chosen times, sending the contents of the semi-active files to the transfer files and moving material from the active files to the semi-active files
(D) transferring all material bearing a date prior to an established minimum period and merging with material previously sent to files.

28. A "tickler file" is used chiefly for
(A) unsorted papers which the file clerk has not had time to file
(B) personnel records
(C) pending matters which should receive attention at some particular time
(D) index to cross-referenced material.

29. The papers in a filing folder are arranged with the most recently dated one in front, and a clerk has been instructed to arrange them according to date in a binder but with the paper of most recent date at the back. The most efficient of the following methods which he might use in performing this task is to

(A) begin at the back of the folder and remove the papers in groups of convenient size for binding, laying each group face down on top of the group pulled just before
(B) begin at the back of the folder and pull the papers one by one, laying each paper face up on top of the one pulled just before
(C) begin at the front of the folder and pull the papers one by one, laying each paper face up on top of the one pulled just before
(D) begin at the front of the folder and pull the papers one by one, laying each paper face down on top of the one pulled just before.

30. Of the following, for which reason are cross-references necessary in filing?
(A) There is a choice of terms under which the correspondence may be filed.
(B) The only filing information contained in the correspondence is the name of the writer
(C) Records are immediately visible without searching through the files
(D) Persons other than file clerks can easily locate material.

31. Of the following, which practice is undesirable in the operation of files?
    (A) handling guides by sides instead of tabs
    (B) mending torn papers before placing them in the files
    (C) using clips for fastening papers belonging together
    (D) placing headings of papers to the left face forward in the file drawer.

32. Of the following, in which situation would the subject filing system furnish an advantage?
    (A) Speed is required in preparing material for the files
    (B) Only inexperienced file clerks are available
    (C) All the papers relating to a given topic or transaction are usually wanted at the same time
    (D) It is considered undesirable to keep an index to the files.

33. Of the following, which statement presents the only disadvantage in maintaining a central file department?
    (A) Elimination of duplication of copies of the original correspondence is effected
    (B) Responsibility for the location of records is placed upon one person
    (C) Elimination of doubt as to the place of filing material of interest to several bureaus is effected
    (D) Variety of the needs of different bureaus exists which calls for different methods of arrangement of records.

34. Of the following, which procedure would be most likely to result in the efficient operation of a filing system?
    (A) permitting access to the files of employees other than file clerks
    (B) permitting personal conversation among file clerks while filing papers
    (C) failing to charge papers taken from the files for quick reference but not removed from the file room
    (D) using short cuts obtained by time and motion studies

35. Of the following, which statement is false?
    (A) An advantage of using a card record system is that flexibility is permitted by the insertion of cards for new records or the transferring of cards of existing records
    (B) In planning the installation of a filing system, the most effectual procedure is to select the filing equipment first and then adapt the filing system to the equipment
    (C) When it is necessary to use a comparatively inexperienced assistant in a large file room, it is better practice to have him remove records from the file rather than to file them
    (D) Papers misfiled often may be found in the folder preceding or following the one in which they belong.

FOUR METHODS OF FILING

(A) Name	(B) Subject
(C) Geographic	(D) Numeric.

Questions 36-42 list seven filing situations which a clerk may meet. On the basis of the information contained in the above box write, in the proper place, to the right of each situation: (A) if you would file the letter by name; (B) if you would file the letter by subject; (C) if you would file the letter by the use of a geographic scheme; (D) if you would file the letter by the use of a numeric scheme.

36. Mr. Jones has written a letter to the Department of Docks, where you are employed.

37. The U. S. Employment Service has requested in writing, information concerning Mr. John J. Smith.

38. An anonymous letter is sent asking that traffic lights be erected on a certain avenue.

39. You have in your possession the case history of a certain individual who is under the care of a public welfare agency in which you are employed.

40. The department in which you are employed has written a letter to a Mr. Isaac Stein.

41. A letter is received by a certain company from a Mr. Reilly, one of its representatives in a certain city. This company has a tremendous turnover in the personnel of its representatives and has representatives in each of 273 cities which are located so as to cover the country completely.

42. A letter is received from a certain company stating that a very high grade of bond paper is available at a low price. The offices of this company are located in southern California. The organization for which you are employed already possesses files labeled "desks, typewriters."

Answer Key

1. A	22. C
2. B	23. A
3. C	24. C
4. C	25. C
5. C	26. B
6. A	27. C
7. C	28. C
8. B	29. C
9. D	30. A
10. B	31. C
11. B	32. C
12. D	33. D
13. D	34. D
14. A	35. B
15. A	36. A
16. B	37. A
17. C	38. B
18. B	39. A
19. C	40. A
20. D	41. C
21. B	42. B

TEST TWO

DIRECTIONS: *One of the five classes of employment, lettered (A) to (E), may be applied to each of the individuals listed below. Place on the answer sheet the capital letter of the class in which that name may best be placed.*

CLASS OF WORK

(A) Clerical   (B) Educational

(C) Investigational   (D) Mechanical

(E) Art

NAME AND OCCUPATION

1. John M. Devine — Stenographer
2. G. D. Wahl — Lawyer
3. Harry B. Allen — Typewriter Repairman
4. M. C. Walton — Elevator Operator
5. Lewis E. Reigner — Typist
6. John G. Cook — Electrician
7. H. B. Allen — Reporter
8. Walter E. Jenkins — Doctor
9. Clifford H. Wrenn — Telephone Operator
10. H. A. Schwartz — Plumber
11. Harry Gruber — Locksmith
12. Ely Fairbanks — Sculptor
13. Abraham Hohing — Radio Repairman
14. Samuel Tapft — Laundry Driver
15. William M. Murray — Advertising Layout Man
16. Hyman E. Oral — Motion Picture Operator
17. L. A. Kurtz — Director of a Nursery School
18. Richard H. Hunter — Painter of Miniatures
19. Lewis F. Kosch — Radio Announcer
20. Marion L. Young — Assistant Director of a University Ext. Program
21. Karl W. Hisgen — Printer
22. E. T. Williams — Varitype Operator
23. H. B. Enderton — Mimeograph Operator
24. Robert F. Hallock — Proofreader
25. Joseph L. Hardin — Detective
26. E. B. Gjelsteen — Social Worker
27. Carter B. Magruder — Coppersmith
28. Wilber R. Pierce — Flutist
29. Russell G. Smith — Carpenter
30. Wilber S. Nye — Singer
31. David Larr — Instructor in Barbering
32. Oliver M. Barton — Band Leader
33. E. Oliver Parmly — Copyholder
34. C. Parul Summerall — Blacksmith
35. Louis Friedersdorff — Chemical Research Worker
36. Daniel E. Healy — Dir. of Worker's Education in an Industrial union
37. Howard Kessinger — Player of Tympani
38. John B. Horton — Cataloguer
39. Frank S. Kirkpatrick — Supervisor of a filing system
40. William H. Bertsch — Oil Burner Installer

Answer Key

1. A	6. D	11. D	16. D	21. D	26. C	31. B	36. B
2. C	7. C	12. E	17. B	22. A	27. D	32. E	37. E
3. D	8. C	13. D	18. E	23. A	28. E	33. A	38. A
4. D	9. A	14. D	19. E	24. A	29. D	34. D	39. A
5. A	10. D	15. E	20. B	25. C	30. E	35. C	40. D

MATCHING LETTERS AND NUMBERS

DIRECTIONS: In this test of clerical ability, Column I consists of sets of numbered questions which you are to answer one at a time. Column II consists of possible answers to the set of questions in Column I. Select from Column II the one possible answer which contains only the numbers and letters, regardless of their order, which appear in the question in Column I. If none of the four possible answers is correct, mark "E" on your answer sheet.

A SAMPLE QUESTION EXPLAINED

COLUMN I: Set of Questions	COLUMN II: Possible Answers
1. 2-Q-P-5-T-G-4-7.	(A) 5-G-8-P-4-Q
	(B) P-R-7-Q-4-2
	(C) Q-5-P-9-G-2
	(D) 4-2-5-P-7-Q
	(E) None of these.

The Answer to the Sample Question is (D). How did we arrive at that solution? First, remember that the instructions tell you to select as your answer the choice that contains only the numbers and letters, regardless of their order, which appear in the question. The answer choice in Column II does not have to contain all of the letters and numbers that appear in the question. But the answer cannot contain a number or letter that does not appear in the question. Thus, begin by checking the numbers and letters that appear in Answer (A). You will note that while 5-G-P-4-Q all appear in the Sample Question, the number 8, which is included in Answer (A), does not appear in the question. Answer (A) is thus incorrect. Likewise, Answer (B) is incorrect as the letter R does not appear in the Sample Question; Answer (C) is incorrect as the number 9 does not appear in the question. In checking Answer (D), however, one notes that 4-2-5-P-7-Q all appear in the Sample Question. (D) is therefore the correct choice. Answer (E) is obviously eliminated.

Now proceed to answer the following test questions on the basis of the instructions given above.

MATCHING LETTERS AND NUMBERS TEST

TIME: 10 Minutes

DIRECTIONS: In this test of clerical ability, Column I consists of sets of numbered questions which you are to answer one at a time. Column II consists of possible answers to the set of questions in Column I. Select from Column II the one possible answer which contains only the numbers and letters, regardless of their order, which appear in the question in Column I. If none of the four possible answers is correct, mark "E" on your answer sheet.

The Answer Key for these test questions will be found at the end of the test.

COLUMN I: Set of Questions	COLUMN II: Possible Answers
1. 6-4-T-G-9-K-N-8	(A) Z-8-K-G-9-7
2. K-3-L-6-Z-7-9-T	(B) 7-N-Z-T-9-8
3. N-8-9-3-K-G-7-Z	(C) L-3-Z-K-7-6
4. L-Z-G-6-4-9-K-3	(D) 4-K-T-G-8-6
5. 9-T-K-8-3-7-N-Z	(E) None of these.

Set of Questions	Possible Answers
6. 2-3-P-6-V-Z-4-L	(A) 3-6-G-P-7-N
7. T-7-4-3-P-Z-9-G	(B) 3-7-P-V-4-T
8. 6-N-G-Z-3-9-P-7	(C) 4-6-V-Z-2-L
9. 9-6-P-4-N-G-Z-2	(D) 4-7-G-Z-T-3
10. 4-9-7-T-L-P-3-V	(E) None of these.

COLUMN I:	COLUMN II:
Set of Questions	*Possible Answers*

11. Q-1-6-R-L-9-7-V

12. 8-W-2-Z-P-4-H-O

13. N-J-3-T-K-5-F-M

14. 5-T-H-M-O-4-Q-J

15. 4-Z-X-8-W-O-2-L

(A) F-3-N-K-J-4

(B) Q-H-4-O-5-M

(C) O-W-2-Z-4-8

(D) R-9-V-1-Q-6

(E) None of these.

Set of Questions   *Possible Answers*

16. S-2-L-8-U-Q-7-P

17. 4-M-O-6-T-F-W-1

18. J-M-4-X-W-Z-5-8

19. H-Q-2-9-T-I-K-7

20. 8-M-Z-V-4-P-5-Q

(A) 9-Q-T-K-2-7

(B) F-O-1-4-W-M

(C) U-2-8-P-Q-S

(D) Z-M-4-5-8-Q

(E) None of these.

Answer Key

1.D	6.C	11.D	16.C
2.C	7.D	12.C	17.B
3.A	8.A	13.E	18.E
4.E	9.E	14.B	19.A
5.B	10.B	15.C	20.D

CODING ABILITY

DIRECTIONS: The codes given in Column I below begin and end with a capital letter and have an eight digit number in between. You are to arrange the codes in Column I according to the following rules.

1. Arrange the codes in alphabetical order, according to the first letter.

2. When two or more codes have the same first letter, arrange the codes in alphabetical order according to the last letter.

3. When two or more of the codes have the same first and last letters, arrange the codes in numerical order, beginning with the lowest number.

The codes in Column I are numbered (1) through (5). Column II gives you a selection of four possible answers. You are to choose from Column II the lettered choice which gives the correct listing of the codes in Column I arranged according to the above rules.

A SAMPLE QUESTION EXPLAINED

COLUMN I:
Set of Codes

COLUMN II:
Possible Answers

1. (1) E75044127B
    (2) B96399104A
    (3) B93939086A
    (4) B47064465H
    (5) B99040922A

(A) 4, 1, 3, 2, 5
(B) 4, 1, 2, 3, 5
(C) 4, 3, 2, 5, 1
(D) 3, 2, 5, 4, 1

In the Sample question, the four codes starting with B should be placed before the code starting with E. The codes starting with B and ending with A should be placed before the code starting with B and ending with H. Then the codes starting with B and ending with A should be listed in numerical order, beginning with the lowest number. The correct way to arrange the codes therefore is:

(3) B93939086A
(2) B96399104A
(5) B99040922A
(4) B47064465H
(1) E75044127B

Since the order of arrangement is 3, 2, 5, 4, 1,---the answer to the Sample question is (D). Now proceed to answer the following test questions according to the above instructions.

CODING ABILITY TEST

TIME: 15 Minutes

DIRECTIONS: The codes given in Column I below begin and end with a capital letter and have an eight digit number in between. You are to arrange the codes in Column I according to the following rules.

1. *Arrange the codes in alphabetical order, according to the first letter.*
2. *When two or more codes have the same first letter, arrange the codes in alphabetical order according to the last letter.*
3. *When two or more of the codes have the same first and last letters, arrange the codes in numerical order, beginning with the lowest number.*

The codes in Column I are numbered (1) through (5). Column II gives you a selection of four possible answers. You are to choose from Column II the lettered choice which gives the correct listing of the codes in Column I arranged according to the above rules.

The Answer Key for these test questions will be found at the end of the test.

COLUMN I: Set of Codes		COLUMN II: Possible Answers	
1.	(1) S55126179E	(A)	1, 5, 2, 3, 4
	(2) R55136177Q	(B)	3, 4, 1, 5, 2
	(3) P55126177R	(C)	3, 5, 2, 1, 4
	(4) S55126178R	(D)	4, 3, 1, 5, 2
	(5) R55126180P		
2.	(1) T64217813Q	(A)	4, 1, 3, 2, 5
	(2) I64217817O	(B)	2, 4, 3, 1, 5
	(3) T642178180	(C)	4, 1, 5, 2, 3
	(4) I64217811Q	(D)	2, 3, 4, 1, 5
	(5) T64217816Q		
3.	(1) C83261824G	(A)	2, 4, 1, 5, 3
	(2) C78361833C	(B)	4, 2, 1, 3, 5
	(3) G83261732G	(C)	3, 1, 5, 2, 4
	(4) C88261823C	(D)	2, 3, 5, 1, 4
	(5) G83261743C		

	COLUMN I: *Set of Codes*		COLUMN II: *Possible Answers*

4. (1) A11710107H
    (2) H17110017A
    (3) A11170707A
    (4) H17170171H
    (5) A11710177A

(A) 2, 1, 4, 3, 5
(B) 3, 1, 5, 2, 4
(C) 3, 4, 1, 5, 2
(D) 3, 5, 1, 2, 4

5. (1) R26794821S
    (2) O26794821T
    (3) M26794827Z
    (4) Q26794821R
    (5) S26794821P

(A) 3, 2, 4, 1, 5
(B) 3, 4, 2, 1, 5
(C) 4, 2, 1, 3, 5
(D) 5, 4, 1, 2, 3

6. (1) D89143888P
    (2) D98143838B
    (3) D89113883B
    (4) D89148338P
    (5) D89148388B

(A) 3, 5, 2, 1, 4
(B) 3, 1, 4, 5, 2
(C) 4, 2, 3, 1, 5
(D) 4, 1, 3, 5, 2

7. (1) W62455599E
    (2) W62455090F
    (3) W62405099E
    (4) V62455097F
    (5) V62405979E

(A) 2, 4, 3, 1, 5
(B) 3, 1, 5, 2, 4
(C) 5, 3, 1, 4, 2
(D) 5, 4, 3, 1, 2

8. (1) N74663826M
    (2) M74633286M
    (3) N76633228N
    (4) M76483686N
    (5) M74636688M

(A) 2, 4, 5, 3, 1
(B) 2, 5, 4, 1, 3
(C) 1, 2, 5, 3, 4
(D) 2, 5, 1, 4, 3

9. (1) P97560324B
    (2) R97663024B
    (3) P97503024E
    (4) R97563240E
    (5) P97652304B

(A) 1, 5, 2, 3, 4
(B) 3, 1, 4, 5, 2
(C) 1, 5, 3, 2, 4
(D) 1, 5, 2, 3, 4

10. (1) H92411165G
     (2) A92141465G
     (3) H92141165C
     (4) H92444165C
     (5) A92411465G

(A) 2, 5, 3, 4, 1
(B) 3, 4, 2, 5, 1
(C) 3, 2, 1, 5, 4
(D) 3, 1, 2, 5, 4

COLUMN I: Set of Codes		COLUMN II: Possible Answers	

11. (1) X90637799S
    (2) N90037696S
    (3) Y90677369B
    (4) X09677693B
    (5) M09673699S

(A) 4, 3, 5, 2, 1
(B) 5, 4, 2, 1, 3
(C) 5, 2, 4, 1, 3
(D) 5, 2, 3, 4, 1

12. (1) K78425174L
    (2) K78452714C
    (3) K78547214N
    (4) K78442774C
    (5) K78547724M

(A) 4, 2, 1, 3, 5
(B) 2, 3, 5, 4, 1
(C) 1, 4, 2, 3, 5
(D) 4, 2, 1, 5, 3

13. (1) P18736652U
    (2) P18766352V
    (3) T17686532U
    (4) T17865523U
    (5) P18675332V

(A) 1, 3, 4, 5, 2
(B) 1, 5, 2, 3, 4
(C) 3, 4, 5, 1, 2
(D) 5, 2, 1, 3, 4

Answer Key

1.C	4.D	7.D	10.A
2.B	5.A	8.B	11.C
3.A	6.A	9.C	12.D
			13.B

DATA INTERPRETATION

These questions are all from actual, previous examinations. They have been carefully chosen to provide you with the best possible practice for the questions you face on your test. These questions also give a good indication of what to expect. Careful practice will prepare you well for this type of question. The Data Interpretation questions take various forms. There are charts, tables, and graphs, each with different types. For example, a graph may be a circle, line, bar, or combination of these types. Please note that the tables and charts cover a variety of fields. No previous knowledge of the subject is required. Base your answers solely on the table or chart shown. Get a good, general idea of what the data means by looking it over before answering each set of questions. Always refer back to the data when responding to the questions.

A SAMPLE QUESTION ANALYZED

CHART NO. I

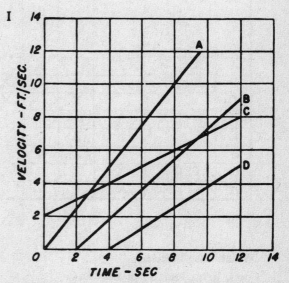

Look at the two columns of data below:

Time sec.	Velocity ft./sec.
0	2
2	3
4	4
6	5
8	6
10	7

// // // //
A B C D

Which one of the lines on the graph at the right most closely represents the data in these two columns?

An examination of the graph shows that time values are indicated along the horizontal scale, and velocity values along the vertical scale. If we observe the velocity value at zero time, we see that the A line has a value of 0 velocity, and the C line a value of 2 ft./sec. No values are shown at 0 time for lines B and D. Hence line C is the only one which shows a velocity of 2 ft. sec. at 0 time.

Similarly at 2 sec. the velocity value for line B is 0, for line A is 2.5, and for line C, 3. Here again C is the only line which corresponds to the data in the table. At 4 sec. the velocity value for line D is 0, for line B is 1.9, for line C is 4, and for line A is 5. Here also line C is the only one that gives the value shown in the table. The same process can be repeated for time values 6, 8, and 10 sec., all of which show that line C is the only one corresponding to the values given in the table.

223

DATA INTERPRETATION TEST

TIME: 10 Minutes

DIRECTIONS: All the questions in this test refer to the following chart. Read each question carefully and answer it on the basis of the chart. Select the best case and mark the correct letter on the answer sheet.

The Answer Key for these test questions will be found at the end of the test.

HOSPITAL CARE FOR PATIENTS

Case	Rent	Food	Shelter	Light	Fuel	Milk	Clothing	Household Supplies	Medical Care	Cod Liver Oil	Hospitalization	Fare	Cash Allowance
A	X	X	X		X		X				X		
B	X	X			X	X		X					
C		X		X		X		X	X	X			
D	X	X	X		X			X					
E			X	X			X		X			X	X
F			X		X		X		X				
G	X	X	X	X			X				X		
H	X		X				X					X	

Which case received:

1. Food, light, and hospitalization?

2. Medical service, shelter, clothing, and fuel?

3. Rent, food, shelter, fuel and household supplies?

4. Fuel, shelter, clothing, no hospitalization, but medical service?

5. Rent, shelter, no household supplies, no hospitalization, but fare?

6. Food, milk, household supplies, no fuel, but medical service?

7. Shelter, clothing, light, no cod liver oil, but medical service?

8. Shelter, clothing, no medical service, no cash allowance, but light?

9. Food, shelter, fuel, but no hospitalization?

10. Rent, fuel, milk, and household supplies?

CONSOLIDATE YOUR KEY ANSWERS HERE

1._____   4._____   7._____   9._____

2._____   5._____   8._____   10._____

3._____   6._____

Answer Key

1. G	4. F	6. C	8. G
2. F	5. H	7. E	9. D
3. D			10. B

ARITHMETIC COMPUTATIONS

TO SCORE HIGH ON MATH TESTS

1. SCHEDULE YOUR STUDY. Set a definite time and stick to it. Enter Arithmetical Computations on your Study Schedule.

2. PLAN on taking different types of Computation Tests in each study period. Keep alert to the differences and complications. That will help keep you bright and interested.

3. DO YOUR BEST and work fast to complete each test before looking at our Correct Answers. Keep pushing yourself, and use the help this book provides, for checking purposes only.

4. RECORD YOUR TIME for each test next to your score. Your schedule may allow you to take the tests again. And you may want to see how your speed and accuracy have improved.

5. REVIEW YOUR ERRORS. This is a must for every study session. Allow time for redoing every incorrect answer. The good self-tutor is a good self-critic. He learns most from his mistakes. And never makes them again.

6. DON'T GUESS AT ANSWERS. Because each practice test, like the actual examination, requires a multiple-choice answer, you might be tempted to pick up speed by approximating the answers. This is fatal. Carefully work out your answer to each question. Then choose the right answer. Any other way is certain to create confusion, slow you down, lower your score.

7. CLARITY & ORDER. Write all your figures clearly, in neat rows and columns. And this includes the figures you have to carry over from one column to—another. Don't make mistakes because of lack of space and cramped writing. Use scratch paper wherever necessary.

8. SKIP THE PUZZLERS. If a single question gives you an unusual amount of trouble, go on to the next question. Come back to the tough one after you have done all the others and still have time left over.

9. STUDY THE SAMPLE SOLUTIONS. Note how carefully we have worked out each step. Get into this habit in doing all the practice tests. You'll quickly find that it's a time-saver . . . a high-scoring habit.

Sample Questions and Detailed Solutions

DIRECTIONS: Each question has five suggested answers lettered A, B, C, D, and E. Suggested answer E is NONE OF THESE. Blacken space E only if your answer for a question does not exactly agree with any of the first four suggested answers. When you have finished the two questions, compare your answers with the answer key at the end of the test.

Sample 1. Divide:

$$4.6\overline{)233.404}$$

(A) 50.74
(B) 52.24
(C) 57.30
(D) 58.24
(E) None of these

Sample II. Multiply:

$$\begin{array}{r} 2\,946 \\ \times\,7.007 \end{array}$$

(A) 21,642.622
(B) 20,642.622
(C) 41,244.001
(D) 20,641.622
(E) None of these

SOLUTION I.

$$\begin{array}{r}
50.74 \\
4/6.\overline{)233/4.04} \\
230 \\
\hline
340 \\
322 \\
\hline
184 \\
184 \\
\hline
\end{array}$$

Since the answer is clearly 50.74, blacken A on the answer sheet. Do not mark any of the other letter choices. There is only one correct answer.

SOLUTION II.

$$\begin{array}{r}
2\,946 \\
\times\,7.007 \\
\hline
20\,622 \\
00\,00 \\
000\,0 \\
20622 \\
\hline
20,642.622 \\
\end{array}$$

The answer is 20,642.622, which is answer choice B. This answer is similar to answer choices A and D, but it is not the same. So you must be careful not to let the A and D choices confuse you. Blacken only B on your answer sheet.

Answer Key

1. A   2. B

MULTIPLICATION AND ADDITION TEST

Time Allowed: 10 minutes

DIRECTIONS: *In this test you are asked to do two of the fundamental operations in arithmetic: addition and multiplication. They are closely related in that multiplication is really a succession of additions. For the multiplication problems, blacken the space under A if the given answer is correct. Blacken the space under B if the answer is incorrect. For the addition problems, blacken the space under D if the given answer is correct. Blacken the space under E if the answer is incorrect. We suggest that you do all of the multiplication problems before going on to addition. You should be able to work more accurately and quickly that way.*

MULTIPLICATION

1) $16 \times 4 = 64$	2) $69 \times 8 = 552$
3) $27 \times 3 = 71$	4) $46 \times 5 = 51$
5) $79 \times 2 = 158$	6) $58 \times 4 = 222$

Answer Sheet

1 Ⓐ Ⓑ Ⓒ Ⓓ Ⓔ
2 Ⓐ Ⓑ Ⓒ Ⓓ Ⓔ
3 Ⓐ Ⓑ Ⓒ Ⓓ Ⓔ
4 Ⓐ Ⓑ Ⓒ Ⓓ Ⓔ
5 Ⓐ Ⓑ Ⓒ Ⓓ Ⓔ
6 Ⓐ Ⓑ Ⓒ Ⓓ Ⓔ
7 Ⓐ Ⓑ Ⓒ Ⓓ Ⓔ
8 Ⓐ Ⓑ Ⓒ Ⓓ Ⓔ
9 Ⓐ Ⓑ Ⓒ Ⓓ Ⓔ
10 Ⓐ Ⓑ Ⓒ Ⓓ Ⓔ

WORK SPACE

7) $15 \times 3 = 35$	8) $28 \times 6 = 168$
9) $49 \times 7 = 343$	10) $89 \times 9 = 801$

ADDITION

WORK SPACE

1)
$$\begin{array}{r} 68 \\ 30 \\ 46 \\ +52 \\ \hline 206 \end{array}$$

2)
$$\begin{array}{r} 44 \\ 57 \\ 60 \\ +32 \\ \hline 193 \end{array}$$

3)
$$\begin{array}{r} 37 \\ 63 \\ 12 \\ +78 \\ \hline 190 \end{array}$$

4)
$$\begin{array}{r} 24 \\ 43 \\ 72 \\ +57 \\ \hline 197 \end{array}$$

5)
$$\begin{array}{r} 20 \\ 59 \\ 66 \\ +81 \\ \hline 236 \end{array}$$

6)
$$\begin{array}{r} 48 \\ 42 \\ 77 \\ +16 \\ \hline 184 \end{array}$$

7)
$$\begin{array}{r} 34 \\ 28 \\ 65 \\ +41 \\ \hline 168 \end{array}$$

8)
$$\begin{array}{r} 94 \\ 36 \\ 89 \\ +64 \\ \hline 283 \end{array}$$

9)
$$\begin{array}{r} 25 \\ 40 \\ 66 \\ +31 \\ \hline 152 \end{array}$$

10)
$$\begin{array}{r} 52 \\ 17 \\ 25 \\ +64 \\ \hline 158 \end{array}$$

MULTIPLICATION

11) 67
 × 3
 191

12) 54
 × 7
 378

13) 67
 × 6
 412

14) 29
 × 8
 222

15) 36
 × 5
 190

16) 78
 × 4
 312

17) 18
 × 4
 72

18) 25
 × 7
 165

19) 47
 × 6
 282

20) 88
 × 4
 352

21) 68
 × 5
 330

22) 53
 × 8
 414

23) 64
 × 3
 192

24) 28
 × 9
 242

25) 82
 × 8
 656

WORK SPACE

Answer Sheet

11 Ⓐ Ⓑ Ⓒ Ⓓ Ⓔ
12 Ⓐ Ⓑ Ⓒ Ⓓ Ⓔ
13 Ⓐ Ⓑ Ⓒ Ⓓ Ⓔ
14 Ⓐ Ⓑ Ⓒ Ⓓ Ⓔ
15 Ⓐ Ⓑ Ⓒ Ⓓ Ⓔ
16 Ⓐ Ⓑ Ⓒ Ⓓ Ⓔ
17 Ⓐ Ⓑ Ⓒ Ⓓ Ⓔ
18 Ⓐ Ⓑ Ⓒ Ⓓ Ⓔ
19 Ⓐ Ⓑ Ⓒ Ⓓ Ⓔ
20 Ⓐ Ⓑ Ⓒ Ⓓ Ⓔ
21 Ⓐ Ⓑ Ⓒ Ⓓ Ⓔ
22 Ⓐ Ⓑ Ⓒ Ⓓ Ⓔ
23 Ⓐ Ⓑ Ⓒ Ⓓ Ⓔ
24 Ⓐ Ⓑ Ⓒ Ⓓ Ⓔ
25 Ⓐ Ⓑ Ⓒ Ⓓ Ⓔ

ADDITION

11) 44
 68
 75
 + 38
 225

12) 26
 64
 39
 + 24
 163

13) 58
 64
 27
 + 67
 216

14) 65
 34
 48
 + 92
 249

15) 11
 18
 85
 + 42
 156

16) 33
 26
 94
 + 35
 178

17) 88
 64
 38
 + 46
 226

18) 29
 63
 11
 + 84
 187

19) 54
 36
 29
 + 63
 182

20) 48
 75
 63
 + 68
 254

21) 75
 62
 32
 + 64
 223

22) 38
 82
 46
 + 54
 220

23) 12
 43
 65
 + 57
 187

24) 46
 58
 42
 + 23
 179

25) 28
 94
 35
 + 32
 199

WORK SPACE

Answer Key

1. A-E	8. A-D	15. B-D	22. B-D
2. A-D	9. A-E	16. A-E	23. A-E
3. B-D	10. A-D	17. A-E	24. B-E
4. B-E	11. B-D	18. B-D	25. A-E
5. A-E	12. A-E	19. A-D	
6. B-E	13. B-D	20. A-D	
7. B-D	14. B-E	21. B-E	

SUBTRACTION AND DIVISION TEST

Time Allowed: 10 minutes

DIRECTIONS: *Subtraction and division are two of the basic operations in arithmetic. This test will help you gain proficiency in both these diminution processes, and thereby in many others. For the division problems, blacken the space under A if the given answer is correct. Blacken the space under B if the answer is incorrect. For the subtraction problems, blacken the space under D if the given answer is correct. Blacken the space under E if the answer is incorrect. For this test the space under C will not be blackened. We suggest that you do all the division problems before going on to subtraction. Although the processes are related, you should be able to work more accurately and quickly if you do the test this way.*

SUBTRACTION

1) 16 −11 = 5
2) 23 −18 = 15
3) 55 −29 = 16
4) 61 −32 = 39
5) 32 −19 = 13
6) 77 −51 = 26
7) 48 −39 = 9
8) 53 −25 = 38
9) 86 −47 = 49
10) 66 −52 = 14
11) 38 −17 = 21
12) 94 −43 = 51
13) 69 −31 = 38
14) 99 −19 = 70
15) 57 −32 = 15
16) 35 −14 = 21

Answer Sheet

1 Ⓐ Ⓑ Ⓒ Ⓓ Ⓔ
2 Ⓐ Ⓑ Ⓒ Ⓓ Ⓔ
3 Ⓐ Ⓑ Ⓒ Ⓓ Ⓔ
4 Ⓐ Ⓑ Ⓒ Ⓓ Ⓔ
5 Ⓐ Ⓑ Ⓒ Ⓓ Ⓔ
6 Ⓐ Ⓑ Ⓒ Ⓓ Ⓔ
7 Ⓐ Ⓑ Ⓒ Ⓓ Ⓔ
8 Ⓐ Ⓑ Ⓒ Ⓓ Ⓔ
9 Ⓐ Ⓑ Ⓒ Ⓓ Ⓔ
10 Ⓐ Ⓑ Ⓒ Ⓓ Ⓔ
11 Ⓐ Ⓑ Ⓒ Ⓓ Ⓔ
12 Ⓐ Ⓑ Ⓒ Ⓓ Ⓔ
13 Ⓐ Ⓑ Ⓒ Ⓓ Ⓔ
14 Ⓐ Ⓑ Ⓒ Ⓓ Ⓔ
15 Ⓐ Ⓑ Ⓒ Ⓓ Ⓔ
16 Ⓐ Ⓑ Ⓒ Ⓓ Ⓔ

DIVISION

1) $5\overline{)30}$ = 6
2) $2\overline{)18}$ = 8
3) $5\overline{)25}$ = 4
4) $7\overline{)35}$ = 5
5) $4\overline{)12}$ = 4
6) $8\overline{)24}$ = 4
7) $6\overline{)24}$ = 4
8) $7\overline{)49}$ = 7
9) $4\overline{)32}$ = 9
10) $5\overline{)35}$ = 7
11) $9\overline{)81}$ = 8
12) $7\overline{)42}$ = 7
13) $7\overline{)28}$ = 4
14) $5\overline{)40}$ = 8
15) $8\overline{)16}$ = 2
16) $4\overline{)16}$ = 3

WORK SPACE

SUBTRACTION

17) 61 −19 = 42
18) 78 −51 = 26
19) 64 −28 = 26

20) 36 −16 = 20
21) 83 −38 = 55
22) 43 −12 = 31

23) 87 −79 = 8
24) 55 −31 = 23
25) 80 −14 = 76

26) 93 −40 = 53
27) 79 −64 = 5
28) 28 −12 = 16

29) 70 −34 = 46
30) 98 −83 = 15
31) 69 −37 = 42

32) 47 −33 = 14
33) 60 −49 = 11
34) 73 −28 = 45

35) 21 −16 = 4
36) 88 −77 = 11
37) 97 −59 = 39

38) 53 −29 = 25
39) 31 −19 = 12
40) 77 −49 = 28

DIVISION

17) $7\overline{)21}$ = 4
18) $2\overline{)14}$ = 7
19) $7\overline{)56}$ = 8

20) $5\overline{)45}$ = 8
21) $9\overline{)72}$ = 9
22) $7\overline{)14}$ = 2

23) $5\overline{)20}$ = 4
24) $7\overline{)63}$ = 9
25) $3\overline{)12}$ = 4

26) $5\overline{)15}$ = 2
27) $4\overline{)20}$ = 4
28) $9\overline{)63}$ = 7

29) $8\overline{)32}$ = 3
30) $8\overline{)56}$ = 7
31) $4\overline{)24}$ = 6

32) $9\overline{)54}$ = 5
33) $8\overline{)40}$ = 6
34) $4\overline{)28}$ = 7

35) $6\overline{)54}$ = 9
36) $6\overline{)18}$ = 4
37) $8\overline{)48}$ = 7

38) $3\overline{)18}$ = 6
39) $6\overline{)36}$ = 7
40) $9\overline{)27}$ = 4

WORK SPACE

Answer Sheet

17 Ⓐ Ⓑ Ⓒ Ⓓ Ⓔ
18 Ⓐ Ⓑ Ⓒ Ⓓ Ⓔ
19 Ⓐ Ⓑ Ⓒ Ⓓ Ⓔ
20 Ⓐ Ⓑ Ⓒ Ⓓ Ⓔ
21 Ⓐ Ⓑ Ⓒ Ⓓ Ⓔ
22 Ⓐ Ⓑ Ⓒ Ⓓ Ⓔ
23 Ⓐ Ⓑ Ⓒ Ⓓ Ⓔ
24 Ⓐ Ⓑ Ⓒ Ⓓ Ⓔ
25 Ⓐ Ⓑ Ⓒ Ⓓ Ⓔ
26 Ⓐ Ⓑ Ⓒ Ⓓ Ⓔ
27 Ⓐ Ⓑ Ⓒ Ⓓ Ⓔ
28 Ⓐ Ⓑ Ⓒ Ⓓ Ⓔ
29 Ⓐ Ⓑ Ⓒ Ⓓ Ⓔ
30 Ⓐ Ⓑ Ⓒ Ⓓ Ⓔ
31 Ⓐ Ⓑ Ⓒ Ⓓ Ⓔ
32 Ⓐ Ⓑ Ⓒ Ⓓ Ⓔ
33 Ⓐ Ⓑ Ⓒ Ⓓ Ⓔ
34 Ⓐ Ⓑ Ⓒ Ⓓ Ⓔ
35 Ⓐ Ⓑ Ⓒ Ⓓ Ⓔ
36 Ⓐ Ⓑ Ⓒ Ⓓ Ⓔ
37 Ⓐ Ⓑ Ⓒ Ⓓ Ⓔ
38 Ⓐ Ⓑ Ⓒ Ⓓ Ⓔ
39 Ⓐ Ⓑ Ⓒ Ⓓ Ⓔ
40 Ⓐ Ⓑ Ⓒ Ⓓ Ⓔ

Answer Key

1. A-D
2. B-E
3. B-E
4. A-E
5. B-D
6. B-D
7. A-D
8. A-E
9. B-E
10. A-D
11. B-D
12. B-D
13. A-D
14. A-E
15. A-E
16. B-D
17. B-D
18. A-E
19. A-E
20. B-D
21. B-E
22. A-D
23. A-D
24. A-E
25. A-E
26. B-D
27. B-E
28. A-D
29. B-E
30. A-D
31. A-E
32. B-D
33. B-D
34. A-D
35. A-E
36. B-D
37. B-E
38. A-E
39. B-D
40. B-D

COMPUTATIONAL SPEED TEST

Time Allowed: 10 minutes

DIRECTIONS: Each question has five suggested answers lettered A, B, C, D, and E. Suggested answer E is NONE OF THESE. Blacken space E only if your answer for a question does not exactly agree with any of the first four suggested answers. When you have finished all the questions, compare your answers with the answer key at the end of the test.

ANSWERS

1) Multiply:
   896
   × 708

   (A) 643,386
   (B) 634,386
   (C) 634,368
   (D) 643,368
   (E) None of these

2) Divide:
   9 / 4266

   (A) 447
   (B) 477
   (C) 474
   (D) 475
   (E) None of these

3) Add:
   $125.25
   .50
   70.86
   + 6.07

   (A) $201.68
   (B) $202.69
   (C) $200.68
   (D) $202.68
   (E) None of these

4) Subtract:
   $1,250.37
   — 48.98

   (A) $1,201.39
   (B) $1,201.49
   (C) $1,200.39
   (D) $1,201.38
   (E) None of these

5) Divide:
   29 / 476.92

   (A) 16.4445
   (B) 17.4445
   (C) 16.4555
   (D) 17.4455
   (E) None of these

Answer Sheet

1 Ⓐ Ⓑ Ⓒ Ⓓ Ⓔ
2 Ⓐ Ⓑ Ⓒ Ⓓ Ⓔ
3 Ⓐ Ⓑ Ⓒ Ⓓ Ⓔ
4 Ⓐ Ⓑ Ⓒ Ⓓ Ⓔ
5 Ⓐ Ⓑ Ⓒ Ⓓ Ⓔ
6 Ⓐ Ⓑ Ⓒ Ⓓ Ⓔ
7 Ⓐ Ⓑ Ⓒ Ⓓ Ⓔ
8 Ⓐ Ⓑ Ⓒ Ⓓ Ⓔ
9 Ⓐ Ⓑ Ⓒ Ⓓ Ⓔ
10 Ⓐ Ⓑ Ⓒ Ⓓ Ⓔ

WORK SPACE

ANSWERS

6) Multiply:
   7962.27
   × .06

   (A) 4777.362
   (B) 477.6732
   (C) 4787.632
   (D) 477.7362
   (E) None of these

7) Add:
   28
   19
   17
   + 24

   (A) 87
   (B) 88
   (C) 90
   (D) 89
   (E) None of these

8) Divide:
   3.7 / 2339.86

   (A) 632.4
   (B) 62.34
   (C) 642.3
   (D) 63.24
   (E) None of these

9) Add:
   4 ½
   5 ¾
   + 3 ⅔

   (A) 13 10/13
   (B) 12 ¾
   (C) 13 ⅔
   (D) 12 ½
   (E) None of these

10) Multiply:
    45,286
    × 4 1/5

    (A) 190,021 1/5
    (B) 190,234
    (C) 190,201 1/5
    (D) 190,202 2/5
    (E) None of these

ANSWERS

ANSWERS

11) Subtract:

$$8\ \tfrac{1}{6}$$
$$-5\ \tfrac{2}{3}$$

(A) 3 ⅔
(B) 2 ⅓
(C) 3 ⅙
(D) 2 ½
(E) None of these

16) Multiply:

$$7\ \text{ft.}\ 4\ \text{in.}$$
$$\times\ 6\ \text{in.}$$

(A) 582 sq. in.
(B) 825 sq. in.
(C) 528 sq. in.
(D) 568 sq. in.
(E) None of these

Answer Sheet

11 Ⓐ Ⓑ Ⓒ Ⓓ Ⓔ

12 Ⓐ Ⓑ Ⓒ Ⓓ Ⓔ

13 Ⓐ Ⓑ Ⓒ Ⓓ Ⓔ

14 Ⓐ Ⓑ Ⓒ Ⓓ Ⓔ

15 Ⓐ Ⓑ Ⓒ Ⓓ Ⓔ

16 Ⓐ Ⓑ Ⓒ Ⓓ Ⓔ

17 Ⓐ Ⓑ Ⓒ Ⓓ Ⓔ

18 Ⓐ Ⓑ Ⓒ Ⓓ Ⓔ

19 Ⓐ Ⓑ Ⓒ Ⓓ Ⓔ

20 Ⓐ Ⓑ Ⓒ Ⓓ Ⓔ

12) Multiply:
$$1/9 \times \tfrac{2}{3} \times \tfrac{7}{8} =$$

(A) 6/108
(B) 7/108
(C) 14/27
(D) 14/108
(E) None of these

17) 1/5 of 2 9 5 =

(A) 55
(B) 49
(C) 57
(D) 59
(E) None of these

13) Divide:
$$4\ \tfrac{1}{3}\ /\ \tfrac{1}{4}$$

(A) 3/52
(B) 5/52
(C) 17 ⅓
(D) 12/52
(E) None of these

18) Subtract:

$$26.456$$
$$-2.6465$$

(A) 24.8095
(B) 23.0895
(C) 24.8059
(D) 23.8095
(E) None of these

14) Find 6 ⅔%
of $13.50.

(A) $.89
(B) $.91
(C) $.88
(D) $.95
(E) None of these

19) Multiply:
$$6/7 \times 48.14 =$$

(A) 40.27
(B) 41.26
(C) 40.26
(D) 41.28
(E) None of these

15) Reduce 11/16
to a decimal.

(A) .8675
(B) .6875
(C) .6785
(D) .6578
(E) None of these

20) Add:
$$.84 + 7.2 + .008 =$$

(A) 8.048
(B) 7.148
(C) 7.048
(D) 8.148
(E) None of these

WORK SPACE

Answer Key

1. C	6. D	11. D	16. C
2. C	7. B	12. B	17. D
3. D	8. A	13. A	18. D
4. A	9. E	14. E	19. E
5. E	10. C	15. B	20. A

WORD PROBLEMS TEST

Time Allowed: 10 minutes

DIRECTIONS: The following arithmetic word problems have been devised to make you think with numbers. In each question, the arithmetic is simple, but the objective is to comprehend what you have to do with the numbers and/or quantities. Read the problem carefully and choose the correct answer from the five choices that follow each question.

The Answer Key for these test questions will be found at the end of the test.

1. Add the following: 40¢, $2.75, $186.21, $24,865, $.74, $8.42, $2,475.28, $11,998.24.

   (A) $38,537.04   (B) $39,537.04
   (C) $38,533.40   (D) $39,573.40
        (E) None of these

2. Perform the indicated operations and express your answer in its simplest form: ⅝ divided by 20/3 times 7/19 divided by 63/38 times 16/21 divided by 1/14.

   (A) 2/9   (B) ½
   (C) ⅓   (D) 5/9
        (E) None of these

3. Perform the indicated operations: .020301 times 2.15 divided by .00000063.

   (A) 69218.19   (B) 69821.19
   (C) 69281.91   (D) 69281.19
        (E) None of these

4. Add the following fractions: 1½, 2 1/16, 9⅓, 2¼, 6 1/5.

   (A) 21 8/20   (B) 21½
   (C) 20   (D) 20 9/20
        (E) None of these

5. Perform the indicated operations and express your answer in inches: 12 feet, minus 7 inches, plus 2 feet 1 inch minus 7 feet, minus 1 yard, plus 2 yards 1 foot 3 inches.

   (A) 130 inches   (B) 128 inches
   (C) 129 inches   (D) 131 inches
        (E) None of these

6. Add:
   7 years, 3 months
   5 years, 6 months
   8 years, 11 months

   (A) 20 yrs.   (B) 20 yrs. 8 mos.
   (C) 21 yrs. 9 mos. (D) 21 yrs. 8 mos.
        (E) None of these

7. Find the cost of 2 dozen boxes of pencils at $3.60 per ¼ dozen boxes.

   (A) $28.80   (B) $29.50
   (C) $20.88   (D) $28.08
        (E) None of these

8. When 5.1 is divided by 0.017 the quotient is

   (A) 30   (B) 300
   (C) 3,000   (D) 30,000
        (E) None of these

9. One percent of $23,000 is

   (A) $.023   (B) $2.30
   (C) $23   (D) $2300
        (E) None of these

10. The sum of $82.79; $103.06 and $697.88 is, most nearly,

    (A) $1628   (B) $791
    (C) $873   (D) $1395
         (E) None of these

11. The sum of 2345 and 4483 is

    (A) 6288   (B) 6828
    (C) 6882   (D) 8628
         (E) None of these

12. The difference between 2876 and 1453 is

    (A) 1342
    (B) 1324
    (C) 1234
    (D) 1423
    (E) None of these

13. If each of 5 sections has 15 cans, the total for all five sections is

    (A) 70
    (B) 65
    (C) 60
    (D) 80
    (E) None of these

14. The area of a street 100 yards long and 30 yards wide is

    (A) 3,000 sq. yds.
    (B) 3,500 sq. yds.
    (C) 2,500 sq. yds.
    (D) 130 sq. yds.
    (E) None of these

15. Five tons of snow will weigh how many pounds?

    (A) 1,000 lbs.
    (B) 10,000 lbs.
    (C) 100 lbs.
    (D) 5,000 lbs.
    (E) None of these

16. If a man earns $12,000 a year, approximately how much is his weekly pay?

    (A) $180
    (B) $200
    (C) $220
    (D) $240
    (E) None of these

17. A man who works 8 hours a day for 6 days will work a total of how many hours?

    (A) 40 hrs.
    (B) 45 hrs.
    (C) 50 hrs.
    (D) 47 hrs.
    (E) None of these

18. If a load of snow contains 3 tons, it will weigh how many lbs.?

    (A) 3,000 lbs.
    (B) 1,500 lbs.
    (C) 12,000 lbs.
    (D) 6,000 lbs.
    (E) None of these

19. A section of pavement which is 10 feet long and 8 feet wide contains how many square feet?

    (A) 80 sq. ft.
    (B) 92 sq. ft.
    (C) 800 sq. ft.
    (D) 18 sq. ft.
    (E) None of these

20. If a man mops 13 halls each day for 15 days, he will have mopped a total of how many halls?

    (A) 165 halls
    (B) 190 halls
    (C) 200 halls
    (D) 175 halls
    (E) None of these

21. If you divided 56 pounds of soap powder equally among 8 men, each man would get how many pounds of soap powder?

    (A) 6 lbs.
    (B) 7 lbs.
    (C) 8 lbs.
    (D) 5 lbs.
    (E) None of these

22. The sum of 284.5, 3016.24, 8.9736, and 94.15 is, most nearly,

    (A) 3402.9
    (B) 3403.0
    (C) 3403.9
    (D) 4036.1
    (E) None of these

23. If 8394.6 is divided by 29.17, the result is most nearly

    (A) 288
    (B) 347
    (C) 2880
    (D) 3470
    (E) None of these

24. If two numbers are multiplied together, the result is 3752. If one of the two numbers is 56, the other number is

    (A) 41
    (B) 15
    (C) 109
    (D) 76
    (E) None of these

25. The sum of the fractions $\frac{1}{4}$, $\frac{2}{3}$, $\frac{3}{8}$, $\frac{5}{6}$, and $\frac{3}{4}$ is

    (A) 20/33
    (B) 1 19/24
    (C) 2¼
    (D) 2⅞
    (E) None of these

Answer Key

1. B	8. B	15. B	22. C
2. A	9. E	16. E	23. A
3. D	10. C	17. E	24. E
4. E	11. B	18. D	25. D
5. C	12. D	19. A	
6. D	13. E	20. E	
7. A	14. A	21. B	

CIVIL SERVICE TEST TUTORS

TITLE	NUMBER	PRICE	TITLE	NUMBER	PRICE
Account Clerk (order BOOKKEEPER–ACCOUNT CLERK or BEGINNING OFFICE WORKER)			Bus Mechanic (order BUS MAINTAINER–BUS MECHANIC)		
			BUS OPERATOR–CONDUCTOR	05489-1	8.00
ACCOUNTANT-AUDITOR	05544-8	10.00	Captain Fire Department (order FIREFIGHTER PROMOTION EXAMINATIONS)		
Administrative Assistant (order PRINCIPAL ADMINISTRATIVE ASSOCIATE–ADMINISTRATIVE ASSISTANT)			Captain Police Department (order POLICE PROMOTION EXAMINATIONS)		
Administrative Manager (order STAFF POSITIONS–METHODS ANALYST–SENIOR ADMINISTRATIVE ASSISTANT–ADMINISTRATIVE MANAGER)			CARPENTER	05406-9	8.00
			CASE WORKER	04979-0	8.00
			CASHIER–HOUSING TELLER	00703-6	8.00
			CIVIL ENGINEERING TECHNICIAN	04267-2	10.00
AMERICAN FOREIGN SERVICE OFFICER	04219-2	8.00	CIVIL SERVICE ARITHMETIC AND VOCABULARY	04872-7	8.00
APPRENTICE MECHANICAL TRADES	00571-8	6.00	CIVIL SERVICE CLERICAL PROMOTION TESTS	06186-3	8.00
ASSISTANT ACCOUNTANT	05613-4	8.00	CIVIL SERVICE HANDBOOK	05166-3	5.00
Associate Staff Analyst (order STAFF ANALYST–ASSOCIATE STAFF ANALYST)			CIVIL SERVICE TESTS FOR BASIC SKILLS JOBS	06187-1	8.00
Audit Clerk (order BEGINNING OFFICE WORKER or SENIOR CLERICAL SERIES)			CIVIL SERVICE TYPING TESTS	06184-7	8.00
			Civilian Police Aide (order POLICE ADMINISTRATIVE AIDE–CIVILIAN POLICE AIDE)		
Auditor (order ACCOUNTANT–AUDITOR)			Clerical Promotion Tests (order CIVIL SERVICE CLERICAL PROMOTION TESTS)		
AUTO MECHANIC–AUTOMOTIVE SERVICEMAN	05397-6	8.00	Clerk (order BEGINNING OFFICE WORKER or FEDERAL CLERK–STENO–TYPIST or FEDERAL OFFICE ASSISTANT GS 2–4		
Automotive Serviceman (order AUTO MECHANIC–AUTOMOTIVE SERVICEMAN)			Clerk–Carrier (Postal Service) (order POST OFFICE CLERK–CARRIER)		
Battalion Chief (order FIREFIGHTER PROMOTION EXAMINATIONS)			Clerk–Typist (order FEDERAL CLERK–STENO–TYPIST)		
BEGINNING OFFICE WORKER	05404-2	8.00			
BOOKKEEPER–ACCOUNT CLERK	05398-4	8.00			
Bridge and Tunnel Officer (order SPECIAL OFFICER–SENIOR SPECIAL OFFICER–BRIDGE AND TUNNEL OFFICER)			COMPLETE GUIDE TO U.S. CIVIL SERVICE JOBS	05245-7	4.00
			Conductor (order BUS OPERATOR–CONDUCTOR)		
BUILDING CUSTODIAN–BUILDING SUPERINTENDENT	05405-0	8.00	CORRECTION OFFICER	05322-4	8.00
Building Groundskeeper (order CIVIL SERVICE TESTS FOR BASIC SKILLS JOBS)			Court Clerk (order COURT OFFICER–SENIOR COURT OFFICER–COURT CLERK)		
Building Porter (order CIVIL SERVICE TESTS FOR BASIC SKILLS JOBS)			COURT OFFICER–SENIOR COURT OFFICER–COURT CLERK	05615-0	9.00
Building Superintendent (order BUILDING CUSTODIAN–BUILDING SUPERINTENDENT)			Custodial Assistant (order CIVIL SERVICE TESTS FOR BASIC SKILLS JOBS)		
BUS MAINTAINER–BUS MECHANIC	00111-9	8.00	Deputy Sheriff (order HOME STUDY COURSE FOR SCORING HIGH ON LAW ENFORCEMENT TESTS)		

TITLE	NUMBER	PRICE
Detective–Investigator (order *HOME STUDY COURSE FOR SCORING HIGH ON LAW ENFORCEMENT TESTS*)		
DISTRIBUTION CLERK, MACHINE–LETTER SORTING MACHINE OPERATOR	05648-7	8.00
ELECTRICIAN–ELECTRICIAN'S HELPER	05492-1	8.00
Electrician's Helper (order *ELECTRICIAN–ELECTRICIAN'S HELPER*)		
Elevator Operator (order *CIVIL SERVICE TESTS FOR BASIC SKILLS JOBS*)		
FEDERAL CLERK–STENO–TYPIST	05407-7	8.00
FEDERAL OFFICE ASSISTANT GS 2–4	05490-5	8.00
File Clerk (order *BEGINNING OFFICE WORKER* or *FILE CLERK–GENERAL CLERK*)		
FILE CLERK–GENERAL CLERK	05408-5	8.00
FIREFIGHTER, F.D.	05170-1	8.00
FIREFIGHTER PROMOTION EXAMINATIONS	05611-8	10.00
FOOD SERVICE SUPERVISOR	04819-0	8.00
General Clerk (order *FILE CLERK–GENERAL CLERK*)		
GENERAL TEST PRACTICE FOR 101 U.S. JOBS	05246-5	6.00
Handyman (order *MAINTENANCE WORKER*)		
HOME STUDY COURSE FOR CIVIL SERVICE JOBS	05413-1	8.00
HOME STUDY COURSE FOR SCORING HIGH ON LAW ENFORCEMENT TESTS	05410-7	9.00
Hospital Attendant–Messenger (order *CIVIL SERVICE TESTS FOR BASIC SKILLS JOBS*)		
Housing Caretaker (order *CIVIL SERVICE TESTS FOR BASIC SKILLS JOBS*)		
Housing Officer (order *POLICE OFFICER* including *TRANSIT AND HOUSING OFFICER*)		
Housing Teller (order *CASHIER–HOUSING TELLER*)		
HOW TO GET A CLERICAL JOB IN GOVERNMENT	05647-9	8.00
HOW TO PASS EMPLOYMENT TESTS	05537-5	6.95
Letter Sorting Machine Operator (order *DISTRIBUTION CLERK, MACHINE–LETTER SORTING MACHINE OPERATOR*)		
Lieutentant Fire Department (order *FIREFIGHTER PROMOTION EXAMINATIONS*)		
Lieutenant Police Department (order *POLICE PROMOTION EXAMINATIONS*)		
MACHINIST–MACHINIST'S HELPER	05621-5	8.00
Machinist's Helper (order *MACHINIST–MACHINIST'S HELPER*)		
MAIL HANDLER, U.S. POSTAL SERVICE	05247-3	6.00
MAINTENANCE WORKER– MECHANICAL MAINTAINER	05764-5	8.00
MANAGEMENT ANALYST– ASSISTANT–ASSOCIATE	03864-0	8.00
Management Analyst Assistant (order *MANAGEMENT ANALYST–ASSISTANT– ASSOCIATE*		
Management Analyst Associate (order *MANAGEMENT ANALYST– ASSISTANT–ASSOCIATE*)		
MASTERING WRITING SKILLS FOR CIVIL SERVICE ADVANCEMENT	05774-2	8.00
MECHANICAL ABILITY TESTS	05769-6	8.00
MECHANICAL APTITUDE AND SPATIAL RELATIONS TESTS	05150-7	8.00
Mechanical Maintainer (order *MAINTENANCE WORKER– MECHANICAL MAINTAINER*)		
Medical Aide (order *MEDICAL TECHNICIAN–MEDICAL ASSISTANT–MEDICAL AIDE*)		
Medical Assistant (order *MEDICAL TECHNICIAN– MEDICAL ASSISTANT–MEDICAL AIDE*)		
MEDICAL TECHNICIAN–MEDICAL ASSISTANT–MEDICAL AIDE	05370-4	8.00
Methods Analyst (order *STAFF POSITIONS–METHODS ANALYST–SENIOR ADMINISTRATIVE ASSISTANT–ADMINISTRATIVE MANAGER*)		
MOTORMAN	00061-9	6.00
NURSE–REGISTERED NURSE–PRACTICAL NURSE–PUBLIC HEALTH NURSE (also order *NURSE'S AIDE HANDBOOK*)	05248-1	8.00
NURSE'S AIDE HANDBOOK (also order *NURSE–REGISTERED NURSE–PRACTICAL NURSE–PUBLIC HEALTH NURSE*)	05858-7	10.00
OFFICE AIDE	04704-6	8.00

TITLE	NUMBER	PRICE	TITLE	NUMBER	PRICE
Office Assistant (order *FEDERAL CLERK–STENO–TYPIST*)			Professional Administrative Career Examination (order *TEST PREPARATION FOR PROFESSIONAL AND ADMINISTRATIVE POSITIONS IN THE FEDERAL SERVICE*)		
OFFICE ASSOCIATE	04855-7	8.00			
OFFICE HANDBOOK FOR CIVIL SERVICE EMPLOYEES	05605-3	8.00	Public Health Nurse (order *NURSE–REGISTERED NURSE– PRACTICAL NURSE–PUBLIC HEALTH NURSE* and *NURSE'S AIDE HANDBOOK*)		
Office Machines Operator (order *FEDERAL CLERK– STENO–TYPIST* or *FEDERAL OFFICE ASSISTANT GS 2–4*)					
Park Service Worker (order *CIVIL SERVICE TESTS FOR BASIC SKILLS JOBS*)			*RAILROAD CLERK*	05643-6	8.00
			RAILROAD PORTER	05637-1	8.00
Parole Officer (order *PROBATION OFFICER–PAROLE OFFICER*)			*REAL ESTATE ASSESSOR– APPRAISER–REAL ESTATE MANAGER*	00563-7	10.00
Patrol Inspector (order *HOME STUDY COURSE FOR SCORING HIGH ON LAW ENFORCEMENT TESTS*)			Real Estate Manager (order *REAL ESTATE ASSESSOR– APPRAISER–REAL ESTATE MANAGER*)		
Payroll Clerk (order *BEGINNING OFFICE WORKER*)			*REFRIGERATION LICENSE MANUAL*	02726-6	12.00
POLICE ADMINISTRATIVE AIDE–CIVILIAN POLICE AIDE	05411-5	8.00	Registered Nurse (order *NURSE–REGISTERED NURSE- PRACTICAL NURSE–PUBLIC HEALTH NURSE* and *NURSE'S AIDE HANDBOOK*)		
POLICE OFFICER–TRANSIT AND HOUSING OFFICER (also order *HOME STUDY COURSE FOR SCORING HIGH ON LAW ENFORCEMENT TESTS*)	05130-2	8.00			
			SANITATION WORKER	05491-3	8.00
POLICE PROMOTION EXAMINATIONS	05604-5	12.00	*SCHOOL SECRETARY*	05918-4	8.00
Police Sergeant (order *HOME STUDY COURSE FOR SCORING HIGH ON LAW ENFORCEMENT TESTS* and *SERGEANT, P.D.*)			Security Officer–Inspector (order *HOME STUDY COURSE FOR SCORING HIGH ON LAW ENFORCEMENT TESTS*)		
POST OFFICE CLERK–CARRIER	05388-7	6.95	Senior Administrative Assistant (order *STAFF POSITIONS–METHODS ANALYST–SENIOR ADMINISTRATIVE ASSISTANT–ADMINISTRATIVE MANAGER*)		
Practical Nurse (order *NURSE–REGISTERED NURSE– PRACTICAL NURSE–PUBLIC HEALTH NURSE* and *NURSE'S AIDE HANDBOOK*)					
			SENIOR CLERICAL SERIES	05523-5	8.00
PRACTICE FOR CLERICAL, TYPING AND STENOGRAPHIC TESTS	05616-9	8.00	*SENIOR CLERK–STENOGRAPHER*	01797-X	9.00
PRACTICE FOR PROMOTION TO SUPERVISORY AND ADMINISTRATIVE POSITIONS IN CIVIL SERVICE	05763-7	8.00	Senior Court Officer (order *COURT OFFICER–SENIOR COURT OFFICER–COURT CLERK*)		
			Senior grades of Clerk (order *SENIOR CLERICAL SERIES*)		
PRINCIPAL ADMINISTRATIVE ASSOCIATE–ADMINISTRATIVE ASSISTANT	05617-7	10.00	Senior Special Officer (order *SPECIAL OFFICER–SENIOR SPECIAL OFFICER–BRIDGE AND TUNNEL OFFICER*)		
PRINCIPAL CLERK–PRINCIPAL STENOGRAPHER	05536-7	8.00			
Principal Stenographer (order *PRINCIPAL CLERK–PRINCIPAL STENOGRAPHER*)			*SERGEANT, P.D.* (also see *HOME STUDY COURSE FOR SCORING HIGH ON LAW ENFORCEMENT TESTS*)	05278-3	12.00
Prison Guard (order *CORRECTION OFFICER*)			*SOCIAL SUPERVISOR*	04190-0	10.00
PROBATION OFFICER–PAROLE OFFICER	05619-3	8.00	*SPECIAL OFFICER–SENIOR SPECIAL OFFICER–BRIDGE AND TUNNEL OFFICER*	05614-2	8.00

TITLE	NUMBER	PRICE	TITLE	NUMBER	PRICE
STAFF ANALYST–ASSOCIATE STAFF ANALYST	05522-7	10.00	SUPERVISION COURSE	05618-5	10.00
STAFF POSITIONS–METHODS ANALYST–SENIOR ADMINISTRATIVE ASSISTANT–ADMINISTRATIVE MANAGER	03490-4	6.00	Supervisor (Child Welfare) (order SOCIAL SUPERVISOR)		
STATE TROOPER	05765-3	8.00	TAKING TESTS AND SCORING HIGH	01347-8	5.00
STATIONARY ENGINEER AND STATIONARY FIREMAN	00070-8	9.00	Telephone Operator (order BEGINNING OFFICE WORKER)		
Stationary Fireman (order STATIONARY ENGINEER AND STATIONARY FIREMAN)			TEST PREPARATION FOR PROFESSIONAL AND ADMINISTRATIVE POSITIONS IN THE FEDERAL SERVICE	05921-4	10.00
Statistical Clerk (order BEGINNING OFFICE WORKER)			TEST PREPARATION FOR STENOGRAPHER–TYPIST	05535-9	8.00
Statistics Clerk (order SENIOR CLERICAL SERIES)			Track Worker (order CIVIL SERVICE TESTS FOR BASIC SKILLS JOBS)		
Stenographer (order FEDERAL CLERK–STENO–TYPIST or FEDERAL OFFICE ASSISTANT GS 2–4 or SENIOR CLERK–STENOGRAPHER or STENOGRAPHER–TYPIST GS–2 TO GS–7 or TEST PREPARATION FOR STENOGRAPHER–TYPIST)			TRAFFIC ENFORCEMENT AGENT	05771-8	8.00
			Transcriber (order FEDERAL CLERK–STENO–TYPIST)		
Stenographer (Law) (order SENIOR CLERICAL SERIES)			Transit Officer (order POLICE OFFICER–INCLUDING TRANSIT AND HOUSING OFFICER)		
STENOGRAPHER–TYPIST GS-2 TO GS-7	05412-3	8.00	Typing Tests (order CIVIL SERVICE TYPING TESTS)		
Stores Clerk (order SENIOR CLERICAL SERIES)			Typist (order FEDERAL OFFICE ASSISTANT GS 2–4)		
SUPERVISING CLERK–STENOGRAPHER–OFFICE ASSOCIATE	04309-1	8.00	VOCABULARY BUILDER AND VERBAL APTITUDE TEST GUIDE	05807-2	6.95
			VOCABULARY, SPELLING, AND GRAMMAR	05806-4	6.95

ARCO CIVIL SERVICE TEST TUTORS

Government service, the nation's largest field of employment, provides jobs to millions of civilian workers—about 1 out of 6 employed persons in the United States.

Since 1937, Arco has prepared millions of people for tests covering hundreds of Federal, State and Local Government positions.

Each ARCO CIVIL SERVICE TEST TUTOR offers:

- **In-depth information on how to apply for a Civil Service job**
- **Study techniques**
- **Complete review and explanation for all question types appearing on the exam**
- **Full-length exams, using previous official test questions, for practice**
- **Helpful hints for scoring high on the test**

If you are thinking about a career in Government service, there is an Arco book that will help you reach your goal!

A complete list of ARCO CIVIL SERVICE TEST TUTORS appears on the preceding pages.

ARCO IS THE LEADER IN CIVIL SERVICE TEST PREPARATION BOOKS